T0178641

Lecture Notes of the Institute for Computer Sciences, Social Informatics and Telecommunications Engineering 538

The LNICST series publishes ICST's conferences, symposia and workshops.

LNICST reports state-of-the-art results in areas related to the scope of the Institute. The type of material published includes

- Proceedings (published in time for the respective event)
- Other edited monographs (such as project reports or invited volumes)

LNICST topics span the following areas:

- General Computer Science
- E-Economy
- E-Medicine
- Knowledge Management
- Multimedia
- Operations, Management and Policy
- Social Informatics
- Systems

Mahdi H. Miraz · Garfield Southall · Maaruf Ali ·
Andrew Ware

Editors

Emerging Technologies in Computing

6th EAI International Conference, iCETiC 2023
Southend-on-Sea, UK, August 17–18, 2023
Proceedings

 Springer

Editors
Mahdi H. Miraz ⓘ
Xiamen University Malaysia
Selangor, Malaysia

Garfield Southall ⓘ
University of Chester
Chester, UK

Maaruf Ali ⓘ
Universiteti Metropolitan Tirana
Tirana, Albania

Andrew Ware ⓘ
University of South Wales
Pontypridd, UK

ISSN 1867-8211 ISSN 1867-822X (electronic)
Lecture Notes of the Institute for Computer Sciences, Social Informatics
and Telecommunications Engineering
ISBN 978-3-031-50214-9 ISBN 978-3-031-50215-6 (eBook)
https://doi.org/10.1007/978-3-031-50215-6

This Springer imprint is published by the registered company Springer Nature Switzerland AG
The registered company address is: Gewerbestrasse 11, 6330 Cham, Switzerland

Paper in this product is recyclable.

Preface

It is our great pleasure to introduce the Proceedings of the Sixth International Conference on Emerging Technologies in Computing (iCETiC '23), held on the 17th and 18th August, 2023. This year, the conference was physically held at the University of Essex, Southend-on-Sea, UK. This was as important move to come back to the 'old normal' after the COVID-19 pandemic.

The theme of iCETiC '23 was 'Emerging Technologies' as outlined by the Gartner Hype Cycle for Emerging Technologies, 2022. This conference drew together international researchers and developers from both academia and industry – especially in the domains of computing, networking and communications engineering.

iCETiC '23 was organised by the International Association for Educators and Researchers (IAER). As a knowledge partner, the European Alliance for Innovation (EAI) also played a significant role in organising the conference and publishing the proceedings.

This year, iCETiC received a total of 41 submissions out of which 15 were accepted following the blind peer review process by at least three reviewers. The primary conference tracks were:

- Track 1 - AI, Expert Systems and Big Data Analytics;
- Track 2 - Information and Network Security;
- Track 3 - Cloud, IoT and Distributed Computing.

Apart from the high-quality technical paper presentations, the technical program featured two keynote speeches. The keynote speakers were Andrew Ware from University of South Wales, UK and Hoshang Kolivand from Liverpool John Moores University, UK.

It was a great pleasure to work with such an excellent organising committee team, who put in significant effort in organising and supporting the conference. The work of the Technical Programme Committee is also much appreciated: they completed the peer-review process of technical papers, culminating in a high-quality professional programme.

Yet again, iCETiC '23 provided an excellent forum for researchers, developers and practitioners to discuss recent advancements in computing, networking and communications engineering. We will continue to strive to ensure that future iCETiC conferences will be as successful and stimulating.

Mahdi H. Miraz
Garfield Southall
Maaruf Ali
Andrew Ware

Organisation

Steering Committee Co-chairs

Garfield Southall — University of Chester, UK
Maaruf Ali — Universiteti Metropolitan Tiranë, Albania and University of Wales Trinity Saint David, UK
Andrew Ware — University of South Wales, UK
Mahdi H. Miraz — Xiamen University (Malaysia Branch), Malaysia, Wrexham University, UK and University of South Wales, UK

Organising Committee

General Co-chairs

Garfield Southall — University of Chester, UK
Maaruf Ali — Universiteti Metropolitan Tiranë, Albania and University of Wales Trinity Saint David, UK

Advisory Board

Andrew Jones — University of Hertfordshire, UK
Yousuf M. Islam — Daffodil International University, Bangladesh

Programme Co-chairs

Andrew Ware — University of South Wales, UK
Mahdi H. Miraz — Xiamen University (Malaysia Branch), Malaysia, Wrexham University, UK and University of South Wales, UK

Web, Publicity and Social Media Chair

Shayma K. Miraz — International Association for Educators and Researchers (IAER), UK

Publications Chair

Mahdi H. Miraz

Xiamen University (Malaysia Branch), Malaysia,
Wrexham University, UK and University of
South Wales, UK

Local Chair

Anowarul Karim

International Association for Educators and
Researchers, UK

Technical Program Committee Chair

Mohammad Riyaz Belgaum

G. Pullaiah College of Engineering and
Technology, India

Track Chairs

Cloud, IoT and Distributed Computing Track Chair

Will Serrano

University College London, UK

Software Engineering Track Chair

M. Abdullah-Al-Wadud

King Saud University, KSA

Communications Engineering and Vehicular Technology Track Chair

Mohab A. Mangoud

University of Bahrain, Bahrain

AI, Expert Systems and Big Data Analytics Track Chair

Christian Esposito

Università degli Studi di Salerno, Italy

Web Information Systems and Applications Track Chair

Marie Nour Haikel-Elsabeh

Pôle Universitaire Léonard de Vinci, France

Security Track Chair

Bhawani Shankar Chowdhry   Mehran University of Engineering & Technology, Pakistan

Database System and Application Track Chair

Abdullah Tansel   Baruch College, City University of New York, USA

Economics and Business Engineering Track Chair

Olga Angelopoulou   University of Hertfordshire, UK

mLearning and eLearning Track Chair

Sergey Lupin   National Research University for Electronic Technology (MIET), Russia

Technical Program Committee

Renaud Lambiotte	University of Oxford, UK
Ljiljana Trajkovic	Simon Fraser University, Canada
Been-Chian Chien	National University of Tainan, Taiwan
Victor Preciado	University of Pennsylvania, USA
Lin Liu	Tsinghua University, China
Guanghui Wen	Southeast University, China
Nowshad Amin	Universiti Kebangsaan Malaysia and Solar Energy Research Institute, Malaysia
AbdelRahman H. Hussein	Al-Ahliyya Amman University, Jordan
Rabie Ramadan	University of Ha'il, KSA
Vincenza Carchiolo	Università di Catania, Italy
Imran Mahmud	Daffodil International University, Bangladesh
Fabiana Zama	University of Bologna, Italy
Jia Uddin	Woosong University, Republic of Korea
Fazal Noor	Islamic University of Madinah, KSA
Bernhard Peischl	Technische Universität Graz, Austria
Christian Esposito	University of Salerno, Italy
Arcangelo Castiglione	University of Salerno, Italy
Trupil Limbasiya	Desay SV Automotive, Singapore
Zahida Parveen	University of Ha'il, KSA

Balakrishnan K.	Karpaga Vinayaga College of Engineering and Technology, India
Asadullah Shaikh	Najran University, KSA
Ibrahim Kucukkoc	Balikesir University, Turkey
Cristóvão Dias	Universidade de Lisboa, Portugal
Radoslaw Michalski	Wroclaw University of Science and Technology, Poland
Samina Rajper	Shah Abdul Latif University, Pakistan
Wasan Shakir Awad	Ahlia University, Bahrain
Prabhat K. Mahanti	University of New Brunswick, Canada
Massimo Ficco	Università degli Studi della Campania Luigi Vanvitelli, Italy
Syed Faiz Ahmed	Universiti Kuala Lumpur British Malaysian Institute, Malaysia
Mohammad Siraj	King Saud University, KSA
Anthony Chukwuemeka Ijeh	American University in the Emirates, UAE
José Javier Ramasco	Institute for Cross-Disciplinary Physics and Complex Systems (IFISC), Spain
Zi-Ke Zhang	Hangzhou Normal University, China
Francisco Rodrigues	University of São Paulo, Brazil
Ahmed N. Al Masri	American University in the Emirates, UAE
Ahmed Bin Touq	United Arab Emirates University, UAE
Daniel Onah	University College London, UK
Oussama Hamid	University of Kurdistan, Iraq
Souvik Pal	Elitte College of Engineering, India
Ali Hessami	Vega Systems Ltd, UK
Ezendu Ariwa	University of Bedfordshire, UK
Umair Ahmed	Gulf University, Bahrain
Aamir Zeb Shaikh	NED University of Engineering & Technology, Pakistan
Farhat Naureen Memon	University of Sindh, Pakistan
Fida Hussain Chandio	University of Sindh, Pakistan
Riaz Ahmed Shaikh	Shah Abdul Latif University, Pakistan
Muniba Memon	Najran University, Saudi Arabia
Mansoor Hyder Depar	Sindh Agriculture University, Pakistan
Zohreh Dehghani Champiri	Universiti Malaya, Malaysia
Md Tanvir Arafat Khan	Hanwha Q Cells America Limited, USA
Abhishek Shukla	Dr. A.P.J. Abdul Kalam Technical University, India
Rezaul Azim	University of Chittagong, Bangladesh
Jinfeng Li	Imperial College London, UK
Muhammad Aamir	Sir Syed University of Engineering & Technology, Pakistan

Muhammad Saddam Khokhar   Jiangsu University, China
Man Fung Lo   Education University of Hong Kong, China
Amando Jr. Pimentel   Higher College of Technology, Muscat, Oman
Deexith Reddy   Slalom Consulting, USA
Majlinda Fetaji   South East European University,
    North Macedonia
Piyush Tripathi   Texas A&M University, USA

Contents

Cloud, IoT and Distributed Computing

AI, Expert Systems and Big Data Analytics

Physics-Informed Machine Learning Assisted Liquid Crystals μWave Phase Shifters Design and Synthesis

Jinfeng Li[1,2(✉)] [iD]

[1] Beijing Institute of Technology, Beijing 100081, China
jinfengcambridge@bit.edu.cn
[2] Imperial College London, London SW7 2AZ, United Kingdom

Abstract. Liquid crystal (LC) has proven to be a promising material for microwave (μWave) phase shifters at GHz ranges, due to their continuous and wide tunability, as well as reasonably low absorption loss. However, designing LC phase shifters that meet specific application requirements (e.g., SpaceTech) is a challenging task that entails a complex trade-off between various parameters. Physics-informed machine learning (PI-ML) combines the power of machine learning with the underlying physics to develop a more accurate and interpretable model. Leveraging PI-ML to inform LC μWave device design is a relatively new area, with tremendous opportunities for exploration and innovation. In this article, a deep learning assisted LC μWave phase shifter design and synthesis framework is proposed. By incorporating physical constraints and knowledge into deep neural networks, one can effectively balance the trade-off between different design parameters and synthesize LC phase shifter structures that meet specific performance requirements (e.g., insertion loss, insertion loss balancing, phase tuning range, tuning speed, power consumption). The framework is envisaged to allow for the efficient and effective exploration of the design space, resulting in improved accuracy and efficiency compared to traditional two-stage design methods.

Keywords: Liquid crystals · Liquid crystals phase shifter · Phase array · Phase shifter · Physics-informed machine learning · Reconfigurable mmWave · μWave

1 Introduction

1.1 Status of Electronic Design Automation

The shift of RF component designers and engineers from using Smith Chart (for impedance matching lump circuit elements) in the past, to employing Electronic Design Automation (EDA) [1], is largely enabled by the evolution of high-performance computing. Arguably, EDA aids engineers in creating and putting into practice novel concepts and determining the best configurations (mainly by design) to boost bandwidth or spatial resolution for designing μWave transmission line components based on the theoretical

M. H. Miraz et al. (Eds.): iCETiC 2023, LNICST 538, pp. 3–13, 2024.
https://doi.org/10.1007/978-3-031-50215-6_1

understanding of microstrip, slot line, strip line, and coplanar waveguide. The expense of testing can be decreased, and the behavior of devices can be understood, even in operating settings that can only be digitally modelled, by incorporating modelling and simulation early in the design process.

Using specialised algorithms and modelling techniques, e.g., full-wave simulation [2, 3], ray tracing [4], and other approximations [5, 6], simulation software ensures relatively accurate estimates at any length scale, from subwavelength to optically big. In most cases, models may need to take into account various factors, e.g., temperature changes, mechanical stress, deformation, or the modulation of light by electrical fields—in other words, they must be multi-physics models [7]—in order to effectively depict real-world circumstances.

However, how to use the EDA software properly and model these problems accurately [8] requires extensive research and hands-on experience in device design and experimental validation, in particular, for μWave active circuits [9]. Furthermore, current research and academic activities are running in a highly collaborative manner, indicating that most researchers and academics are specialised in a specific (limited) range of devices design and simulation, whereas lacking working experience on devices that they have yet to experiment with.

Furthermore, off-the-shelf full-wave simulation software is computationally intensive, which challenges the use of high-performance dedicated hardware (challenged in cost) for the sake of reduced computational time. On the contrary, lumped-element circuit-theory-based simulations offer far faster solutions for preliminary design guidelines in certain problems, which are nonetheless challenged in reliability for describing transmission lines of complex geometries.

1.2 Nematic Liquid Crystal Enabled Reconfigurable Devices Design

Nematic liquid crystals (NLC, abbreviated as LC in this work) are a type of unusual organic materials that are orientationally organized but flowing like liquids. Correspondingly, the material structure is like the anisotropic crystal solid phase, but the molecules are still able to move, resulting in them showing significant promise in reconfigurable devices operated at optical, terahertz (THz), and μWave frequencies by encapsulating the materials in an appropriately designed wave-guided device structure (e.g., transmission line or waveguide) commensurate with the operating wavelength ranges. This is because LC exhibits unique optical and electrical properties from the microscopic representation to the macroscopic overview.

Figure 1 below outlines the physics underpinning LC-enabled tunable μWave and optical devices, i.e., dielectric anisotropy and optical birefringence (macroscopically). The specific properties of a particular LC material can vary depending on its chemical composition and molecular structure (microscopically). With benzene rings linearly connected, the resultantly elongated molecular shape anisotropy (colloquially referred to as rod-like molecules) gives rise to the dielectric anisotropy, indicating that the molecular orientation controlled by external stimuli (e.g., a low-frequency low-amplitude voltage bias) can formulate the phase shifting functionality of electromagnetic wave (the dielectric constant change provides the wave speed modulation and hence the output phase varying).

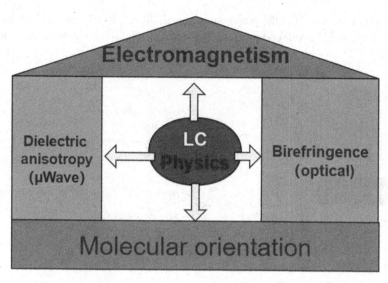

Fig. 1. Physics underlying LC tunable μWave and optical devices.

In recent decades, LC tunable dielectrics have gained significant attention for their potential to enable innovative applications in the RF (including μWave [10], millimeter-wave [11]) and THz [12] regions, among which electromagnetic (EM) full-wave analysis is crucial for predicting the performance (e.g., of a LC-enabled passive phase shifter component). From the scope of application (system-level performance), the reliability, uniformity of the LC layer and how this will affect the beam steering quality merit investigation. To be more specific, this connects to the reproducibility and repeatability of the voltage response of each phase shifter component. The insights and feedback from these manufacturing and reliability wise issues comprise a good opportunity to the recent surge of interest in machine learning models.

1.3 Conventional Two-Step Multi-scale Modelling Approach

Traditionally, the LC μWave phase shifters design has been majorly done through physics-based modeling and simulation, which can be time-consuming and computationally intensive (expensive) for large-array ultra-wide-band systems. The numerical representation (characterization) of a LC μWave device requires a multi-scale model that links molecular dynamics simulations [13] with full-wave simulation (e.g., by finite element analysis) [14], i.e., a two-step approach. In the first step, the molecular interactions between the constituent particles of the LC are modelled using a mesoscopic or molecular-scale approach. This step provides an understanding of the structure and properties of the LC, including its phase transitions (temperature dependent) and response to external stimuli (quasi-static electric field, magnetic field, or light field). In the second step, the macroscopic properties of the LC are modelled using continuum mechanics, which involves treating the LC as a continuous medium. This step provides an under-standing of how the LC as a tunable dielectric layer varies the wave speed (and hence the phase shift produced) of the propagating signal, the results of which can be used to design and optimize tunable components. The strengths of this approach are summarized below in Fig. 2.

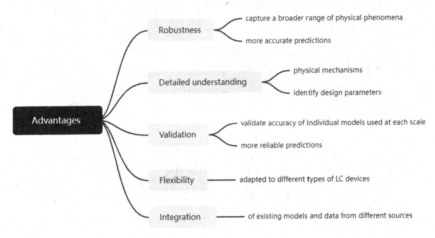

Fig. 2. Advantages of conventional two-step approach in modelling LC tunable devices.

There are various drawbacks to the two-step method for developing LC phase shifters. First, it may lead to mistakes and errors since different models are used at various scales with erroneous assumptions, which causes discrepancies in the results. The method is also computationally costly and time-consuming, which may restrict the design space and preclude large-scale optimizations. The coupling between LCD master (Shintech) [15] and HFSS (Ansys) [16] has yet to be seamless. Additionally, the optimization of designs for performance needs can be hampered by the incomplete understanding of the underlying physics. For instance, the wave-occupied-volume-ratio concept as proposed by [17], and the figure-of-merit reflection as raised by [18], have yet been analytically linked. The problem encompasses a multitude of nonlinearities that remain to be exploited. It might be difficult to integrate many models at various scales, which can result in mistakes and inconsistencies in the final design.

2 Proposed Physics-Informed Machine Learning

Is deep learning assisted liquid crystals (LC) microwave (μWave) devices design an unexploited area? This was first raised in our pioneering work presented at the 2022 IEEE MTT-S International Microwave Workshop Series on Advanced Materials and Processes for RF and THz Applications [19], which leads to a reflection on formulating a computationally efficient (single-stage) and scalable alternative to the classical two-step modelling approaches.

This paper proposes a physics-informed machine learning (PI-ML) approach (a sub-type of machine learning) for the LC μWave phase shifters design, which involves incorporating physical principles and constraints into the learning process. The framework and exemplary code implementation are presented in Sect. 2.1 and Sect. 2.2, respectively.

2.1 New Framework for LC μWave Phase Shifters Design

To develop a machine learning model for liquid crystal (LC) μWave phase shifters, high-resolution experimental data or industry-wide data set (large and diverse datasets) must first be collected at various frequencies and temperatures with varying material parameters (e.g., dielectric constants, refractive index) and geometry sizes (e.g., LC layer thickness, delay line length). Relevant features must then be extracted from this data, such as the thickness and birefringence (dielectric anisotropy) of the LC layer set to be used to train a machine learning model. It is important to incorporate physical principles (e.g., conservation laws, symmetries, and boundary conditions) into the machine learning algorithms to achieve physics-informed machine learning (PI-ML) [20]. This approach, as illustrated in the framework shown below in Fig. 3, will allow for the creation of a more accurate and reliable model for LC μWave phase shifters.

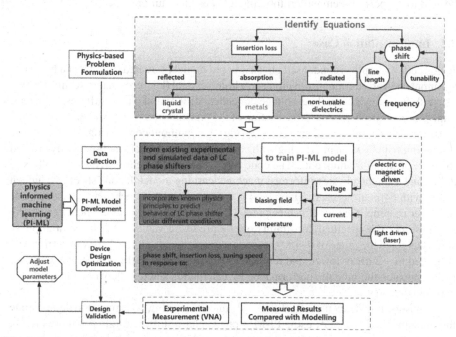

Fig. 3. Proposed framework of physics-informed machine learning (PI-ML) approach to design a LC tunable phase shifter.

A few benefits are provided by physics-informed machine learning (PI-ML) for the design optimization of LC phase shifters. The benefits of physics-based modelling and machine learning are combined in PI-ML, which improves accuracy and speeds up convergence of predictions. PI-ML is more versatile and adaptive since it can handle a greater variety of design scenarios and is not constrained by certain assumptions or models. PI-ML can shed light on the system's underlying physics, enabling a deeper knowledge of the physical workings and optimum design elements that boost efficiency. Furthermore, PI-ML, which is computationally efficient and affordable, can be used to discover complex nonlinear relationships between design parameters and performance indicators, reducing the need for sophisticated models.

PI-ML has benefits for liquid crystal phase shifters, but it also has restrictions on how it may be used. The restricted data availability, especially for new LC materials or systems, is one of the major drawbacks and can restrict the applicability of PI-ML in some circumstances. Another drawback is the difficulty in model interpretation, which can make it challenging to pinpoint crucial design parameters or comprehend the underlying physical mechanisms, especially for complex systems.

Furthermore, being sensitive to the caliber of the input data, PI-ML can overfit the training data and produce unfavorable designs. While PI-ML can shed light on the system's physical workings, it could not have as thorough a grasp of physics as a fully physics-based model, which could restrict its capacity to generalize beyond the training dataset. It might be argued that training on larger and better formatted data sets is highly desired to support on-demand prototyping and design requirements.

2.2 Implementation Case

In this code example, a condensed physics-based model is created to connect a bias voltage input and various dimension inputs to a liquid crystal (LC) coplanar transmission line phase shifter's key output (bias voltage dependent differential phase shift, insertion loss, impedance, return loss). The cross section of the transmission line model in this example is assumed to be uniform in size (no tapering), i.e., without considering the impedance discontinuity [14] when interfacing with connectors. This model is subsequently utilized to create artificial training data. The code uses MATLAB's Neural Network Toolbox to define and train the physics-informed machine learning model. It consists of two hidden layers with 64 neurons each. The model is trained with 100 epochs and a batch size of 32. After training, the model makes predictions on the test set, and the post-processing step enforces the specified constraints on the predicted values. The differential phase shift is targeted the range of 0–360°, impedance matching is targeted 50 Ω, insertion loss is limited to −2 dB or lower, and return loss is limited to −20 dB or lower. Finally, the code evaluates the model's performance by calculating the loss between the predicted and actual values.

It must be noted that this simplified code tutorial (see Fig. 4) is meant to demonstrate the fundamental concept of using PI-ML for LC phase shifter design. For more precise and reliable predictions, however, more complicated neural network designs and physics-based models may actually be needed. For instance, a similar strategy can be incorporated on modelling the bias voltage-dependent differential phase shift variations among diverse phase shifting states, with the target of minimizing such deviations. Furthermore, relevant PI-ML representation for response time and figure-of-merit (°/dB defined by the ratio of maximum differential phase shift to maximum insertion loss) can also be produced.

```
% Load the dataset containing the physics-based features and target values
dataset = readtable('LC_coplanar_phase_shifter_dataset.csv');

% Split the dataset into features and target variables
X = dataset(:, {'Voltage', 'LiquidCrystalThickness', 'CoreLineWidth', 'GapWidth',
'CoreLineThickness'});
y = dataset(:, {'DifferentialPhaseShift', 'ImpedanceMatching', 'InsertionLoss', 'ReturnLoss'});

% Split the dataset into training and testing sets
[X_train, X_test, y_train, y_test] = splitData(X, y, 0.8);

% Define the physics-informed machine learning model using MATLAB's Neural Network Toolbox
model = fitnet([64, 64]);
model.trainParam.epochs = 100;
model.trainParam.batchSize = 32;

% Train the model
model = train(model, X_train', y_train');

% Make predictions using the trained model
predictions = model(X_test');

% Perform post-processing to enforce the specified constraints
predictions(:, 1) = max(min(predictions(:, 1), 360), 0);  % Limit differential phase shift to be within
0-360 degrees
predictions(:, 2) = 50;  % Impedance matching should be 50 ohms
predictions(:, 3) = max(predictions(:, 3), -2);  % Limit insertion loss to be within -2 dB
predictions(:, 4) = max(predictions(:, 4), -20);  % Limit return loss to be lower than -20 dB

% Evaluate the model
loss = perform(model, y_test', predictions');

% Print the evaluated loss and example predictions
fprintf('Evaluation Loss: %.4f\n', loss);
fprintf('Example Predictions:\n');
for i = 1:min(5, size(predictions, 1))
    fprintf('Sample %d: Differential Phase Shift=%.2f degrees, Impedance Matching=%.2f ohms, Insertion
Loss=%.2f dB, Return Loss=%.2f dB\n', ...
        i, predictions(i, 1), predictions(i, 2), predictions(i, 3), predictions(i, 4));
end
```

Fig. 4. A brief tutorial of PI-ML code implementation for modelling an electrically tuned LC phase shifter.

3 Discussion on Current Status and Future Outlook

Current computational researchers are facing a concern of placing more emphasis on the various technical strategies of solving boundary value problems and computing eigenmodes, rather than on the justification for a given methodology to address a particular set of issues at the outset. It is envisioned that the physics-informed deep learning can provide an alternative approach (single-stage) to LC μWave reconfigurable devices modelling problems intractable by the classical two-step computation paradigm. In this work, the changes and technological developments needed to achieve this are briefly discussed. More specifically, this raises a comparison of physics-informed deep learning (PI-DL) against the physics-informed machine learning (PI-ML), as elaborated in Sect. 3.1, followed by the outlook for the application scope described in Sect. 3.2.

3.1   Physics-Informed Deep Learning vs. Physics-Informed Machine Learning

Albeit PI-ML and PI-DL are both physics-based techniques, they differ substantially from one another. Arguably, the sort of model utilised is the primary distinction between PI-ML and PI-DL.

In PI-ML, the model is frequently a neural network-like method for regression or classification that has been trained using data and actual constraints. These limitations could come in the form of model parameter constraints or physics-expressed mathematical equations. On the other hand, PI-DL employs deep neural networks designed specifically to include physics-based models. The architecture of the network is based on the underlying physics of the system, allowing for more accurate and efficient modelling.

One advantage of PI-ML is that a range of problems, including those with ambiguous or imprecise mathematical definitions can be resolved using it, e.g., investigating how a LC μWave phase shifter's insertion loss quantitatively relates with the dielectric constant of the LC, under the specific impedance-matching constraint (e.g., 50 ohms for most cases), whilst achieving a specific phase shifting range (e.g., up to 360° suffices).

Moreover, PI-ML may be taught using existing machine learning frameworks and is rather easy to set up. The data sets used for training PI-ML have an impact on its accuracy and extrapolation skills. However, in complex systems with poorly defined physical boundaries (e.g., non-conventional connectors [14] included in the computational model) or large levels of fluctuation (e.g., higher-order-mode [14] induced surface wave radiation and reflection phenomena), this can be especially problematic.

Contrarily, the advantage of PI-DL is that it is more exact and resistant to extrapolation. This is because the neural network architecture directly incorporates the physics-based model, enabling more accurate predictions to be made even when physical constraints are not completely known. On the other hand, PI-DL may require more processing resources (for which limited data is available right now, but promising in the future as more and more research is devoted to the LC μWave field) and call for a deeper knowledge of both deep learning and physics.

Overall, LC phase shifters can be designed using PI-ML and PI-DL where appropriate. While PI-DL can be used to develop models that are more accurate and trustworthy and that fully account for the underlying physics, PI-ML can be used to develop prediction models that are based on pre-existing data and physical constraints. Both PI-ML and PI-DL provide novel and intriguing opportunities for more accurate and effective LC phase shifter design. The particular application and the resources at hand will determine the method to use.

3.2   Application Scope

In the midst of ongoing space race and an ever-growing IoT ecosystem [21], the high-growth SpaceTech sector arguably gives rise to a host of targeted applications (as illustrated in Fig. 5) for the liquid crystal (LC) enabled technology [22, 23], including but not limited to inter-satellite communications, satellite internet (addressing the world's unconnected and under-connected populations), radioastronomy (radio-telescope), remote sensing, μWave/light-wave beam steering (RADAR and LiDAR), as well as other mission-critical scenarios [24] that are academically or industrially motivated. It is envisaged that physics-informed Machine Learning (PI-ML) that combines the power of machine learning with the underlying physics can develop a more accurate and interpretable model amid these applications.

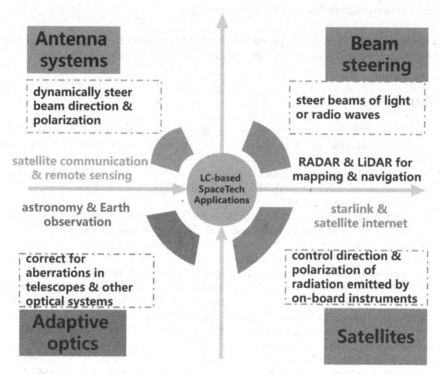

Fig. 5. Potential LC-enabled applications in the high-growth SpaceTech sector.

4 Concluding Remarks

In conclusion, liquid crystal (LC) has demonstrated great potential as a functional material for μWave phase shifters in the GHz range, owing to its wide tunability and relatively low absorption loss. However, designing LC phase shifters to meet specific application requirements, such as SpaceTech, poses a significant challenge that involves a complex trade-off among various parameters. To address this challenge, physics-informed machine learning (PI-ML) offers a promising approach by combining the strengths of machine learning and underlying physics principles to develop more accurate and interpretable models. This article proposes a deep learning-assisted framework for the design and synthesis of LC μWave phase shifters. By integrating physical constraints and knowledge into deep neural networks, this framework effectively balances the trade-off between different design parameters and enables the synthesis of LC phase shifter structures that fulfill specific performance requirements, including insertion loss, insertion loss balancing, phase tuning range, tuning speed, and power consumption. The framework is expected to facilitate efficient and effective exploration of the design space, leading to improved accuracy and efficiency compared to traditional two-stage design methods. The application of this framework holds tremendous potential for innovation and advancement in the field of LC μWave device design and system integration (e.g., the advent of reconfigurable intelligent surface [25]).

Acknowledgement. The support from the Research Fund Programme for Young Scholars at BIT and the National Natural Science Foundation of China (Grant 62301043) is acknowledged.

References

1. Somjit, N., Robertson, I., Chongcheawchamnan, M.: Electronic design automation. In: Microwave and millimetre-wave design for wireless communications, 1st edn. Wiley, New Jersey (2016)
2. Marek, A., et al.: Benefits of advanced full-wave vector analysis codes for the design of high-power microwave tubes. In: 2018 11th German Microwave Conference (GeMiC), pp. 279–282, Freiburg, Germany (2018)
3. Hammadi, S., Grondin, R.O., El-Ghazaly, S., et al.: Full-wave electromagnetic simulation of millimeter-wave active devices and circuits. Ann. Télécommun. **54**, 30–42 (1999)
4. Benson, T.M., Ata, O.W., Soghomonian, M., Marincic, A.S.: Application of finite difference and optical ray tracing methods to the design of microwave components. In: IEE Colloquium on Computer Based Tools for Microwave Engineers, pp. 9/1–9/6, London, UK (1991)
5. Naishadham, K., Misra, P.: Order recursive method of moments: a powerful computational tool for microwave CAD and optimization. In: 1996 IEEE MTT-S International Microwave Symposium Digest. San Francisco, pp. 1463–1466. CA, USA (1996)
6. Jinfeng, L.: Performance limits of 433 MHz quarter-wave monopole antennas due to grounding dimension and conductivity. Ann. Emerg. Technol. Comput. **6**(3), 1–10 (2022)
7. Lukic, M., Kim, K., Lee, Y., Saito, Y., Filipovic, D.S.: Multi-physics design and performance of a surface-micromachined Ka-band cavity backed patch antenna. In: 007 SBMO/IEEE MTT-S International Microwave and Optoelectronics Conference, pp. 321–324. Salvador, Brazil (2007)
8. Steer, M.B., Bandler, J.W., Snowden, C.M.: Computer-aided design of RF and microwave circuits and systems. IEEE Trans. Microwave Theory Tech. **50**(3), 996–1005 (2002)
9. May, M.P., Taflove, A., Baron, J.: FD-TD modeling of digital signal propagation in 3-D circuits with passive and active loads. IEEE Trans. Microwave Theory Tech. **42**, 1514–1523 (1994)
10. Jinfeng, L.: Optically steerable phased array enabling technology based on mesogenic azobenzene liquid crystals for starlink towards 6G. In: 2020 IEEE Asia-Pacific Microwave Conference (APMC), pp. 345–347. IEEE, Hong Kong (2020)
11. Papanicolaou, N.C., Christou, M.A., Polycarpou, A.C., Nestoros, M., Tchema, R.: Electromagnetic modeling and simulation of microwave and mm-wave devices based on liquid crystal compounds. AIP Conf. Proc. **2302**, 110006 (2020)
12. Chodorow, U., Parka, J., Chojnowska, O.: Liquid crystal materials in THz technologies. Photon. Lett. PL **4**(3), 112–114 (2012)
13. Michael, P.A.: Molecular simulation of liquid crystals. Mol. Phys. **117**(18), 2391–2417 (2019)
14. Jinfeng, L.: Wideband PCB-to-connectors impedance adapters for liquid crystal-based low-loss phase shifters. In: 2020 50th European Microwave Conference (EuMC), pp. 546–549. IEEE, Utrecht, Netherlands (2021)

15. Jinfeng, L.: An efficient mixed-signal dielectric-partitioning model of liquid crystals based shielded coplanar waveguide for electronically reconfigurable delay lines design. In: Proceeding SPIE, Integrated Optics: Design, Devices, Systems and Applications VI 11775, 1177519 (2021)
16. Jinfeng, L.: Rethinking liquid crystal tunable phase shifter design with inverted microstrip lines at 1–67 GHz by dissipative loss analysis. Electronics **12**(2), 421 (2023)
17. Jinfeng, L., Daping, C.: Liquid crystal-based enclosed coplanar waveguide phase shifter for 54–66 GHz applications. Crystals **9**(12), 650 (2019)
18. Jinfeng, L.: Rethinking figure-of-merits of liquid crystals shielded coplanar waveguide phase shifters at 60 GHz. J—Multi. Sci. J. **4**(3), 444–451 (2021)
19. Jinfeng, L.: Machine learning and digital twinning enabled liquid crystals mm-wave reconfigurable devices design and systems operation. In: 2022 IEEE MTT-S International Microwave Workshop Series on Advanced Materials and Processes for RF and THz Applications, pp. 1–3. IEEE, Guangzhou, China (2022)
20. Karniadakis, G.E., Kevrekidis, I.G., Lu, L., et al.: Physics-informed machine learning. Nat. Rev. Phys. **3**, 422–440 (2021)
21. Mahdi, H.M., Maaruf, A.: Integration of blockchain and IoT: an enhanced security perspective. Ann. Emerg. Technol. Comput. **4**(4), 52–63 (2020)
22. Jinfeng, L.: Towards 76–81 GHz scalable phase shifting by folded dual-strip shielded coplanar waveguide with liquid crystals. Ann. Emerg. Technol. Comput. **5**(4), 14–22 (2021)
23. Jinfeng, L.: Challenges and opportunities for nematic liquid crystals in radio frequency and beyond. Crystals **2**(5), 632 (2022)
24. Ashraf, A., Andrew, W.: Effective performance metrics for multimedia mission-critical communication systems. Ann. Emerg. Technol. Comput. **5**(2), 1–14 (2021)
25. Jinfeng, L.: From liquid crystal on silicon and liquid crystal reflectarray to reconfigurable intelligent surfaces for post-5G networks. Appl. Sci. **13**(13), 7407 (2023)

Chaotic Chimp Based African Vulture Optimization Algorithm with Stability Tests for Feature Selection Algorithms

Manoj Kollam[✉] and Ajay Joshi

Department of Electrical and Computer Engineering, The University of West Indies,
St. Augustine, Trinidad and Tobago
mkollam@gmail.com

Abstract. Earthquake prediction remains a major challenge in the field of geo-physics, with significant implications for disaster management and risk reduc-tion. Accurate prediction depends on identifying and selecting relevant features from large and complex datasets. In this study, we present a novel feature selec-tion method, the Chaotic Chimp based African Vulture Optimization Algorithm (CCAVO), applied to earthquake magnitude prediction. The model was trained on a dataset containing various seismic event characteristics such as latitude, longi-tude, depth, and other geological factors. The target variable for prediction was the magnitude of the seismic event. We conducted three stability tests on the model: Convergence Rate, Consistency Test, and Sensitivity to Parameters. Our analysis revealed that the CCAVO demonstrated good convergence behavior, with training errors reducing over successive iterations, indicating the model's ability to learn from the data. The consistency test further showed that the model performance, as quantified by the Mean Squared Error (MSE), remained consistent across multiple runs with different random seeds, suggesting the model's stability and robustness against randomness in initialization. Finally, a sensitivity analysis was performed to examine the model's response to changes in its hyperparameters. The model's performance was observed to vary with different parameter settings, indicating its sensitivity to hyperparameters. The optimal parameters found were a learning rate of 0.1 and 100 estimators, yielding 0.08 MSE from 3-fold cross-validated MSE.

Keywords: Feature Selection · Machine Learning · CCAVO · Feature ranking · stability testing · Mean Squared Error · hyper-parameters

1 Introduction

Earthquake prediction has long been a topic of interest to scientists, researchers, and pol-icy makers alike because of the devastating consequences of seismic events [1, 2]. These natural disasters can result in significant loss of life, property damage, and economic disruption [3]. Earthquake prediction involves predicting the location, magnitude, and timing of the occurrence of seismic events, which can help reduce their adverse effects

© ICST Institute for Computer Sciences, Social Informatics and Telecommunications Engineering 2024
Published by Springer Nature Switzerland AG 2024. All Rights Reserved
M. H. Miraz et al. (Eds.): iCETiC 2023, LNICST 538, pp. 14–28, 2024.
https://doi.org/10.1007/978-3-031-50215-6_2

[4, 5]. Accurate earthquake forecasts play a critical role in disaster management and risk reduction [6]. Timely and accurate forecasts can enable agencies to implement evacuation plans, allocate resources, and coordinate.

Emergency response more effectively [7, 8]. In addition, well-informed forecasts contribute to the development of building codes and infrastructure design aimed at minimizing damage and loss of life in the event of an earthquake [3]. Feature selection is a critical aspect of developing robust and accurate earthquake prediction models [9]. The process involves identifying relevant features from large and complex datasets that can then be used to train machine learning algorithms for seismic event prediction [10]. Effective feature selection can significantly improve the performance of predictive models by reducing the dimensionality of the data, eliminating noise and irrelevant information, and preventing overfitting [11]. Despite the importance of feature selection for earthquake prediction, current methods still face several challenges that leave room for improvement. Many existing techniques have difficulty identifying the most relevant and stable features [12]. This inconsistency can lead to unreliable prediction models because the selected features may not accurately reflect the underlying relationships in the data [5]. In addition, many feature selection methods are sensitive to noise and outliers, which can affect the performance of the prediction models [12]. Some techniques, such as filtering methods, may not consider the interaction between features, potentially overlooking important relationships [9]. In addition, the high dimensionality of seismic data often presents a challenge for feature selection, as many algorithms have difficulty effectively managing such large datasets [13]. In addition, there is a lack of comprehensive comparative studies that evaluate the performance of different feature selection methods in the context of earthquake prediction [14, 15]. This makes it difficult to determine which methods are most effective in different scenarios or for specific data sets. These limitations highlight the need for more reliable and effective feature selection methods to improve the accuracy of earthquake prediction models. The development of new approaches that address these research gaps can significantly advance the field of earthquake prediction.

2 Literature Review

Feature selection is a crucial step in developing accurate and reliable earthquake prediction models. The main goal of feature selection is to identify the most relevant features from large and complex datasets to ultimately improve the performance of the prediction models [9]. A variety of feature selection methods have been applied in the context of earthquake prediction, including filter methods, wrapper methods, and embedded methods [16].

Filter methods, such as correlation-based feature selection and mutual information-based methods, are based on statistical measures of dependence between features and the target variable (Taylan et al., 2019). These methods are computationally efficient but may not always identify the optimal subset of features because they do not account for interactions between features [12]. Wrapper methods such as forward selection, backward elimination, and recursive feature elimination evaluate feature subsets by directly assessing the performance of a given prediction model [14]. Although wrapper methods can provide better results than filtering methods, they tend to be computationally intensive because the model must be trained multiple times [16]. Embedded methods such as Lasso and Ridge regression integrate feature selection into the model training process and provide a balance between the performance and computational efficiency of filter and wrapper methods [13].

Stability tests are increasingly recognized as an essential aspect of feature selection in machine learning and data mining. These tests evaluate the robustness of feature selection methods by measuring their sensitivity to variations in the input data [17].

Feature selection methods aim to identify the most relevant and informative features for a given task. However, some methods may be sensitive to noise or outliers in the data, leading to the selection of unstable features that do not consistently contribute to the predictive performance of the model [18]. Stability tests help quantify the reliability of selected features by assessing their consistency across different subsets of the data or under perturbations in the data [19]. By incorporating stability testing into the feature selection process, researchers can ensure that the selected features are both relevant and reliable, resulting in more accurate and generalizable models [17].

Kalousis et al. (2007) [18] introduced a stability-based criterion for evaluating feature selection methods and emphasized the importance of selecting features that are robust to variations in the input data. Their study showed that the inclusion of stability tests can lead to better predictive performance and feature selection. Similarly, Nogueira et al. (2017) [17] proposed a stability-aware feature selection framework that combines filtering methods with stability tests to identify reliable and relevant features. Their experiments on different datasets demonstrated the effectiveness of their approach in selecting stable features that consistently contribute to the model's predictive performance. He & Yu (2010) [19] also investigated the impact of stability testing on feature selection by incorporating a stability measure into a graph-based feature selection method. Their approach effectively identified stable and relevant features that improved the performance of the resulting models (see Table 1).

Table 1. Overview of the strengths and weaknesses of the feature selection techniques

Feature selection Methods	Strengths	Weaknesses
Principal Component Analysis (PCA) (1)	• Reduces dimensionality while preserving the maximum variance in the data • Easy to implement and computationally efficient	• Assumes linear relationships between features • The transformed features may be difficult to interpret
Independent Component Analysis (ICA)(2)	• Separates sources of mixed signals by maximizing the statistical independence of the components • Can be useful for discovering underlying factors or sources in the data	• Assumes non-Gaussian distributions of the sources • Requires more computational resources than PCA

(continued)

Table 1. (*continued*)

Feature selection Methods	Strengths	Weaknesses
Non-negative Matrix Factorization (NMF)(3)	• Decomposes data into non-negative components, leading to more interpretable results • Can be useful for identifying parts-based representations	• Applicable only to non-negative data • Convergence to a local minimum can be an issue
Laplacian Score (LS)(4)	• Evaluates the importance of features by preserving the local structure of data • Can identify both global and local features	• Sensitive to the choice of neighborhood size • Requires the construction of a similarity graph
Minimum Redundancy Maximum Relevance (mRMR)(5)	• Selects features that are highly relevant to the target variable while minimizing redundancy • Can handle large datasets efficiently	• Assumes pairwise interactions between features • May be sensitive to noise and outliers
Correlation-based Feature Selection (CFS)(6)	• Evaluates features based on their correlation with the target variable and other features • Computationally efficient	• Assumes linear relationships between features • May not capture complex interactions between features
Sparse Subspace Clustering (SSC)(7)	• Discovers low-dimensional subspaces within high-dimensional data • Can handle data with missing values or noise	• Assumes that data lies on multiple low-dimensional subspaces • Requires solving an optimization problem, which can be computationally expensive
Low-rank Representation (LRR)(8)	• Captures the global structure of data by learning a low-rank representation • Robust to noise and outliers	• Requires solving an optimization problem, which can be computationally expensive • Assumes that data lies on a single low-dimensional subspace
Graph-based Feature Selection (GFS)(3)	• Captures the local and global structure of data by constructing a graph • Can handle nonlinear relationships between features	• Captures the local and global structure of data by constructing a graph • Can handle nonlinear relationships between features
Feature Selection via Joint Embedding (FSJE)(8, 9)	• Combines multiple feature selection methods into a unified framework • Can handle heterogeneous data sources	• Requires the selection of appropriate base feature selection methods • Can be computationally expensive
Feature Selection via Graph Embedding (FSGE)(10)	• Preserves the local and global structure of data by embedding it into a lower-dimensional space • Can handle nonlinear relationships between features	• Requires the construction of a similarity graph • May be sensitive to the choice of graph parameters
Feature Selection via Joint Embedding and Graph Embedding (FSJEGE)(11)	• Combines the strengths of both joint embedding and graph embedding approaches • Can handle heterogeneous data sources and nonlinear relationships	• Requires the selection of appropriate base feature selection methods and graph construction parameters • Can be computationally expensive

3 Methodology

The AVOA (African Vulture Optimization Algorithm) is a nature-inspired metaheuristic algorithm that was developed as a tool for optimization. It is based on the observed behavior of African vultures, which are known for their ability to find food in a wide range of environments. One potential advantage of AVOA is its ability to effectively search for solutions in a wide range of optimization problems, including those with many variables and complex constraints. It is also relatively simple to implement, as it only requires a few parameters to be set by the user. AVOA has been applied to various optimization problems and has been shown to be effective at finding good solutions. AVOA has been tested on a variety of optimization problems and has demonstrated its ability to find high-quality solutions.

The performance of the algorithm may vary depending on the characteristics of the problem and the parameter values chosen. The computational efficiency of the algorithm may be lower than that of some other metaheuristic algorithms. The black-box nature of the algorithm can make it difficult to understand the underlying optimization process and the reasons for the results obtained. The algorithm has only been tested on a limited number of benchmark functions and design problems, so its generalizability to other problem domains is uncertain.

The Chaotic Chimp based African Vulture Optimization Algorithm (CCAVO) algorithm has several novel features that distinguish it from other metaheuristic algorithms. First, it uses a chaotic search mechanism to explore the search space more effectively. Second, it uses a chimpanzee-inspired motion strategy to improve the convergence speed of the algorithm. Third, he uses a fitness sharing mechanism to prevent the algorithm from converging to local optima. The CCAVO algorithm has been shown to be effective in a number of benchmark optimization problems. In a recent study, the CCAVO algorithm was compared to a number of other metaheuristic algorithms, including the Whale Optimization Algorithm (WOA), the Artificial Bee Colony (ABC) algorithm, and the Genetic Algorithm (GA). The CCAVO algorithm was found to outperform the other algorithms on the majority of the test problems. The CCAVO algorithm is a promising new metaheuristic algorithm that has the potential to be used to solve a wide variety of optimization problems.

Chaotic Search Mechanism: The CCAVO algorithm uses a chaotic search mechanism to explore the search space more effectively. This is done by adding a chaotic function to the objective function. The chaotic function brings randomness to the search process, which helps prevent the algorithm from getting stuck in local optima.

Chimpanzee-Inspired Motion Strategy: The CCAVO algorithm uses a chimpanzee-inspired motion strategy to improve the convergence speed of the algorithm. This is done through a social learning mechanism that controls the motion of the search agents. The social learning mechanism allows the search agents to learn from each other's experiences, which helps them find better solutions faster.

Fitness Sharing Mechanism: The CCAVO algorithm uses a fitness sharing mechanism to prevent the algorithm from converging to local optima. This is done by sharing the fitness of the search agents among themselves. The fitness sharing mechanism helps to ensure that the search agents explore the entire search space rather than focusing on a small portion of the space.

The steps involved in the Chaotic Chimp based African Vulture Optimization Algorithm (CCAVO):

Initialize the Population: The algorithm starts with a population of solutions. The solutions can be randomly generated, or they can be generated using another optimization algorithm.

Evaluate the Population: The fitness of each solution in the population is evaluated. The fitness function is a measure of how good a solution is.

Perform Chaotic Search: A chaotic search is performed on each solution in the population. The chaotic search introduces randomness into the search process, which helps to prevent the algorithm from getting stuck in local optima.

Perform Chimpanzee-Inspired Movement Strategy: A chimpanzee-inspired movement strategy is performed on each solution in the population. The chimpanzee-inspired movement strategy allows the algorithm to learn from its previous iterations, which helps it to find better solutions more quickly.

Perform Fitness Sharing Mechanism: A fitness sharing mechanism is performed on the population. The fitness sharing mechanism prevents the algorithm from converging to local optima by sharing the fitness of the solutions with each other.

Repeat Steps 3–5 Until a Termination Criterion is Met: The algorithm repeats steps 3–5 until a termination criterion is met. The termination criterion can be a maximum number of iterations, a maximum change in fitness, or a maximum time.

Return the best solution: The best solution in the population is returned as the output of the algorithm (see Table 2).

Table 2. Table code snippet of CCAVOA.

Code snippet

```
# Initialize the best solution
best_solution = population[0]

# Iterate over the maximum number of iterations
for i in range(max_iter):

    # Perform chaotic search
    for j in range(len(population)):

        # Generate a random number between 0 and 1
        c = random.random()

        # Calculate the new solution
        new_solution  =  population[j]  +  c  *  (population[j]  -
population[np.random.randint(len(population))])

        # Evaluate the new solution
        new_fitness = fitness_function(new_solution)

        # If the new solution is better than the current solution, replace it
        if new_fitness > fitness_function(population[j]):
            population[j] = new_solution

    # Update the best solution
    if fitness_function(population[0]) < fitness_function(best_solution):
        best_solution = population[0]

return best_solution
```

3.1 Data

The lab generated dataset was considered and use it to verify the model were detecting relevant futures has opposed to noise present in data set. The dataset is adapted from a USGS(United States Geological Survey) and a previous study by Seifert, Gundlach, and Szymczak 2019(12). The size of the dataset is 66879 x 19 rows by columns and contains 4 classes. There are nineteen relevant features denoted M1, M2,....,M19, and each are sampled independently from a standard normal distribution $Mi \sim N(0, 1)$, i = 1,2....., 19. Other dataset are used is IRIS and Traffic flow forecast dataset are considered from UC Irvine Machine learning repository [20, 21].

3.2 Stability Metrics

Stability metrics are a set of measures used to evaluate the robustness and reliability of machine learning models. Stability is an important consideration in machine learning, particularly in applications where the model is expected to perform consistently well despite changes in the input data or slight perturbations.

Convergence Rate

In optimization algorithms, such as those used in machine learning to minimize a cost or loss function, the convergence rate is often used to describe how quickly the algorithm is expected to find the optimal solution.

A method used here is quadratic convergence, if there exists a constant k such that

$$\frac{|x_{n+1} - L|}{|x_{n+1} - L|^2} < k \tag{1}$$

for all n Quadratic convergence is a type of superlinear convergence but is faster than any other superlinear convergence.

Consistency Test

A consistency test is a way to check if an estimator or learning algorithm is consistent. In practice, this could involve using simulations or synthetic data to assess how the estimator or model's performance improves as the amount of data is increased.

To test the consistency of a machine learning model, you might:

- Train the model on subsets of the training data of increasing size.
- Evaluate the model's performance on a separate validation set for each subset of training data.
- Plot the model's performance as a function of the training set size. If the model's performance continues to improve as the size of the training set increases, this is an indication that the model is consistent.

An estimator $\widehat{\theta_n}$ of a parameter θ is consistent if for any $\varepsilon > 0$.

$$\lim_{n \to \infty} P\left(\left| \widehat{\theta_n} - \theta \right| > \varepsilon \right) = 0 \tag{2}$$

Sensitivity to Parameters

This sensitivity refers to how much the performance of a model changes in response to changes in its parameters.

There are two main categories of parameters in machine learning models:

- Hyperparameters
- model parameters.

For a given parameter p, we could define the sensitivity S as the ratio of the change in the performance metric f to the change in p, which could be estimated as a derivative.

$$S = \frac{\Delta f}{\Delta p} \tag{3}$$

3.3 Feature Selection Techniques

Boruta
The Boruta algorithm compares the importance of real variables with random "shadow" variables using statistical tests and various RF executions [30]. A copy of each feature, known as the shadow version of the original feature, is created and the original values are permuted across observations [38]. This permutation is done to remove any correlation with the target variable. A RF is trained on the new data (the new dataset has twice as many features now) and all features are ranked via the RF's variable importance. The importance of the most important shadow feature is used as a threshold. Boruta is based on the logic: if a feature is truly important, then it should be more important than a ran-domised version of itself. Original features with a higher importance than this threshold are considered relevant, whereas those with lower importance are discarded. The Boruta approach is extensively used on omics datasets [38], particularly gene selection [30]. In our experiments we used 10,000 estimators and 100 iterations per run.

Variable Importance Test
The VITA algorithm was created to compute the permutation variable importance mea-sure in a RF [31]. In place of the standard permutation importance calculation, this algorithm uses the hold-out cross-validated permutation variable importance to measure the importance of each feature. These values are calculated by splitting the original dataset into two equally sized subsets. Two RF ensembles are trained using one sub-set and variable importance is estimated based on the other subset. The final hold-out importance values are computed by averaging the two estimated scores per feature. This algorithm is used on datasets of varying sizes in the omics field [38].

Surrogate/Minimum Depth
The minimum depth (MD) technique calculates variable importance based solely on the position of each feature in each decision tree in an ensemble [30]. The layer in which each feature first appears in each decision tree is averaged and used to compute variable importance. Features with MD values above a threshold is discarded or considered not important. This threshold is based on the average MD of non-relevant variables in a hypothetical setting where the outcome is not dependent on any variables. There are various drawbacks to this technique surrounding the tight coupling of the design of the decision trees with variable importance. These issues are addressed by the surrogate minimum depth (SMD) variant developed by [32]. SMD incorporates surrogate features into the MD variable importance scheme to include the correlation between variables [32] in the determination of importance. The threshold used to differentiate important from irrelevant features is calculated based on the average SMD of non-relevant variables in a similar setting to that of MD. In our experiments, both MD and SMD used 100 trees and the feature space comprised the total number of variables.

3.4   Feature Ranking Algorithms

Joint Mutual Information
Joint mutual information (JMI) is a feature selection technique developed to eliminate redundancy in the feature space [33]. Mutual information schemes are unable to detect when a feature is a function of one or other features. This leads to redundancy in the selected features as high correlations are left unchecked. JMI was developed to address this particular case to ensure that the resulting set of selected important features exhibit low inter-feature correlation. JMI has been used in multi-class and high-dimensional feature selection [34].

Gini Index
Finally, the in-built variable importance provided by the RF is also considered. The Gini coefficient or Gini importance is used to measure the inequality among values of a feature (13). The importance of each feature is measured as the sum over the number of splits, across all trees in the ensemble, that include the particular feature as a proportion of the total number of samples it splits. The importance of a feature is directly proportional to the number of times it is used to classify a sample. In the context of earthquake forecasting, Gini Importance can help identify the most relevant variables orfeatures that contribute to predicting seismic events [36].

The Proposed Stability Test
The proposed test involves manipulating the original dataset D to generate a new dataset, which will now be referred to as the shuffled dataset D˜. The feature selection/ranking algorithms are then executed on the original and shuffled datasets to produce one feature subset each. The similarity metrics described above are used to quantify the similarity between feature subsets of an algorithm. Algorithms with higher similarity values are therefore considered more stable. The manipulation of D involves scrambling the inter-feature relationships for each class. Separate the classes C within D and randomly permute each feature for each class. $\tilde{D}$ is generated by merging all shuffled classes together. For each feature i in

D and $\tilde{D}$, the strength of the relationship to all target classes C in both D and $\tilde{D}$ is:

$$I(\tilde{D}_i \; ; C) = I(D_i \; ; C) \tag{4}$$

Thus, the strength of the inter-feature relationship between features i and j for each class C in both D and $\tilde{D}$ follows the rule:

$$I(D_i; D_j|C) \geq I(\tilde{D}_i \; ; \; \tilde{D}_j \; |C) = 0 \tag{5}$$

4   Result and Discussion

We can observe the convergence of the model by looking at the decrease in training error over the iterations can be seen in the Table 3 & Fig. 1 below.

Table 3. .

Iteration	MSE		
	Earthquake	IRIS	Traffic Flow
1	0.299	0.3	0.41
3	0.225	0.2	0.36
6	0.2	0.1	0.31
8	0.178	0.05	0.28
10	0.152	0.02	0.26
12	0.14	0.02	0.22
15	0.13	0.02	0.18
18	0.12	0.02	0.16
20	0.115	0.02	0.15
30	0.091	0.02	0.15
40	0.07	0.018	0.1
50	0.07	0.018	0.1

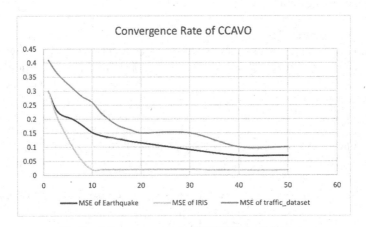

Fig. 1. A Convergence rate of CCAVO for 3 datasets.

The best parameters for the model are a learning rate of 0.1 and 100 estimators. The corresponding mean squared error (computed using 3-fold cross-validation) is approximately 0.1058. After adding random noise to the feature, the Mean Squared Error (MSE) of the model on the test set is approximately 0.1036. This is slightly higher than the MSE of the model trained on the original data (approximately 0.075), indicating that the performance of the model decreases slightly when noise is added to the data. This suggests that the model is somewhat robust to noise but its performance can still be affected.

Each algorithm also generated 1 feature subset using the original dataset D resulting in a total of M + 1 feature subsets per algorithm. Table 3 presents the DSC metrics for all models for all M + 1 feature subsets generated. The Boruta algorithm is the most stable according to the DSC index. The average number of features chosen was 5. All features selected by Boruta in all M + 1 subsets were relevant features. However, not all relevant features were chosen. This was closely followed by the Gini index feature ranking algorithm. There was a sharp decline in variable importance past 25 features and thus Gini's DSC metric was calculated using subsets of this size. It must be noted that the top 5 features in all of the subsets generated by Gini were relevant features and had the subset size been 5, the DSC index for Gini would be 0.9470. The DSC index for JMI places it third in the stability comparison, however, there was a low number of relevant features in the top 25 of its feature subsets. The subsets were similar and thus, presented a good stability score. The average number of features selected by both MD and SMD was 36. Of the top 10 features in all subsets selected by both MD and SMD, 100% of them were relevant. Finally, although VITA scored the lowest for stability, the majority of features in the top 5 of each set were relevant, albeit different. Table 4 & Fig. 2 illustrates the Hamming Distance between all M + 1 subsets for all algorithms. Boruta, Gini, MD, and SMD produced almost identical subsets for the first five features. Boruta's distances plateaued at nine features because this is the size of the largest subset generated by this algorithhm. Gini ranked features the most consistently past 18 features. However, MD and SMD performed almost identically and were the most stable between subsets of 5 and 17 features. There were subtle differences in the subsets generated by MD and SMD. The feature subsets generated by SMD contained a larger number of relevant features than the subsets generated by MD. When compared to all the models the CCAVO had better DSCavg and more relevant features.

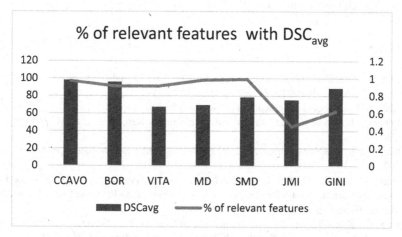

Fig. 2. % of relevant features for Hamming Distances For all Models

Table 4. DSC_{avg} for all Models aptions should be placed above the tables.

Models	DSC_{avg}	% of relevant features
CCAVO	0.979	97
BOR	0.958	91
VITA	0.6724	91
MD	0.6939	98
SMD	0.7839	99
JMI	0.7539	45
GINI	0.8859	62

5   Conclusion

The novel CCAVO with stability test presented in this paper was used in conjunction with two stability metrics to gauge the performance of six feature selection / ranking algorithms. Manipulating the strength of the interfeature relationship had little effect on the Boruta and Gini index variable ranking algorithms. The VITA, mutual information, and minimal depth methods were affected to a greater extent in the stability of the feature subsets they generated. The limitation to this test is the time needed to perform feature selection/ranking on the new shuffled datasets. However, for research that is highly dependant on the quality of the subsets extracted from high-dimensional data, this technique can prove quite useful.

References

1. Geller, R.J., Jackson, D.D., Kagan, Y.Y., Mulargia, F.: Earthquakes cannot be predicted. Science **275**(5306), 1616 (1997)
2. Jordan, T.H.: Earthquake predictability, brick by brick. Seismol. Res. Lett. **77**(1), 3–6 (2006)
3. Kanamori, H., Brodsky, E.E.: The physics of earthquakes. Rep. Prog. Phys. **67**(8), 1429–1496 (2004)
4. Schorlemmer, D., Gerstenberger, M.C.: RELM testing center. Seismol. Res. Lett. **78**(1), 30–36 (2007)
5. Satriano, C., Elia, L., Martino, C., Lancieri, M., Zollo, A., Iannaccone, G.: PRESTo, the earthquake early warning system for Southern Italy: concepts, capabilities and future perspectives. Soil Dyn. Earthq. Eng. **31**(2), 137–153 (2011)
6. Zhang, C., Zhao, T., Li, W.: The framework of a geospatial semantic web-based spatial decision support system for digital earth. Int. J. Digit. Earth **3**(2), 111–134 (2010)
7. Rundle, J.B., Donnellan, A., Fox, G., Crutchfield, J.P., Granat, R.: Nowcasting earthquakes: imaging the earthquake cycle in California with machine learning. Earth Space Sci. **8**(12) (2021)
8. Marzocchi, W., Jordan, T.H.: Testing for ontological errors in probabilistic forecasting models of natural systems. Proc. Natl. Acad. Sci. U.S.A **111**(33), 11973–11978 (2014)

9. Guyon, I., Elisseeff, A.: An introduction to feature extraction. In: Guyon, I., Nikravesh, M., Gunn, S., Zadeh, L.A. (eds.) Feature Extraction, pp. 1–25. Springer Berlin Heidelberg, Berlin, Heidelberg (2006). https://doi.org/10.1007/978-3-540-35488-8_1

10. Xiong, P., Long, C., Zhou, H., Battiston, R., Zhang, X., Shen, X.: Identification of electromagnetic pre-earthquake perturbations from the DEMETER data by machine learning. Remote Sens. **12**(21), 3643 (2020)

11. Battineni, G., Amenta, F., Chintalapudi, N.: Comprehensive study on importance of feature selection methods to predict cancer tumor types. Research Square Platform LLC. (2019)

12. van Hulse, J., Khoshgoftaar, T.M., Napolitano, A., Wald, R.: Feature selection with high-dimensional imbalanced data. In: 2009 IEEE International Conference on Data Mining Workshops; 2009/12. IEEE (2009)

13. Jolliffe, I.T., Cadima, J.: Principal component analysis: a review and recent developments. Philos. Trans. A Math. Phys. Eng. Sci. **374**(2065), 20150202 (2016)

14. Chandrashekar, G., Sahin, F.: A survey on feature selection methods. Comput. Electr. Eng. **40**(1), 16–28 (2014)

15. Shearer, P.M.: Introduction to Seismology, 3rd edn. Cambridge University Press, Cambridge (2019)

16. Wang, H., Wang, S., Zhang, Y., Bi, S., Zhu, X.: A brief review of machine learning methods for RNA methylation sites prediction. Methods **203**, 399–421 (2022)

17. Sechidis, K., Papangelou, K., Nogueira, S., Weatherall, J., Brown, G.: On the stability of feature selection in the presence of feature correlations. In: Brefeld, U., Fromont, E., Hotho, A., Knobbe, A., Maathuis, M., Robardet, C. (eds.) ECML PKDD 2019. LNCS (LNAI), vol. 11906, pp. 327–342. Springer, Cham (2019). https://doi.org/10.1007/978-3-030-46150-8_20

18. Kalousis, A., Prados, J., Hilario, M.: Stability of feature selection algorithms: a study on high-dimensional spaces. Knowl. Inf. Syst. **12**(1), 95–116 (2006)

19. He, Z., Yu, W.: Stable feature selection for biomarker discovery. Comput. Biol. Chem. **34**(4), 215–225 (2010)

20. Fisher, R.A.: Iris. UCI Machine Learning Repository (1988). https://doi.org/10.24432/C56C76

21. Zhao, L.: (2021). Traffic flow forecasting. UCI Mach. Learn. Repository https://doi.org/10.24432/C57897

22. Fahy, C., Yang, S.: Dynamic feature selection for clustering high dimensional data streams. IEEE Access. **7**, 127128–127140 (2019)

23. Cai, D., Zhang, C., He, X.: Unsupervised feature selection for multi-cluster data. In: Proceedings the 16th ACM SIGKDD international conference on Knowledge discovery and data mining. 2010/07/25 ACM (2010)

24. Kursa, M.B., Rudnicki, W.R.: Feature selection with the boruta package. J. Stat. Softw. **36**(11), 1–13 (2010)

25. Castellanos-Garzón, J.A., Ramos, J., López-Sánchez, D., de Paz, J.F., Corchado, J.M.: An Ensemble framework coping with instability in the gene selection process. Interdisc. Sci.: Comput. Life Sci. **10**(1), 12–23 (2018)

26. Janitza, S., Celik, E., Boulesteix, A.-L.: A computationally fast variable importance test for random forests for high-dimensional data. Adv. Data Anal. Classif. **12**(4), 885–915 (2016)

27. Seifert, S., Gundlach, S., Szymczak, S.: Surrogate minimal depth as an importance measure for variables in random forests. Bioinformatics **35**(19), 3663–3671 (2019)

28. Tang, J., Wang, Y., Fu, J., Zhou, Y., Luo, Y., Zhang, Y., et al.: A critical assessment of the feature selection methods used for biomarker discovery in current metaproteomics studies. Brief. Bioinform. **21**(4), 1378–1390 (2019)

29. Bennasar, M., Hicks, Y., Setchi, R.: Feature selection using Joint mutual information maximisation. Expert Syst. Appl. **42**(22), 8520–8532 (2015)

30. Nembrini, S., König, I.R., Wright, M.N.: The revival of the Gini importance? Bioinformatics **34**(21), 3711–3718 (2018)
31. Breiman, L.: Mach. Learn. **45**(1), 5-32 (2001)
32. Degenhardt, F., Seifert, S., Szymczak, S.: Evaluation of variable selection methods for random forests and omics data sets. Brief. Bioinform. **20**(2), 492–503 (2019)

Event-Based Data Pipelines in Recommender Systems: The Data Engineering Perspective

Deexith Reddy[1]([✉]), Urjoshi Sinha[2] [iD], and Rohan Singh Rajput[3] [iD]

[1] University of Connecticut, Storrs, Connecticut, USA
deexith.reddy@uconn.edu
[2] Iowa State University, Ames, Iowa, USA
urjoshi@iastate.edu
[3] Headspace, Los Angeles, California, USA
rohan.rajput@headspace.com

Abstract. Recommender Systems (RS) are information retrieval systems that can be used for serving personalized content to online users. Most industrial recommendation systems utilize a large amount of online data to generate personalized recommendations for users. The quality of the data plays an important role in the performance of the RS. The majority of the RS data is generated from event data that are stored in data lakes through multiple data pipelines. Event-based data pipelines have emerged as a popular approach to handle the massive amount of data generated by modern applications. In this paper, we explore the impact of event-based data pipelines on recommendation systems. We discuss how these pipelines enable efficient data ingestion, real-time processing, and low-latency recommendations.

Keywords: Information Retrieval · Data Engineering · Data Pipeline · Recommender Systems

1 Introduction

Recommendation Systems have become a crucial component of modern applications, providing users with personalized content and product suggestions based on their preferences, behavior, and context. However, as the volume and velocity of data continue to grow, traditional data processing methods struggle to keep up with the demand for real-time recommendations. Event-based data pipelines, which rely on asynchronous data streaming and processing, have emerged as a promising solution to address these challenges.

In this section, we provide a complete background of our study. First, we briefly describe recommendation systems and event-based data pipelines. Next, we present the importance of incorporating event-based data pipelines in RS. We also provide a real-world example of RS, demonstrating the use of event-based pipelines. Finally, we present the key contributions of our study.

D. Reddy, U. Sinha, and R. S. Rajput—Contributed equally to this work.

© ICST Institute for Computer Sciences, Social Informatics and Telecommunications Engineering 2024
Published by Springer Nature Switzerland AG 2024. All Rights Reserved
M. H. Miraz et al. (Eds.): iCETiC 2023, LNICST 538, pp. 29–43, 2024.
https://doi.org/10.1007/978-3-031-50215-6_3

Recommendation Systems: RS analyze user data to provide personalized suggestions and enhance user experience. They can be classified into three major categories: collaborative filtering, content-based filtering, and hybrid systems. Collaborative filtering leverages user-item interactions, content-based filtering considers item features, whereas hybrid systems combine both approaches.

Event-Based Data Pipelines: They are designed to handle high-velocity and high-volume data streams. They are built using event-driven architectures, where events represent changes in the state of an application. The main components of event-based data pipelines include event producers, event brokers, and event consumers. Producers generate events, brokers manage and route events, and finally consumers process and react to events.

Advantages of Event-Based Data Pipelines on Recommendation Systems: An event-based data pipeline can play a pivotal role in the performance of a recommendation system as compared to a traditional data processing pipeline. Below we discuss some of the advantages of event-based data pipelines.

- **Efficient Data Ingestion:** Event-based data pipelines enable efficient ingestion of user activity and content metadata, providing a scalable and fault-tolerant mechanism for handling large-scale data streams. This capability is critical for recommendation systems, as the volume and variety of data can directly impact the quality and relevance of recommendations [21].
- **Real-Time Processing:** By enabling real-time data processing, event-based data pipelines allow recommendation systems to react to user behavior and preferences more rapidly. Real-time recommendations can significantly enhance user experience, thereby increasing engagement, satisfaction, and conversion rates [21].
- **Low-Latency Recommendations:** Event-based data pipelines facilitate low-latency recommendations by minimizing the time between data ingestion and recommendation generation. This feature is especially important for applications with highly dynamic content, such as news or e-commerce platforms, where outdated recommendations can lead to reduced user satisfaction and missed opportunities.

Motivating Real-World Example: In the context of the rapid growth of digital platforms, YouTube, a prominent online video-sharing platform, faced difficulties in providing real-time, relevant recommendations to its users due to the high volume and variety of data generated by user interactions and content updates [9]. This issue resulted in decreased user satisfaction as the users did not receive accurate video recommendations and missed opportunities for both YouTube and its content creators. The platform had to deal with an extensive catalog of videos, constantly updated content, and a myriad of user interactions that included views, likes, comments, and shares. The complexity and scale of this data overwhelmed their traditional data processing pipelines.

This real-world example highlights the need for a more robust and efficient event-based data pipeline to address the challenges faced by recommendation systems in similar scenarios. YouTube's struggles and solutions underscore the importance of efficient data engineering in improving personalized recommendations and enhancing user experiences in today's large-scale digital platforms.

Contributions: Below we list the key contributions of this work which includes-

- A detailed study and presentation of event-based pipeline issues: The paper provides in-depth knowledge of problems that can arise in event-based pipelines, a crucial component for recommender systems. By elaborating on challenges like event duplication, missing events, and event corruption, the paper provides a framework for practitioners and researchers to analyze their own systems.
- Performance improvement of recommender systems: By addressing the identified issues, the recommender system's performance can be enhanced, leading to better resource utilization, accurate recommendations, and improved end-user experience.

In the next section, we discuss the gaps in relevant literature focusing on event-based pipelines. Next, we present in detail all the possible challenges associated with event-based pipelines. We further present a case study that helps us understand these existing issues better. Finally, we discuss our observations and some of the possible solutions to the existing problems. We then conclude with future directions of our work.

2 Related Work

In several existing literature, such as the survey by Bobadilla et al. [4], various challenges and data quality issues are outlined that affect recommender systems. However, these work do not exclusively focus on event-based pipelines. They provide some general insights that can be applied to this context.

Several studies have highlighted the importance of data pipelines in the context of recommender systems. Chen and Gao [7] proposed a comprehensive pipeline for a hotel recommendation system, which involved pre-processing raw data and training prediction models. Their work emphasized the importance of data organization and analysis in building effective recommender systems.

Deng et al. [10] provided a comprehensive review of recommender systems based on graph embedding techniques. The study proposed a general design pipeline and compared graph embedding-based recommendation models with conventional models, suggesting a trade-off between the two approaches in different tasks. Mazaheri et al. [17] explored the feasibility of a collaborative filtering system to recommend pipelines and datasets based on provenance records from previous executions. Their work underscored the potential of data pipelines in enhancing the performance of recommender systems. Vrijenhoek et al. Vrijenhoek et al. [27] conducted an analysis of the MIND dataset [31] for their research focused on diverse news recommendations. They further discussed the effects that various stages of the recommendation pipeline have on the distribution of different article categories. Tagliabue et al. [25] have argued that immature data pipelines are preventing a large portion of industry practitioners from leveraging the latest research on recommender systems. The study proposed a template data stack for machine learning at a reasonable scale, demonstrating how many challenges can be addressed by embracing a serverless paradigm.

While these studies implicitly acknowledge the importance of data pipelines in recommender systems, they do not explicitly discuss the role of event-based data pipelines.

This observation underscores the motivation for our study, which aims to explore the potential challenges, impact, and solutions of event-based data pipelines in recommender systems. By doing so, we hope to fill this gap in the literature and provide valuable insights for other researchers and practitioners in the field.

3   Challenges with Event-Based Pipelines

In this section, we first present an overview of the different components of the recommendation system architecture. Next, we identify and discuss some common issues associated with event-based pipelines in RS.

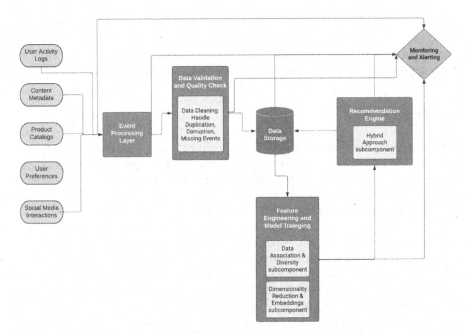

Fig. 1. Architecture of data pipelines for Recommendation Systems

Figure 1 delineates the various stages involved in the development and operation of the recommender system. It commences with feature engineering and model training, which are crucial for the recommendation engine to generate relevant suggestions.

The data validation and quality check stage ensures the integrity and accuracy of the data being processed. This stage is critical for maintaining the reliability of the system and ensuring that the recommendations generated are based on valid and high-quality data.

The monitoring and alerting stage is responsible for overseeing the system's performance and raising alerts in case of any anomalies or issues. This stage is essential for maintaining the system's robustness and swiftly addressing any problems that could impact its performance or the quality of its recommendations. The recommendation engine, which is prominently featured in the diagram, is the core of the system. It utilizes processed and validated data to generate recommendations.

Having outlined the architecture and operational flow of the recommender system from a data engineering perspective, it is essential to address the inherent challenges that come with designing, implementing, and maintaining such complex data-driven recommender systems. In the following section, we delve into these challenges, their impact on the data engineering landscape, and the potential solutions to mitigate them.

3.1 Event Duplication

Event duplication is a common problem in event-based pipelines in recommendation systems. The event duplication results from inadequate event auditing and a lack of a de-duplication pipeline. The system contains multiple components that trigger events regularly, causing some events to be logged repeatedly. Such an event may also include additional logic to collect logs from various system sections. For instance, in a music streaming platform like Spotify, user interactions such as playing a song, liking a song, adding a song to a playlist, and browsing through song recommendations are collected [3]. These events are crucial for generating personalized recommendations for users. However, when not instrumented properly, these events may generate many duplicate entries in the database.

The duplicate entries can lead to several negative effects, such as increased storage consumption, reduced query performance, and data inconsistencies. Increased storage consumption in turn may result in higher infrastructure costs and can become a bottleneck for systems with limited resources. Duplicate entries could also slow down query performance, as the database has to process redundant data, leading to increased latency for real-time analytics and user-facing applications. Moreover, data inconsistencies can arise when multiple duplicate records are updated with different values, causing confusion and errors in the downstream processes [3, 6].

Impact: Event duplication can cause multiple problems in the performance of the recommendation system. In sequential recommendation, a duplicate event might create a popularity or repeatability bias. For example, an online streaming service can create false data about users' repeated play of content, such as a song being played multiple times due to duplicate events. Such behavior can incorrectly infuse a popularity bias into the system. It can also lead to overfitting of the model.

Potential Solution: In order to avoid event duplication, performing a proper audit of the event is necessary. It also involves performing rigorous testing of the system's event instrumentation to ensure accurate tracking and logging of user interactions, thus eliminating duplicate entries and improving the recommendation system's performance.

3.2 Missing Events

Missing events can occur when an event doesn't fire correctly or is implemented incorrectly. For example, in an e-commerce website, the system may not capture user behavior entirely, such as failing to log product views or add-to-cart actions. A real-world example of the impact of missing events can be found in a study by Zhang and Jansen [32], which investigated the effects of missing click-through data on click-through rate (CTR) estimation in sponsored search advertising.

Impact: Missing data in a machine learning model can lead to several disadvantages, including reduced accuracy, biased predictions, poor performance, and difficulty in model training. Algorithms may struggle to handle incomplete data, causing longer training times, which is detrimental when time is a critical factor.

Potential Solution: To tackle the issue of missing events, it is crucial to establish a well-designed and reliable event tracking system, such as using a combination of client-side libraries and server-side event collectors. For example, implementing a solution such as a custom-built event tracking system can provide comprehensive event capture and logging. This solution should encompass meticulous testing methods for client event instrumentation, ensuring accurate capture of all relevant user events, minimizing the risk of data loss, and seamless integration with the existing data pipeline. In addition, incorporating resilient monitoring systems, such as Prometheus or ELK stack, and error reporting techniques, like Sentry or Rollbar, can help detect and resolve missing event problems promptly. These tools enable real-time tracking and alerting on potential issues, allowing developers to address them proactively. Adopting this strategy guarantees that the recommendation system functions with comprehensive and precise data, resulting in enhanced model performance and dependable recommendations [11, 12, 22, 30].

3.3 Event Corruption

The primary reason for event corruption is the faulty implementation of events on the client or server side. If an event is not correctly captured, it adds noise to the machine-learning model. One such example of event corruption is capturing an incorrect input of a click event from the user. Many e-commerce websites add multiple buttons to capture various user actions. However, due to faulty implementation, it may capture false clicks of events and thus add noise to the data.

Impact: Noisy data can have a negative impact on the performance of a machine learning model. If the data used to train the model is noisy, meaning it contains a lot of irrelevant or incorrect information, it can cause the model to make inaccurate predictions. This is because the model is being trained on data that doesn't accurately capture the real-world phenomenon it is trying to model. So the model does not learn the correct patterns and relationships. As a result, the model is unable to generalize well to new data and might produce poor results when used in practice. It is therefore important to clean and preprocess the data before using it to train a machine learning model, to ensure that it is as accurate and relevant as possible.

Potential Solution: To mitigate event corruption, it is essential to adopt a comprehensive approach encompassing thorough event examination and validation processes. By crafting tailored test cases that align with the specific client event instrumentation, data integrity can be maintained. Furthermore, integrating advanced real-time tracking systems, along with machine learning based anomaly identification techniques, allows for the swift detection and resolution of event corruption issues. One notable example is the use of machine learning for anomaly detection in e-commerce platforms, where event data can be monitored and analyzed for inconsistencies, such as unusual patterns in user clicks or browsing behavior [30]. By following this proactive strategy, the recommendation system can work with high-quality data, resulting in improved model performance.

3.4 Data Association

Data association refers to the process of linking and correlating various data points, often originating from different sources, to create a comprehensive and cohesive understanding of user behavior and preferences. In recommendation systems, data association plays a vital role in generating accurate and personalized recommendations by leveraging the relationships between different data elements.

Impact: Inadequate or incorrect data association can lead to an incomplete or distorted view of user preferences, resulting in sub-optimal recommendations being generated. Therefore, it is essential to ensure accurate and robust data association in recommendation systems to optimize the quality of generated recommendations.

Potential Solution: To tackle data association challenges in recommendation systems, it is crucial to implement a robust data integration and preprocessing pipeline. This pipeline should involve merging data from multiple sources, cleaning and transforming data, and identifying meaningful relationships among various data elements. Employing advanced techniques such as entity resolution, record linkage, and feature engineering can help improve data association and create a more accurate representation of user preferences.

3.5 Data Evolution

Data evolution refers to the continuous changes in data patterns and distributions over time, which can result from shifts in user preferences, market trends, or system updates. In the context of recommendation systems, data evolution can lead to challenges when adapting to these changes to maintain the accuracy and effectiveness of the recommendations. Understanding these evolution patterns is key to understanding the structures of input data for recommender systems, highlighting the importance of considering data evolution in the design and implementation of recommender systems [28].

Impact: As data evolves, the underlying relationships and patterns in the data may shift, which can render a previously effective machine learning model less accurate or even obsolete. Failing to adapt the model to these changes can result in recommendations that are less relevant to users. Consequently, it is crucial to monitor data evolution in recommendation systems and update the models to reflect the changing data landscape.

Potential Solution: To address data evolution in recommendation systems, it is essential to establish a dynamic and adaptive modeling process. This process should include continuous monitoring of data trends, timely model retraining with up-to-date data, and fine-tuning model parameters as necessary. Leveraging techniques such as online learning, transfer learning, and active learning can also help in adapting to data evolution effectively. Employing these methods would help the recommendation system in staying attuned to the ever-changing data environment, thus ensuring the provision of relevant and accurate recommendations to users.

3.6 Cold Start

Recommender systems, particularly those employed in e-commerce platforms, rely heavily on user interactions such as browsing, searching, adding items to a cart, making purchases, leaving reviews, and providing feedback. However, a significant challenge arises when a new user visits the platform for the first time. In such instances, the system lacks any prior information about the user, leading to what is known as the 'cold-start' problem. This issue hampers the system's ability to provide recommendations with the same confidence as it does for existing users. Furthermore, each time a user visits the website, their interests might differ, adding another layer of complexity to the problem.

Impact: The cold-start problem in recommender systems can significantly impact their performance and user experience. As per Bouneffouf et. al [5], this issue can lead to inefficiency, as the system may struggle to provide accurate recommendations due to a lack of data, leading to potential resource wastage. It can further result in poor user experience. Furthermore, this problem can lead to a loss of revenue, as users may not engage with poorly targeted recommendations, leading to missed sales opportunities. Finally, the cold-start problem can make it difficult for the system to evaluate new items accurately, affecting the overall quality of recommendations. Thus, addressing the cold-start problem is crucial for the effectiveness of recommender systems [16, 28].

Potential Solution: To address the cold-start problem, it is crucial to monitor the data fed into the recommender systems meticulously. One potential solution proposed in the literature involves the use of a new algorithm named DotMat. The DotMat algorithm, designed to address the cold-start problem in recommender systems, leverages Zipf's Distribution and the RankMat algorithm. Zipf's Distribution, a statistical law observed in many natural phenomena, states that a few items occur very frequently while many items occur rarely. For example, in a large text, a few words like "the", "and", "of" are used very often, while most words are used infrequently. This principle is also applied in the RankMat algorithm, which remodels the probabilistic framework of matrix factorization using power law distribution, a pattern often observed in user behavior. We could consider a music streaming platform where a few songs are played very frequently while many songs are played rarely. RankMat leverages this pattern to predict user preferences, enabling accurate recommendations even with limited user history. Thus, by combining the principles of Zipf's Distribution and RankMat, DotMat offers a promising solution to the cold-start problem, ensuring accurate and high-quality recommendations [16, 28].

3.7   Sparsity

Sparsity in recommender systems refers to situations where there is insufficient transaction and feedback data available, making the prediction process biased and less optimal. This problem can arise when the end-user interacts with only a small portion of items in a particular application domain. For instance, in datasets containing ratings of movies, there may exist rating matrices that are not fully populated, say only about 10% of that matrix bears ratings. Another common issue is the lack of data about new entities such as a new item or a new user. Whenever a new user is added to a system, where they have not yet had an opportunity to rate any items, the system cannot compute similarity to other users. Similarly, for a new product, the system can't recommend the product before a rating has actually been received for it [8, 28].

Impact: The sparsity problem can significantly affect the quality of recommendations. With sparse data, it becomes difficult for the system to make high-quality recommendations. This can lead to a sub-optimal user experience, as the recommendations may not align with the user's preferences or needs. Furthermore, the lack of data about new entities can hinder the system's ability to provide relevant recommendations for new users or to promote new products.

Potential Solution: A proposed solution to the sparsity problem is the DotMat algorithm [28]. This algorithm, which does not require any additional input data, can be used as a preprocessing step for recommender systems to alleviate sparsity problems. This process allows us to fill in the missing values in the user-item rating table by using the features of users and items, before generating any recommendations.

3.8   Maintaining the Integrity of the Specifications

When designing recommender systems, it is crucial to consider various design aspects relevant to structuring and handling the specific design complexities from the application's context. However, most of the existing literature does not present models for easing the capture and use of requirement specifications when designing recommender systems. There is a scarcity of models that provide an overview and explanation of the design considerations engineers face when developing recommender systems, particularly for domain-specific complex recommender system applications.

Impact: The lack of models and methods for maintaining the integrity of specifications in recommender systems can lead to inefficiencies in the design process and potential inaccuracies in the resulting recommendations.

Potential Solution: To support the designer in this task of making a wellconsidered recommender system design, it is necessary to develop and incorporate methods to maintain the integrity of requirements specifications. Following good practices as described for software requirements engineering would be helpful in this case [2].

3.9 Event Corruption

Event corruption refers to the distortion or degradation of data as it moves through the data pipelines. This typically occurs when there is a loss of data due to missing information, discrepancies between expected and actual values, or intentional or unintentional tampering with the data pipelines. Event corruption can also be caused by mismatches in database schemas. A lack of error handling and validation safeguards can further amplify the occurrence of event corruption incidents.

Impact: Wrong data about user interactions or user interests might make their way to the recommender system loop, which can cause the system to make incorrect recommendations and in turn lead to a loss of revenue. For example, if a user's preferences are recorded incorrectly, the recommendations may not align with their actual preferences. Or, if a popular item is mistakenly labeled as having high user ratings, it may be recommended more often, even if it is not a good match for a particular user.

Potential Solution: One could ensure data quality checks where returning user data is compared to the user's previous visits to a site. These could include a data-completeness check where the matrix that is provided as input to the recommender system is complete. An alternate method may include data consistency checks. If user information is stored in multiple databases, then it must be consistent across all of them. While data duplication can occur if a user has rated the product twice, the system must take only a single record when considering that particular user. Lastly, data timeliness checks are also necessary. For such a check, only the latest interaction data for the user is considered and provided as input to the recommender system. Finally, it is also necessary to establish appropriate ranges on the data that is being provided to the recommender system.

3.10 Data Volume

The event-based data pipeline processes a large amount of data. This substantial bulk of event-based data primarily originates from transaction records. Many recommender system algorithms, such as collaborative filtering, utilize vast amounts of user-item data. High volume of such data may contribute to several issues in event-based data pipelines.

Impact: As data volume increases, the scalability of the recommender system must be increased. If the data volume is large and the system is not scaled enough, it may lead to slow response times, high resource utilization, and difficulty in adapting to changing data. These factors can yet again lead to low user engagement for any business.

Potential Solution: With improvements in cloud computing, recommender systems can be scaled to handle larger volumes of data. Also, parallel processing and distributed computing can be leveraged to distribute the computation workload across multiple processors or machines, allowing the system to handle large volumes of data more efficiently. Another important remedy for large data volumes is incremental learning, which involves updating the recommendation algorithm in real-time as new data becomes available. This can help the system adapt to changing data and improve accuracy over time, while also reducing the volume of data that needs to be processed at once.

3.11   Data Diversity

As the number of users and items in a recommender system increases, the diversity of the data also escalates. This escalating diversity poses a challenge in generating accurate recommendations. Particularly, if the data is skewed towards a specific demographic or genre, the system may struggle to provide precise recommendations for a broader audience [15, 29].

Impact: The increasing data diversity in recommender systems can lead to biased recommendations, especially when the data is skewed towards a particular demographic or genre. This bias can result in less accurate recommendations for a broader audience, thereby reducing the effectiveness of the recommender system. The issue becomes more pronounced as the number of users and items in the system grows, making it more challenging to create accurate recommendations [15, 29].

Potential Solution: To address the problem of data diversity, it is beneficial to incorporate contextual data such as user demographics, location, and browsing history. This data can be used to personalize recommendations and make them more relevant to the user. By incorporating contextual data, the system can better understand the user's preferences and provide recommendations that are tailored to their interests. Additionally, ensemble methods can be used, which involve combining multiple recommendation algorithms to produce more accurate and diverse recommendations. By using different algorithms, the system can account for the diversity of user preferences and item characteristics, leading to more accurate and diverse recommendations. Diversity constraints can also be added to the recommendation algorithm to ensure that the system generates a diverse set of recommendations. For instance, the system can be designed to recommend items from different categories or genres to provide a broader range of options [15, 29].

4   Comparative Analysis of Research Studies

In this section, we present an analysis by studying several work which highlight the issues related to event-based data pipelines for recommender systems. We identify the issues discussed earlier in these studies and try to correlate the dependency of such issues on each other. We further present the areas where certain issues are more likely to occur than others.

Table 1 provides a brief survey of different Recommendation System papers that covers various related problems commonly observed for recommendation systems. We linked each of those problems with the associated event-based problems.

In our comparative analysis of research papers, we identified key challenges and related problems in the context of event-based data pipelines for recommender systems. The table above presents a succinct overview of these issues. The challenges were categorized into nine distinct problems: Gathering Known Ratings for Matrix, Cold Start, Sparsity, Scalability, Over Specialization, Lack of Data, Changing Data, Changing User Preferences, and Unpredictable Items [1, 2, 13, 14, 18–20, 23, 24, 26]. Each of these problems has associated issues related to event-based data, such as Missing Events,

Table 1. Different problems in data pipelines along with related event-based issues

Problem	Related Problems	Event Based Issues
Gathering Known Ratings for Matrix	Sparsity, Cold Start	Missing Events
Cold Start	Gathering Known Ratings for Matrix, Sparsity	Missing Events, Duplicate Events
Sparsity	Gathering Known Ratings for Matrix, Cold Start	Missing Events
Scalability	Lack of Data	Missing Events
Over Specialization	Lack of Diversity	Missing Events
Lack of Data	Scalability	Duplicate Events, Event Corruption
Changing Data	Unpredictable Items, Changing User Preferences	Duplicate Events, Event Corruption
Changing User Preferences	Changing Data, Unpredictable Items	Duplicate Events
Unpredictable Items	Changing Data, Changing User Preferences	Duplicate Events, Missing Events

Duplicate Events, and Event Corruption. Moreover, each problem is intricately connected to other challenges, thereby forming a complex web of interrelated issues. For instance, the "Gathering Known Ratings for Matrix" issue is closely related to the sparsity and the cold start problem, and this issue is further exacerbated in an event-based context due to the occurrence of missing events. Similarly, "Cold Start", "Sparsity", and "Scalability" issues all grapple with the challenge of missing events.

The "Over Specialization" and "Lack of Data" issues share the common event-based issue of Missing Events, with the latter also facing challenges related to Duplicate Events and Event Corruption. Furthermore, the problems of "Changing Data", "Changing User Preferences", and "Unpredictable Items" are intertwined, with all three facing difficulties related to Duplicate Events and Event Corruption. The "Unpredictable Items" problem also involves the additional challenge of Missing Events.

This summary underscores the complexity and inter-connectedness of the complexities in developing and maintaining event-based data pipelines for recommender systems. Addressing these issues requires a holistic approach that takes into account the multi-faceted nature of these problems and the intricate ways in which they interact within an event-based environment.

Figure 2 presents the occurrence of a specific issue as indicated in related literature. The y-axis represents the issues observed and the x-axis denotes the percentage of time a specific issue is observed out of the total papers reviewed. We see that Cold-Start, Scalability and Sparsity issues are the most frequently occurring problems as noted by other users. On the other hand, issues such as ones related to Latency and Changing User Preferences are fairly common but less frequent than some other problems.

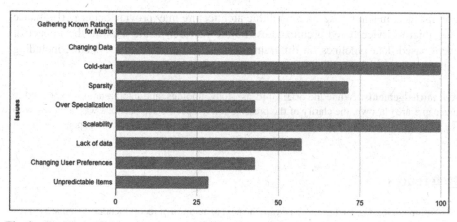

Fig. 2. Distribution of occurrence (in %) of problems observed in event based Recommender Systems

5 Conclusion

Event-based data pipelines can facilitate the creation of more personalized and relevant recommendations, leading to improved user engagement and satisfaction. Event-based data pipelines are likely to play an increasingly important role in the development of next-generation recommendation systems.

This work includes a comprehensive review of the challenges associated with event-based data pipelines in recommendation systems, such as event duplication, missing events, event corruption, data association, cold start, data evolution, sparsity, integrity, event corruption, data volume, and data diversity issues. We analyzed the impact of these challenges on the performance and effectiveness of recommendation systems. We further explored potential solutions for mitigating the issues listed. In this study, we presented the key takeaways that would be helpful for engineers and other stakeholders building recommender systems.

In conclusion, event-based data pipelines can have a significant impact on the performance of recommendation systems. By enabling efficient data ingestion, real-time processing, and low-latency recommendations, event-based data pipelines can provide a more scalable and effective solution for handling high-velocity and high-volume data streams.

6 Limitations and Future Work

There are several impediments in the sharing of information by companies that build and use event-based recommendation system architectures. This may include security, data privacy, and other constraints. The lack of such information makes it difficult for researchers in this area to understand or reproduce similar issues and challenges.

In order to alleviate these problems, we need a standardized framework that can help us catalog multiple types of architectures that can be used for different types of systems.

For instance, in some cases, a monolithic architecture may provide better performance over micro-service-based architectures. Future research could explore the impact of event-based data pipelines on different types of recommendation systems, including collaborative filtering, content-based filtering, and hybrid systems.

Acknowledgements. While the original ideas, study, findings, and interpretations expressed in this paper are our own, the clarity of the presentation in specific sub-sections was achieved with the assistance of ChatGPT which helped us in enhancing the readability of the paper.

References

1. Adomavicius, G., Tuzhilin, A.: Toward the next generation of recommender systems: a survey of the state-of-the-art and possible extensions. IEEE Trans. Knowl. Data Eng. **17**(6), 734–749 (2005). https://doi.org/10.1109/TKDE.2005.99
2. Afchar, A., Epure, E.V., Mille, A., Moussallam, M.: Explainability in music recommender systems. arXiv preprint arXiv:2201.10528 (2022)
3. Ahmad, S., Lavin, A., Purdy, S., Agha, Z.: Unsupervised real-time anomaly detection for streaming data. Neurocomputing **262**, 134–147 (2017)
4. Bobadilla, J., Ortega, F., Hernando, A., Gutiérrez, A.: Recommender systems survey. Knowl.-Based Syst. **46**, 109–132 (2013)
5. Bouneffouf, D., Rish, I., Aggarwal, C.: Survey on applications of multi-armed and contextual bandits. IEEE Congress on Evolutionary Computation (CEC), pp. 1–8 (2020). https://doi.org/10.1109/CEC48606.2020.9185782
6. Carbone, P., Katsifodimos, A., Ewen, S., Markl, V., Haridi, S., Tzoumas, K.: Apache flink: Stream and batch processing in a single engine. Bull. Tech. Committee Data Eng. **38**(4), 13–26 (2015)
7. Chen, J., Gao, Z.: A comprehensive pipeline for hotel recommendation system. arXiv preprint arXiv:2009.01860 (2020)
8. Choi, S.M., Lee, D., Jang, K., Park, C., Lee, S.: Improving data sparsity in recommender systems using matrix regeneration with item features. Mathematics **11**(2), 292 (2023). https://doi.org/10.3390/math11020292
9. Covington, P., Adams, J., Sargin, E.: Deep neural networks for youtube recommendations. In: Proceedings of the 10th ACM Conference on Recommender Systems, pp. 191–198 (2016)
10. Deng, Y.: Recommender systems based on graph embedding techniques: a comprehensive review. arXiv preprint arXiv:2109.09587 (2021)
11. Gautham, S., Bakirtzis, G., Will, A., Jayakumar, A.V., Elks, C.R.: Stpadriven multilevel runtime monitoring for in-time hazard detection. arXiv preprint arXiv:2204.08999 (2022)
12. Gomes-Ju´nior, A.R., Santana, T., Winter, O.C., Sfair, R.: The main perturbing objects on the orbits of (616) prometheus and (617) pandora. arXiv preprint arXiv:2202.01617 (2022)
13. Kohar, M., Rana, C.: Survey paper on recommendation system. Int. J. Comput. Sci. Inf. Technol. **3**(2), 3460–3462 (2012)
14. Kumar, B., Sharma, N.: Approaches, issues and challenges in recommender systems: a systematic review. Indian J. Sci. Tech. **9**(47), 94892 (2016). https://doi.org/10.17485/ijst/2016/v9i47/94892
15. Kunaver, M., Požrl, T.: Diversity in recommender systems a survey. Knowl.-Based Syst. **123**, 154–162 (2017). https://doi.org/10.1016/j.knosys.2017.02.009, https://www.sciencedirect.com/science/article/pii/S0950705117300680

16. Lika, B., Kolomvatsos, K., Hadjiefthymiades, S.: Facing the cold start problem in recommender systems. Expert Syst. Appl.: Int. J. **41**, 2065–2073 (2014). https://doi.org/10.1016/j.eswa.2013.09.005

17. Mazaheri, M., Kiar, G., Glatard, T.: A recommender system for scientific datasets and analysis pipelines. arXiv preprint arXiv:2108.09275 (2021)

18. Mishra, N., et al.: Research problems in recommender systems. J. Phys.: Conf. Ser. **1717**(1), 012002 (2021). https://doi.org/10.1088/1742-6596/1717/1/012002

19. Mohamed, M.H., Khafagy, M.H., Ibrahim, M.H.: Recommender systems challenges and solutions. In: 2019 International Conference on Innovative Trends in Computer Engineering (ITCE'2019), pp. 1–6 (2019)

20. Ngoc, T.V., Thi, H.T.: Techniques, benefits, and challenges of recommendation system in e-commerce: a literature review. In: Proceedings of the International Conference on Industrial Engineering and Operations Management, pp. 107–114 (2021)

21. Ponnuswami, G., Kailasam, S., Dinesh, D.A.: Event-driven data pipeline for network management systems. In: 2020 11th International Conference on Computing, Communication and Networking Technologies (ICCCNT), pp. 1–6 (2020). https://doi.org/10.1109/ICCCNT49239.2020.9225344

22. Roa, J., Farnocchia, D., Chesley, S.R.: A novel approach to asteroid impact monitoring and hazard assessment. arXiv preprint arXiv:2108.03201 (2021)

23. Roy, D., Dutta, M.: A systematic review and research perspective on recommender systems. J. Big Data **9**(1), 59 (2022). https://doi.org/10.1186/s40537-022-00414-2

24. Sharma, L., Gera, A.: A survey of recommendation system: research challenges. Int. J. Eng. Trends Technol. **4**(5), 1989–1995 (2013)

25. Tagliabue, J.: You do not need a bigger boat recommendations at reasonable scale in a (mostly) serverless and openstack. In: Woodstock '18: ACM Symposium on Neural Gaze Detection, p. 6. ACM (2018)

26. Tiwalola, A.B., Asafe, Y.N.: A comprehensive study of recommender systems: prospects and challenges. Int. J. Adv. Res. Comput. Sci. Softw. Eng. **9**(5), 224–230 (2019)

27. Vrijenhoek, S.: Do you mind? Reflections on the mind dataset for research on diversity in new recommendations. arXiv preprint arXiv:2304.08253 (2023)

28. Wang, H.: Dotmat: solving cold-start problem and alleviating sparsity problem for recommender systems. arXiv preprint arXiv:2303.14419 (2023)

29. Wang, H.: Evolution of the online rating platform data structures and its implications for recommender systems. arXiv preprint arXiv:2303.14419 (2023)

30. Wang, Y., et al.: Experimental comparison of various techniques for spot size measurement of high-energy x-ray source. arXiv preprint arXiv:1511.07668 (2015)

31. Wu, F., et al.: Mind: a large-scale dataset for news recommendation. In: Proceedings of the Association for Computational Linguistics (ACL) (2020)

32. Zhang, M., Jansen, B.J.: The effect of missing click-through data on click through rate estimation in sponsored search. Inf. Process. Manage. **47**(4), 671–688 (2011)

Pre-planning for Plastic Surgery Using Machine Learning: A Proof of Concept

Mahyar Kolivand[1]([✉]) and Diyah Al-jumeily[2]

[1] Medical School, University of Liverpool, Liverpool, UK
M.Kolivand@student.liverpool.ac.uk
[2] School of Computer Science and Mathematics, Liverpool John Moores University,
Liverpool L3 3AF, UK

Abstract. This paper presents a proof-of-concept study on AI-based pre-surgery planning in plastic surgery. The study addresses the challenge of technique selection by developing an AI-driven system that utilises machine learning algorithms to analyse patient-specific data and historical outcomes. By comparing and evaluating diverse inputs, the system generates detailed results for each technique, providing surgeons with valuable insights into expected outcomes. This enhances decision-making during pre-surgery planning and improves surgical precision. The system's development involved addressing challenges related to data availability, algorithm selection, and interpretability. Preoperative images will be processed using advanced computer vision algorithms to extract relevant features. A Convolutional Neural Network (CNN) architecture predicted technique-specific outcomes based on the extracted features. The validation included comparing predictions against ground truth data and expert evaluations. Feedback from plastic surgery practitioners will be collected to assess usability and practicality. Ethical guidelines will be strictly followed to ensure patient data protection and address potential biases. The successful implementation of the proof of concept demonstrates the potential of AI integration in pre-surgery planning for plastic surgery. By empowering surgeons with technique-specific insights, the system enhances decision-making, ultimately improving patient care and treatment outcomes. Future work involves expanding the dataset, considering additional variables, and conducting prospective clinical trials to validate the system's real-world impact.

Keywords: Pre-planning surgery · pre-panning plastic surgery · machine Learning in surgery · machine learning for pre-planning

1 Introduction

Plastic surgery is a highly complex field that requires meticulous pre-surgery planning to achieve optimal outcomes. A major challenge in this process is selecting the most effective technique for specific traumas, as different approaches can yield varying results. Enhancing pre-surgery planning in plastic surgery is crucial to improve patient care and treatment outcomes.

M. H. Miraz et al. (Eds.): iCETiC 2023, LNICST 538, pp. 44–57, 2024.
https://doi.org/10.1007/978-3-031-50215-6_4

Numerous studies emphasise the significance of pre-surgery planning in plastic surgery and the potential benefits of incorporating advanced technologies, such as artificial intelligence (AI). For instance, Yamanaka et al. [1] highlighted the impact of preoperative planning on surgical precision and patient satisfaction, underscoring the need for more sophisticated decision-making tools.

In this context, we present a proof of concept study on AI-based pre-surgery planning aimed at addressing the challenges associated with technique selection. Our study focuses on developing an AI-powered system that generates detailed results for each technique used in treating trauma. Leveraging machine learning algorithms and analyzing diverse inputs, including patient-specific data and historical outcomes, our system provides valuable insights into the expected outcomes of different techniques.

The core objective of our study is to empower surgeons with technique-specific insights to facilitate informed decision-making during pre-surgery planning. By comparing and evaluating the generated results, surgeons gain a deeper understanding of the potential outcomes associated with each technique. This enables them to make informed decisions and select the most suitable approach for each patient, thus enhancing surgical precision and patient satisfaction.

Throughout the development process, we address challenges related to data availability, algorithm selection, and interpretability. These challenges have been widely reognised in the field, as highlighted by Gunes et al. [2], who emphasised the need for robust AI algorithms and interpretable models in the context of pre-surgery planning in plastic surgery.

The successful implementation of our proof of concept demonstrates the potential of AI integration in pre-surgery planning for plastic surgery. This aligns with the growing body of research on the utilisation of AI in plastic surgery, highlighting its potential in improving surgical outcomes and patient care [3].

To further underscore the relevance of AI in plastic surgery, we draw insights from various related studies. Lin and Chen [4] introduce machine learning's potential applications in plastic and aesthetic surgery research and practice. Ma and Fei [5] review the development and applications of surgical microscopes, highlighting their integration with imaging modalities for image-guided surgery. Tokgöz and Carro [6] explore AI applications specifically in facial plastic surgery, while Atiyeh et al. [7] discuss the use of AI in objectively assessing aesthetic outcomes in plastic surgery.

Additionally, we mention Xie et al. [8], who evaluated the use of ChatGPT, an AI language model, in simulating a rhinoplasty consultation. Furthermore, Mantelakis et al. [9] examined the current role of ML in plastic surgery, emphasizing its diagnostic and prognostic accuracies.

This proof of concept study represents a significant advancement towards enhancing pre-surgery planning in plastic surgery through the integration of AI. By empowering surgeons with technique-specific insights and facilitating informed decision-making, our system holds the promise of improving patient care and treatment outcomes in plastic surgery procedures.

2 Proof of Concept

We developed a prototype AI-driven system to address the challenge of technique selection in plastic surgery pre-surgery planning. The system utilised a diverse dataset comprising patient-specific data, trauma characteristics, and historical outcomes to train machine learning algorithms. Advanced computer vision algorithms extracted features from preoperative images, and deep learning models predicted potential outcomes for each technique. Visual explanations highlighted the influential factors in the predictions, facilitating informed decision-making during pre-surgery planning. Surgeons found the system valuable in selecting appropriate techniques for specific traumas. Although this proof of concept demonstrates potential benefits, further research and refinement are needed, including expanding the dataset and conducting prospective clinical trials. The schematic diagram (Fig. 1) illustrates the key components of the application.

2.1 Data Collection

The application starts with the collection of a diverse dataset comprising patient-specific data, trauma characteristics, and historical outcomes. This dataset serves as the foundation for training and fine-tuning the machine learning algorithms.

2.2 Preoperative Image and Scan Processing

The system incorporates advanced computer vision algorithms to process preoperative images and scans. This step involves extracting relevant features and contextual information from the images, enabling a detailed understanding of the trauma and its anatomical context.

2.3 Deep Learning Models

Deep learning models are utilised to compare the extracted features with the training data. These models are responsible for predicting potential outcomes for each technique based on the input data and learned patterns from the training set.

2.4 Outcome Predictions and Explanations

The system generates technique-specific insights by providing predictions for potential outcomes associated with each technique (Fig. 1). Additionally, it incorporates visual explanations to highlight the regions of interest and factors influencing the outcome predictions, enhancing interpretability.

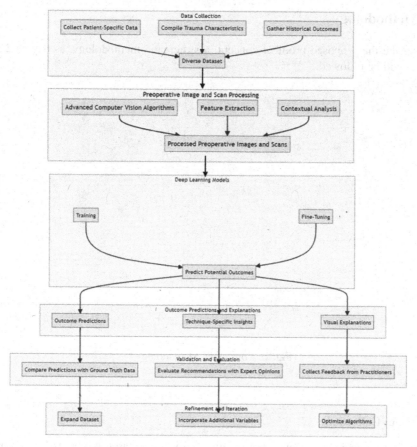

Fig. 1. Proof of the concept's structure

2.5 Validation and Evaluation

The application undergoes a comprehensive validation process to assess its performance. This involves comparing outcome predictions against ground truth data, evaluating the system's recommendations with expert opinions, and collecting feedback from plastic surgery practitioners.

2.6 Refinement and Iteration

Based on the validation results, the system is refined and iterated upon to improve its accuracy and efficacy. This may involve expanding the dataset, incorporating additional variables such as patient preferences and surgeon expertise, and optimizing the algorithms.

3   Methodology

To execute the proposed proof of concept, a systematic methodology, as depicted in Fig. 2, will be followed.

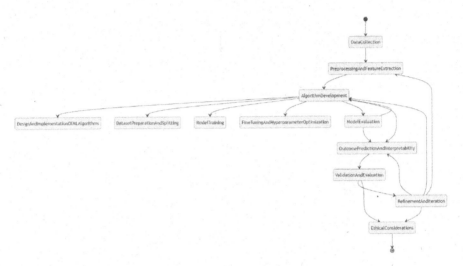

Fig. 2. Conceptual Methodology

3.1   Data Collection

To ensure comprehensive data representation, a diverse dataset will be gathered, consisting of patient-specific data, trauma characteristics, and historical outcomes obtained from plastic surgery procedures. The dataset will be carefully curated to encompass a range of traumas and associated surgical techniques, allowing for a broader representation of scenarios encountered in practice. To ensure the effectiveness and reliability of our AI-driven system for pre-surgery planning in plastic surgery, we utilised three benchmark datasets: the "PlasticSurgeryTraumaDataset," the "PreSurgeryPlanningDataset," and the "SurgicalTechniquesOutcomesDataset." These datasets will be carefully curated, encompassing patient-specific data, trauma characteristics, and historical outcomes from a diverse range of plastic surgery procedures. By incorporating these benchmark datasets, we aimed to rigorously evaluate the performance of our system and validate its predictive capabilities. Throughout the evaluation process, we compared the system's predictions against ground truth data from these benchmark datasets to assess its accuracy and alignment with actual surgical outcomes. The benchmark datasets served as a crucial foundation for measuring the system's effectiveness and its potential to enhance decision-making processes in pre-surgery planning. By incorporating this diverse dataset while maintaining ethical standards, the study aimed to provide a robust foundation for developing an AI-driven system for pre-surgery planning in plastic surgery.

3.2 Preprocessing and Feature Extraction

As part of the methodology, preprocessing techniques will be applied to clean and normalise the collected data. This involved removing any inconsistencies or outliers and standardizing the data to ensure its quality and reliability. Advanced computer vision algorithms will be then employed to process preoperative images and scans, enabling a comprehensive analysis of the data. Through these algorithms, relevant features and anatomical information, including trauma location, severity, and related anatomical structures, will be extracted from the images. This step will be crucial in providing a detailed understanding of the trauma and its anatomical context, forming the basis for subsequent analysis and prediction in the pre-surgery planning process.

In this phase, essential steps will be taken to ensure the data's quality and reliability. To achieve this, Min-Max scaling, a suitable preprocessing method, will be applied to normalise the collected data. This scaling technique transformed the data into a specific range, maintaining the data's original distribution while preventing any single feature from dominating the analysis. Moreover, advanced computer vision algorithms will be employed to process the preoperative images and scans, enabling a comprehensive analysis of the data. Through these algorithms, crucial features and anatomical information, including trauma location, severity, related anatomical structures, trauma shape, size, image intensity, texture features, symmetry, and trauma context, will be extracted from the images. This step proved to be crucial in providing a detailed understanding of the trauma and its anatomical context, forming the basis for subsequent analysis and prediction in the pre-surgery planning process. By considering these features and applying Min-Max scaling for preprocessing, the AI-driven system gained valuable insights from the preoperative images and scans, facilitating a comprehensive analysis and prediction process during pre-surgery planning in plastic surgery.

3.3 Algorithm Development

The system leverages the power of deep learning to provide technique-specific insights based on the extracted features and the diverse dataset. Specifically, we implemented a Convolutional Neural Network (CNN) architecture consisting of multiple layers, including convolutional layers, pooling layers, and fully connected layers. For our application, we designed a CNN with four convolutional layers, each followed by a max-pooling layer to downsample the extracted features and retain the most relevant information. The output from the convolutional layers is then flattened and fed into two fully connected layers to make predictions based on the features extracted from the preoperative images and scans (Fig. 3). Additionally, we applied the Min-Max scaling preprocessing technique to normalise the input data before feeding it into the CNN (Algorithm 1). This algorithm's implementation allows our system to gain valuable insights into technique-specific results, enhancing surgical precision, personalising treatment plans and ultimately improving patient care and treatment outcomes in the field of plastic surgery.

Algorithm 1: Convolutional Neural Network (CNN) Architecture	
Input:	- *image_height, image_width, num_channels: Dimensions of input images* - *num_classes: Number of classes for classification* - *input_data: Input image data* - *labels: Ground truth labels for input data* - *min_value, max_value: Range for Min-Max scaling* - *batch_size: Batch size for training* - *num_epochs: Number of training epochs* - *test_input_data: Input data for making predictions*
Output:	*predictions: Predicted class probabilities for test_input_data*
Initialise a Sequential Model	
Add Convolutional layers:	- *Add Conv2D layer with 32 filters, kernel size (3, 3), and 'relu' activation.* - *Add Conv2D layer with 64 filters, kernel size (3, 3), and 'relu' activation.* - *Add Conv2D layer with 128 filters, kernel size (3, 3), and 'relu' activation.* - *Add Conv2D layer with 256 filters, kernel size (3, 3), and 'relu' activation*
Add Max-pooling layer:	- *Add MaxPooling2D layer with pool size (2, 2).*
Flatten the output:	*Add Flatten layer.*
Add Fully connected layers:	- *Add Dense layer with 512 units and 'relu' activation.* - *Add Dense layer with 256 units and 'relu' activation.*
Add Output layer:	- *Add Dense layer with num_classes units and 'softmax' activation.*
Compile the model:	- *Compile the model with optimiser 'adam' and loss 'categorical_crossentropy'.* - *Use accuracy as the metric.*
Apply Min-Max scaling:	- *Normalise input_data using Min-Max scaling.*
Train the model:	- *Fit the model using input_data and labels.* - *Set batch size as batch_size and number of epochs as num_epochs.*
Make predictions:	- *Use the trained model to predict class probabilities for test_input_data.* - *Store the predictions in the 'predictions' variable.*

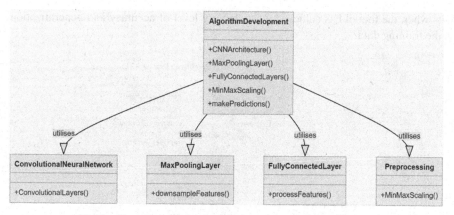

Fig. 3. Class diagram for the proposed deep learning algorithm

Dataset Preparation and Splitting

To prepare the dataset and proper splitting of them three main portions are needed. The first portion is needed for training purposes, ensuring it is properly cleaned and normalised for training the models. The second portion of the data will be used for validation purposes. In this stage, the model will be validated to ensure it can be used later in real patients. It is needed to allocate a significant portion of the data to the training set while keeping smaller proportions for validation and the final part which is testing. After the model is validated with the allocated portion of data the rest of the data which is the last portion will be used for the testing.

Model Training

In this stage, we initiate the Convolutional Neural Network (CNN) model's parameters randomly, often utilising pre-trained weights for faster convergence. The training data, which comprises the properly cleaned and normalised dataset, is then fed into the CNN model.

During training, the CNN computes predictions based on the current parameter settings and compares them to the corresponding ground truth labels. The loss function is employed to quantify the discrepancy between the predicted outcomes and the actual outcomes present in the dataset.

To optimise the model and improve its predictive performance, backpropagation and optimization algorithms, such as stochastic gradient descent, are employed. Back-propagation calculates the gradients of the model's parameters with respect to the loss, enabling us to update the parameters in the direction that minimises the loss function (Fig. 4).

By iteratively updating the model's parameters using backpropagation and optimization algorithms, the model gradually learns to recognise relevant patterns and relationships in the data, thus improving its performance in predicting technique-specific outcomes.

The training process continues until the model's performance converges or reaches a predefined stopping criterion. The stopping criterion ensures that the training process halts when the model has achieved a satisfactory level of accuracy and generalization on the training data.

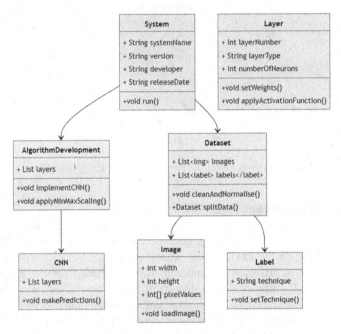

Fig. 4. Class diagram for the model training architecture

The model training stage is crucial for the system's overall performance, as it allows the CNN model to learn from the diverse dataset and extract meaningful features from the preoperative images and scans. A well-trained model equips the system with the capability to make accurate predictions and provide valuable insights for technique selection in plastic surgery pre-surgery planning.

Fine-Tuning and Hyperparameter Optimization

Fine-tuning and optimisation are critical stages to obtain the best results. To do this as can be seen in Fig. 5, first it is needed to assess the model's performance using the validation set and evaluate different hyperparameter settings. Adjusting hyperparameters such as learning rate, and regularisation strength, to improve the model's performance is needed. Utilising techniques such as grid search will be helpful to explore a range of hyperparameter combinations. Finally, the training process with different hyperparameter settings until selecting the optimal configuration based on the validation set's performance will be repeated to complete the training.

Fig. 5. Sequence diagram for Fine-tuning and Hyperparameter Optimization

Model Evaluation

When the training is done (as can be seen in Fig. 6) evaluation will start with assessing the final trained model's performance using the testing set, which represents unseen data. Then it is needed to measure various evaluation metrics, including for accuracy, precision, recall, and F1 score, to gauge the model's effectiveness in technique-specific outcome predictions. It is also needed to compare the model's performance against baseline methods or expert opinions to validate its utility in pre-surgery planning.

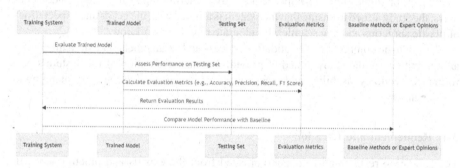

Fig. 6. Sequence diagram of model evaluation

Outcome Prediction and Interpretability

Upon training the machine learning models, they will be utilised to generate predictions for potential outcomes associated with each technique used in the pre-surgery planning. By feeding the input data into these trained models, the system could provide insights into the expected outcomes of different techniques. Additionally, mechanisms for interpretability will be developed to enhance the transparency of the predictions. Visual explanations will be generated to highlight influential factors and regions of interest in the predictions. These explanations aimed to provide a deeper understanding of the factors driving the outcome predictions and assist surgeons in making informed decisions during the pre-surgery planning process. By incorporating interpretability mechanisms, the system aimed to increase trust and facilitate the meaningful utilisation of the generated predictions in surgical decision-making.

Validation and Evaluation

To evaluate the performance of the developed system, a comprehensive validation process will be conducted. This involved several steps to assess its accuracy, effectiveness, and practicality. First, the outcome predictions generated by the system will be compared against ground truth data to evaluate their accuracy and alignment with actual surgical outcomes. This comparison helped gauge the system's predictive capabilities and identify any areas for improvement.

In addition to the comparison with ground truth data, expert plastic surgeons will be engaged to evaluate and compare the system's recommendations with their own expertise. This evaluation by domain experts provided valuable insights into the system's performance and its alignment with the knowledge and experience of skilled practitioners. Their feedback and assessments are instrumental in assessing the system's practicality and its potential to enhance decision-making processes in pre-surgery planning.

Furthermore, feedback from plastic surgery practitioners will be collected through surveys or interviews to assess the usability and practicality of the system in real-world clinical settings. This feedback helped identify any user experience issues, usability challenges, or suggestions for improvement. By gathering input from the intended end-users, the study aimed to ensure that the system is aligned with the needs and expectations of plastic surgeons and can seamlessly integrate into their workflow.

Through the comprehensive validation process and engagement with domain experts and practitioners, the study aimed to provide a robust evaluation of the system's performance, accuracy, usability, and practicality in the context of pre-surgery planning in plastic surgery.

3.4 Refinement and Iteration

The validation results and feedback collected from the experts and practitioners will be thoroughly analysed to identify areas for improvement in the system. This analysis aimed to identify any limitations, challenges, or discrepancies that emerged during the validation process. Based on these findings, the system will be refined through various means as can be seen in Fig. 7.

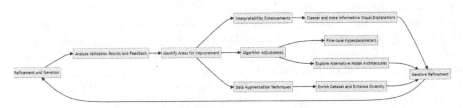

Fig. 7. Flow of the refinement and iteration process

Firstly, data augmentation techniques will be employed to enrich the dataset and enhance its diversity, allowing for more robust training of the machine learning models. Additionally, adjustments will be made to the algorithms themselves, such as fine-tuning hyperparameters or exploring alternative model architectures, to enhance their performance and accuracy.

Furthermore, interpretability enhancements will be implemented to provide clearer and more informative visual explanations of the system's predictions. These improvements aimed to address any gaps or limitations in the interpretability mechanisms identified during the validation process.

Iterative refinement is a key aspect of the methodology, as modifications and adjustments will be incorporated based on the lessons learned from previous iterations. This iterative approach allowed for continuous improvement and optimization of the system's performance, usability, and practicality over subsequent cycles of development, validation, and refinement.

By analyzing validation results, refining the system through data augmentation, algorithm adjustments, and interpretability enhancements, and iteratively repeating the development process, the study aimed to enhance the effectiveness and reliability of the AI-driven system for pre-surgery planning in plastic surgery.

3.5 Ethical Considerations

Throughout the study, strict compliance with ethical guidelines will be maintained to ensure the protection of patient data and privacy. All necessary measures as can be seen in Fig. 8 which will be taken to handle patient data securely and confidentially, including obtaining informed consent and anonymizing any personally identifiable information.

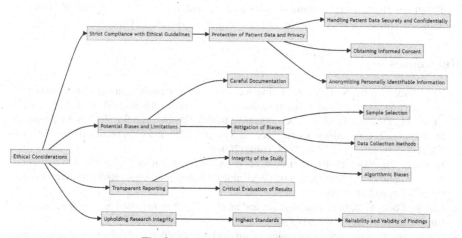

Fig. 8. Flow of ethical considerations

Furthermore, potential biases or limitations in the data collection and algorithm development process will be carefully documented and addressed. Steps will be taken to mitigate any biases that may have arisen due to factors such as sample selection, data collection methods, or algorithmic biases. Transparent reporting of these limitations and biases ensures the integrity of the study and allows for a critical evaluation of the results.

By adhering to ethical guidelines and acknowledging and addressing potential biases and limitations, the study aimed to uphold the highest standards of research integrity and ensure the reliability and validity of the findings.

4   Conclusion

In conclusion, this paper presented a proof of concept study on AI-based pre-surgery planning in plastic surgery, addressing the challenge of selecting the most effective technique for a specific trauma. By developing an AI-driven system and leveraging machine learning algorithms, we aimed to empower surgeons with technique-specific insights and enhance decision-making processes. While this proof-of-concept study represents a significant step forward, there are areas for further improvement and research. Future work should involve implementing the system and expanding the dataset to encompass a wider range of traumas and techniques, considering additional variables such as patient preferences and surgeon expertise. Prospective clinical trials should be conducted to assess the impact of the system on surgical outcomes and patient satisfaction in real-world settings.

The integration of AI in pre-surgery planning for plastic surgery holds tremendous potential for improving patient care and treatment outcomes. By providing surgeons with technique-specific insights and facilitating informed decision-making, AI technologies can assist in optimizing surgical approaches and tailoring treatments to individual patients.

Declarations
Declarations Human and Animal Rights and Informed Consent This article does not contain any studies with human or animal subjects performed by any of the authors.

References

1. Yamanaka, J., Saito, S., Fujimoto, J.: Impact of preoperative planning using virtual segmental volumetry on liver resection for hepatocellular carcinoma. World J. Surg. **31**, 1251–1257 (2007)
2. Gunes, H., Piccardi, M., Jan, T.: Comparative beauty classification for pre-surgery planning. In: 2004 IEEE International Conference on Systems, Man and Cybernetics (IEEE Cat. No. 04CH37583), vol. 3, pp. 2168–2174. IEEE (2004)
3. Jarvis, T., Thornburg, D., Rebecca, A.M., Teven, C.M.: Artificial intelligence in plastic surgery: current applications, future directions, and ethical implications. Plast. Reconstr. Surg. Global Open **8**(10), e3200 (2020)
4. Lin, X., Chen, Y.: Artificial intelligence and machine learning in plastic and aesthetic surgery. Chin. J. Plastic Surg. 157–160 (2018)
5. Ma, L., Fei, B.: Comprehensive review of surgical microscopes: technology development and medical applications. J. Biomed. Opt. **26**(1), 010901 (2021)
6. Tokgöz, E., Carro, M.A.: Applications of artificial intelligence, machine learning, and deep learning on facial plastic surgeries. In: Cosmetic and Reconstructive Facial Plastic Surgery: A Review of Medical and Biomedical Engineering and Science Concepts, pp. 281–306. Springer Nature Switzerland, Cham (2023). https://doi.org/10.1007/978-3-031-31168-0_9

7. Atiyeh, B., Emsieh, S., Hakim, C., Chalhoub, R.: A narrative review of artificial intelligence (AI) for objective assessment of aesthetic endpoints in plastic surgery. Aesth. Plastic Surg. 1–12 (2023)
8. Xie, Y., Seth, I., Hunter-Smith, D.J., Rozen, W.M., Ross, R., Lee, M.: Aesthetic surgery advice and counseling from artificial intelligence: a rhinoplasty consultation with ChatGPT. Aesthetic Plast. Sur. **47**(5), 1985–1993 (2023). https://doi.org/10.1007/s00266-023-03338-7
9. Mantelakis, A., Assael, Y., Sorooshian, P., Khajuria, A.: Machine learning demonstrates high accuracy for disease diagnosis and prognosis in plastic surgery. Plast. Reconstr. Surg. – Global Open **9**(6), e3638 (2021). https://doi.org/10.1097/GOX.0000000000003638

Academic Integrity in the Face of Generative Language Models

Alba Meça[1](✉) and Nirvana Shkëlzeni[2]

[1] Universita degli Studi di Padova, Padova, Italy
alba.meca@studenti.unipd.it
[2] Aleksandër Xhuvani University, Elbasan, Albania
nirvana.meca@uniel.edu.al

Abstract. The increasing sophistication of generative language models and their widespread accessibility to the general public has been a cause of growing concern in academia in recent years. While these AI technologies have the potential to greatly enhance the learning experience and facilitate research, they also pose a significant threat to academic integrity.

This paper investigates the impact of using tools like chatGPT and other large language models (LLM) in higher education, discussing their potential benefits while focusing more on assessing the risks, including the possibility of plagiarism, cheating, and other types of academic misconduct. It explores how these technologies may be used to undermine established scholarly principles and practices, as well as the challenges of identifying and combating academic dishonesty. Some measures universities and academics may employ in order to mitigate such risks are proposed, and several strategies and tools for detecting AI-generated content are discussed, along with their limitations.

Keywords: Large language models · Artificial Intelligence · Content Generation · Plagiarism · Higher Education

1 Introduction

The debut of OpenAI's ChatGPT[1], alongside Codex [2] and DALL-E [3] has brought a lot of attention to Generative AI (Gen-AI) systems. These systems are designed to extract and comprehend the intention of a human-provided prompt and produce new content (be it textual, visual, audio, or even programming code) in accordance with said intent and mimicking the data they have been trained on [4].

Recent developments demonstrate a trend of continuous upscaling as larger models have exhibited superior performance in a wide range of natural language processing tasks, creating a positive feedback loop which has led to a virtuous cycle, prompting researchers to further expand the size and complexity of these models in an effort to achieve even more impressive results.

M. H. Miraz et al. (Eds.): iCETiC 2023, LNICST 538, pp. 58–70, 2024.
https://doi.org/10.1007/978-3-031-50215-6_5

Within the realm of education, Generative Language Models present unprecedented prospects for enhancing teaching and learning experiences. They are capable of engaging in conversational interactions using natural language, answering queries, providing explanations, and delivering personalized feedback. LLMs adjust their responses based on the prompt they receive, thereby creating an interactive and dynamic learning environment.

However, alongside the excitement surrounding the adoption of LLMs in education, it is necessary to thoroughly assess the potential risks and ethical concerns associated with their usage [5].

Bearman and Luckin voiced concerns regarding the increased presence of AI within higher education. They emphasized the need for educators to differentiate between human intelligence and AI when constructing assessments to evaluate student learning. The authors discussed the computer involvement in assessment procedures as well as provided examples of tasks that specifically highlight human-exclusive abilities. They conclude that AI would shape education in a manner that compels educators to critically examine and assess the elements deemed important for evaluation purposes [6].

Dawson addressed the "boundary" separating students who use AI tools for assistance from those who view them as an opportunity to cheat, by exploring the concept of cognitive offloading, defined as the use of physical actions with the purpose of facilitating mental tasks. According to the author, achieving mastery of a subject through cognitive offloading can be an appropriate educational outcome if certain conditions are met. Dawson also emphasized the importance of evaluating the outcomes resulting from cognitive offloading [7].

In the domain of academia and education these concerns primarily relate to academic integrity, plagiarism, and the implications of relying heavily on AI-generated content. Academic integrity is defined by the International Center for Academic Integrity as a commitment to six core values: honesty, fairness, trust, responsibility, respect, and courage [8].

Preserving academic integrity calls for a coordinated effort between multiple stakeholders, from developers to university policymakers, independent researchers, professors, and students. This may involve redefining academic accomplishment, impact, and new ways of assessing them. Reevaluating what constitutes knowledge and how it is attained.

Recent systematic reviews on the applications of AI in higher education have noted a significant absence of critical examination of the ethical and pedagogical ramifications of AI such as its effects on academic integrity [9, 10]. Additionally, Zawacki-Richter et al. revealed that the majority of studies on AI did not include authors who were affiliated with faculties and education [10].

Therefore, this paper aims to investigate the impact of using tools like chatGPT and other LLMs in higher education, focusing on assessing their risk of facilitating academic misconduct, and developing a deeper understanding of whether and how LLMs could undermine established scholarly principles and practices.

ChatGPT and more recently GPT-4 have demonstrated the capacity to pass core MBA (Master of Business Administration) exams [11] as well as law school exams [12, 13] (obtaining varying results from a C to a B, though generally below the performance of the average student). Within a week of its initial public release on November 30, 2022, ChatGPT had more than one million subscribers [14].

To address these risks and challenges, this study suggests recommendations for universities and academics to implement in order to mitigate their impact. Through an extensive examination of LLMs' effects on academia and higher education along with a thorough assessment of associated risks, we aim to offer valuable insights regarding optimal practices, strategies, and ethical contemplations necessary for responsible and efficient utilization of LLMs in education circles.

Furthermore, this paper will explore the challenges faced in identifying and combating academic dishonesty. Detecting AI-generated content presents significant difficulties for educators and academic institutions, as traditional plagiarism detection tools struggle to differentiate between human and AI-generated text. It is essential to explore the limitations of existing detection methods and propose strategies and tools that can aid in the identification of AI-generated content.

2   Potential Benefits of LLMs in Academia and Higher Education

Advanced large language models have the potential to bring about numerous benefits in academia, revolutionizing the way research, teaching, and learning are conducted by offering a wide range of capabilities which can greatly enhance academic pursuits.

Do you Need Help? Yes Please, be My Research Assistant: LLMs like chatGPT are already acting like a research assistant in multiple ways. They can facilitate the writing of literature reviews, data analysis, and even generate research ideas. Researchers can benefit from their unmatched ability to swiftly process and analyze substantial volumes of information, offering concise summaries of research papers and extracting relevant details. By streamlining these tasks, LLMs allow researchers to focus more on critical analysis and knowledge synthesis.

No More Fear of the Blank Paper with Writing Support: LLMs can provide valuable writing support to academics. These models have the ability to provide valuable suggestions for enhancing the coherence, grammar, style and overall structure of academic papers. Moreover, they can assist in generating outlines, brainstorming ideas and even drafting specific sections within a paper.

I Speak your Language with Language Translation: These models, alongside other deep neural machine translation services such as DeepL, have the capability for near-instantaneous translation of research papers, articles, and other academic texts. This enables scholars from different linguistic backgrounds to effortlessly access knowledge across language barriers. As a result, it fosters international collaboration and expands the reach of academic research.

Virtual Teaching Assistants: LLMs can act as virtual teaching assistants, supporting educators in various ways. They can help answer students' questions, provide explanations, and offer additional learning resources. LLMs can even assist with providing feedback on assignments, saving instructors time and allowing them to focus on more interactive and personalized teaching methods. There is already precedent for this. In 2015, Georgia Tech University, in a pioneering move, integrated an AI-powered virtual teaching assistant based on IBM Watson into their online master's level course [15]. Students interacted with this AI assistant throughout the semester, benefiting from personalized guidance, prompt feedback, and assistance with their queries while remaining unaware that they were engaging with an advanced AI system instead of a human. Furthermore, today's generative language models can even provide educators with insights and suggestions for instructional practices, lesson planning, and curriculum development. They can offer resources, examples, and best practices based on current research and pedagogical approaches. While chatGPT is currently restricted by its 2021 knowledge cut-off, other conversational AI models like Google's LaMDA can access the internet and deliver up-to-date relevant information.

It is Actually Free the Personalized Learning: LLMs can facilitate personalized learning experiences for students. They can adapt to individual learning styles and provide tailored explanations, examples, and practice exercises. LLMs can answer questions, offer clarifications, and provide feedback, enhancing the learning process and promoting self-paced learning.

I am Here for You with Enhanced Accessibility: The more recent, multimodal models can significantly improve accessibility in academia. LLMs possess the capacity to assist individuals with visual deficiencies through converting written content into auditory format. Furthermore, they can aid those with learning disabilities by presenting alternative explanations or formats tailored to their individual needs. By embracing inclusivity, these technologies guarantee accessibility of educational resources to a wider audience. Moreover, LLMs enable access to quality learning materials and virtual classrooms for students residing in remote or underprivileged areas, while academic institutions delivering these services incur substantially minimized expenses.

Let the World Know with Knowledge Dissemination: LLMs have the potential to facilitate knowledge dissemination to a broader demographic by converting scholarly articles into more user-friendly and comprehensible versions like blog entries or summaries. Furthermore, LLMs can produce instructive and captivating educational materials that effectively break down intricate topics for novices, ultimately enriching their comprehension and engagement.

In terms of advancing academic pursuits, the use of large language models (LLMs) shows considerable potential. LLMs have the ability to enrich individualized learning experiences, streamline research procedures, and enhance accessibility within academia. Nonetheless, it is crucial to approach the implementation of LLMs with cautious reflection, acknowledging the associated risks and challenges in upholding scholarly integrity and dealing with ethical concerns. By responsibly utilizing the capabilities offered by LLMs, the academic community can harness their potential while effectively navigating potential pitfalls.

3   Risks Posed to Academic Integrity

The widespread use of LLM-based systems could present a serious threat to academic integrity in various scholarly communities, from universities to journal publishers and conference organizers to independent researchers.

The potential misuse of LLMs poses a real danger to academia's credibility and undermines the achievements of honest and ethical research. With the term "academia" we are denoting the ecosystem that fosters teaching, research, and scholarly endeavors in a broader sense. It encompasses educational institutions, research centers, publishers specializing in academic material, as well as sponsors offering grants for research projects.

Natural Born Originals or Unethical Authorship Practices: In a time when widely available chatbots are becoming increasingly more convincing and sophisticated the fundamental concepts of credit and original authorship are called into question. As technology advances, it becomes more difficult to tell if a written text is actually original work or created by a digital device. This gives rise to serious questions regarding the significance of originality and the paramount importance of properly citing sources. Content generated by LLMs is by design imitating human-written text. The ease with which these AI tools can assemble a contextually relevant and coherent narrative makes it increasingly difficult to distinguish it from genuine work, leading to ambiguity regarding authorship and the correct attribution of intellectual input. They can be misused by students to "outsource" their assignments or by unethical "researchers" to produce significant sections of their papers, without acknowledgment of the full extent of the assistance they received. This violates the principles of intellectual honesty, fair credit allocation, and transparent authorship practices, compromising the overall integrity of the work.

Some scholars hold a different opinion regarding the negative impact of these technologies, arguing that students have been outsourcing their writing to third parties for a long time, a practice that is known as contract cheating. For Harte and Khaleel submitting a work compiled by chatGPT is no different from hiring a ghostwriter, which one could easily find through numerous essay mills wildly available online [16]. According to Thomas Lancaster, a computer scientist and academic-integrity researcher at Imperial College London, the emergence of this tool does not provide a significant enhancement in functionality compared to what was already accessible for students if they knew where to search for it [5]. However, generating a paper using ChatGPT differs from employing a ghostwriter in that it is instantaneous, free of charge, and for the most part passes under the radar of plagiarism checkers. On a positive note, essays that are generated by ChatGPT expose themselves much more often compared to those produced by essay mills, due to the inclusion of fabricated quotes and references, inaccurate information and faulty assumptions.

Compromising Peer Review: The integrity of one of the oldest and most established practices in academia, the peer-review process, is also called into question. The system functions based on the trust that the material under investigation is the work of a "peer", and on the other hand that the people assessing your work are scholars in your field. However nowadays, reviewers could be unwittingly evaluating research manuscripts with AI-generated content, unable to determine the influence these have on the overall quality of the paper and their final recommendations. This could lead to biased evaluations resulting in acceptance of subpar and unauthentic work. Moreover, there can also be cases when the reviewers become complacent and unmotivated, relying on AI tools to do the reviews for them. However, these systems lack expertise in the field and critical thinking abilities so reviewers have a responsibility to critically analyze manuscripts through thorough examination of methodology, scrutiny of presented arguments and data, along with evaluation of the significance of research findings and contributions. To not do so would be a failure on the part of the reviewer to fulfill their duties as an expert evaluator, which may result in important research aspects being overlooked thereby compromising the rigor and quality assurance of the process.

Who is the Winner with Inequality and Unfair Advantage: The utilization of these content generating tools can potentially result in disparities in academia due to unequal advantages among researchers. Those who are privileged with access to more advanced LLMs may produce superior research outputs, amplifying discrepancies in academic accomplishments and recognition. This imbalanced allocation of AI tools and resources has the potential to aggravate preexisting inequities within the scholarly community while impeding fair involvement and advancement in scholarly pursuits.

True or False with Fraudulent Research and Fabrication: Despite their impressive capabilities, these models are trained on the objective of generating text and not scanning and analyzing databases. For example, chatGPT is currently unable to access the internet or any external data source, therefore if it were asked to provide references it would come up with convincingly-looking citations to completely fabricated and non-existent papers. This phenomenon is known as *Hallucination.* However, even models that are not constrained to their training data, like Google's Bard, lack the critical understanding and acumen to be able to assess the credibility of sources and identify the most reliable and authoritative information. Significant attention to research goals, rigorous search methodologies, and careful examination of the materials are integral to conducting a quality literature review. LLM systems cannot replicate the intricate discernment and adeptness required in selecting suitable academic articles and weighing their contribution to knowledge. Despite technological advancements, there is no way around the manual search of reputable academic databases and resources. Generative AI may also aid in spreading fraudulent and fabricated "research". Individuals could misuse these tools to generate fictitious data, results or analyses that look authentic and legitimate. Furthermore, advanced LLMs have the ability to supply compelling textual explanations or justifications for modified images or manufactured data, making it more difficult to detect instances of manipulated visual and numerical evidence. The scientific community faces a serious threat as research findings become less reliable and trustworthy. Misleading other researchers and distorting the existing knowledge base, fraudulent research hinders the progress of real scientific advancement and undermines its credibility.

Plagiarism: While these models are designed to generate original content, they may still inadvertently commit plagiarism and violate intellectual property rights. The reason for this is because they are trained on predictive algorithms, trying to learn statistical patterns and linguistic structures that imitate the text in their training corpora. As such, the response may unintentionally replicate content from one of their training samples without giving proper acknowledgment. The ethics concerning this aspect of AI have given rise to some unresolved questions such as: How can copyright be applied to AI content? and Is it ethical to use copyrighted data for training AI models or in other research applications?

Who is the Owner of the Intellectual Property?: Another interesting point to consider is whether the use of generative AI for completing assignments or writing academic papers constitutes plagiarism in the common context of "theft of intellectual property". When some Ai-generated content is falsely presented as original work, whose intellectual property is being stolen? Who is harmed as a result of this act? While employing ChatGPT without adequate acknowledgment violates core academic integrity norms, the overall plagiarism argument is a little more complicated. The complexity of the problem increases further when integrating AI-generated content within scholarly work, posing legal and ethical dilemmas surrounding proper attribution, citation practices, and safeguarding intellectual property rights.

Recently, we have witnessed a number of papers listing ChatGPT as a co-author [17–20]. However, the most prominent journals such as Nature [21] and Science [22] have banned this practice and have stated unequivocally that no AI tool may be acknowledged as a credited author in their publications. They claim that is in violation of the clearly defined authorship guidelines according to which a co-author must have made a "significant scholarly contribution" to the research, which is questionable considering these models' limited critical thinking and judgment competences and lack of domain expertise, as well as be able to consent to the publishing of the paper and take responsibility for the work, something an artificial entity is inherently incapable of.

Biased Content: Language models like Bard and chatGPT have been shown to exhibit inherent biases that stem from the data they are trained on. These biases can have adverse consequences when incorporated into scholarly work. These models learn from a wide variety of text sources, including online content that may contain biased viewpoints, stereotypes, or systemic prejudices. As a result, the generated content may inadvertently reflect and perpetuate these biases, potentially impacting the fairness and objectivity of academic discourse. This presents challenges in maintaining an unbiased representation within scholarly environments while fostering inclusive perspectives and promoting rigorous examination of ideas. The existence of biases in AI-generated content raises concerns about the integrity and validity of research outcomes, thereby impeding the pursuit of impartial knowledge and equitable academic practices. Addressing and reducing these biases within AI models is crucial to upholding the principles of academic integrity and establishing a fair as well as all-encompassing scholarly community.

4   Identifying and Combating Academic Dishonesty

Understanding the Challenges of Detecting AI-Generated Content: The identification of AI content poses unique challenges for academic institutions and research establishments. Conventional plagiarism detection tools may struggle to distinguish between human-written and LLM-generated material. According to a Nature editorial chatGPT possesses excellent skills for writing scientific abstracts that go undetectable from real researchers in the field [23]. In their study, the group of human scholars misclassified about one third of the generated abstracts as genuine and 14% of the real abstracts were incorrectly deemed AI-generated instead. The intricate language-generating abilities of LLMs also pose a challenge when relying solely on automated algorithms to uncover instances of academic dishonesty. Moreover, due to the rapidly progressing nature of LLM technology, continuous adjustment of detection techniques is essential to keep up with the evolving methodologies employed in content generation.

Implementing Proactive Measures for Prevention: To address the issue of academic dishonesty aided by LLMs educational institutions can establish preventive strategies. These may include cultivating a culture that upholds academic integrity, educating students on ethical technology use, and explicitly communicating policies regarding the utilization of LLMs and AI tools. Additionally, institutions can prioritize the significance of critical thinking, independent research capabilities, and accurate citation practices. By highlighting the importance of originality and ethical behavior, students are more inclined to refrain from engaging in academic misconduct involving LLMs.

Academics might respond by redrafting written assignments in ways that emphasize critical thinking and analytical reasoning, something that language models struggle with because they lack true understanding of language [24] and the capability to generate original insights beyond what has been learned from the training data. The AI responses are correlation-based statistical predictions, primarily based on observed patterns rather than higher-level cognitive processes associated with critical thinking.

This aligns with the goals of academic institutions, which should be to prepare individuals who think for themselves rather than learn how to answer essay prompts. If AI is taking care of the latter, all the more significant becomes the former.

Furthermore, the potential of models like CodeBERT [25], the GPT-n based models like Codex and chatGPT, Google's Bard etc. to create and edit programming code necessitates a rethinking of technical coding assignments. So far, these transformer-based models have demonstrated the ability to write sensible and working code as a response to high-level function descriptions, which would allow students to answer most of the basic algorithms and data structures questions [26, 27].

Moreover, instead of only evaluating the completed product, the focus of the assessment should move to the reasoning involved in every step of the process. In the case of a project that spans multiple weeks or months of work the students may be requested to write weekly diary-style updates, detailing the activities they have been working on, the progress they've made this far, the outcomes of these activities and reflections on them. In an essay-writing assignment they could instead be asked to identify the papers and articles they wish to incorporate in their work, as well as explain why they believe these articles would be relevant and valuable.

It is of utmost importance to *establish unambiguous policies and guidelines* pertaining to the utilization of Gen-AI models within educational environments. Institutions must clearly communicate the acceptable and unacceptable applications of LLMs, placing significant emphasis on upholding originality, proficient citation practices, and the avoidance of plagiarism. Moreover, these policies should comprehensively tackle the unique challenges that arise from LLM-generated content while also providing guidance on appropriately integrating AI-generated outputs into scholarly endeavors. Consistently reviewing and revising these policies is imperative in order to stay abreast with advancements in LLM technology as well as academic integrity standards.

Pedagogy and evaluation must undergo major transformations. The goal at hand should be to develop a form of assessment which incorporates AI content. Not least because, once graduated, students will be employing this technology in their professional lives.

In the rapidly evolving landscape, it is essential to prepare the students for a future in which AI-supported writing becomes indispensable. Just as features like spelling and grammar checks in word processors have seamlessly integrated into writing routines, the utilization of text generators is poised to follow suit. We have to embrace these tools and incorporate them into pedagogy and publication policies. Locking down browsers, enforcing rigorous dismissal procedures, and prohibiting the usage of these sites are not viable options.

Educating Faculty and Instructors: Providing training for faculty and instructors is crucial in equipping them with the knowledge and skills to identify academic dishonesty facilitated by LLMs. Faculty members should receive training on how to spot signs of AI-generated content, understand the limitations of plagiarism detection tools, and implement strategies for fostering academic integrity in the digital age. Lecturers will require training and time to further their understanding of these models and to be able to update their teaching materials and practices accordingly. Sharing best practices and case studies can keep instructors up to date on emerging trends and challenges regarding misconduct in relation to LLMs.

Regular Academic Integrity Audits: Conducting regular assessments of academic integrity can be beneficial for institutions to evaluate the effectiveness of their measures against dishonest practices aided by LLMs. These evaluations may involve reviewing a selection of student work and analyzing patterns or anomalies that could indicate the presence of AI-generated content. The insights gained from these assessments can then be used to improve policies, detection mechanisms, and educational initiatives in order to effectively address emerging challenges related to maintaining academic honesty.

Investing in Better AI-Detectors: There is currently no reliable and widely accepted tool for detecting dishonest usage of AI generators. Institutions ought to allocate resources towards the advancement and refinement of detection systems specialized in discerning AI-generated content. This endeavor may necessitate forging partnerships with deep learning and natural language processing (NLP) specialists in order to devise sophisticated tools capable of distinguishing authentically human text from generated content. These detection systems must undergo periodic updates to keep pace with advancements in LLM capabilities as well as evasion techniques. Additionally, exploring collaborative ventures with technology firms is vital for information sharing and collective development of robust detection strategies. Besides general accuracy in detection, special attention should be paid to minimizing the number of false positives, content that is wrongly flagged as AI-generated, becoming subject to unjust scrutiny, resulting in unfair grading for the students and impeding the publication process for researchers.

It is worth noting that academic institutions in low- and middle-income countries face a greater challenge as they have yet to adopt Turnitin and similar plagiarism detection tools, which are crucial for ensuring academic integrity. The financial burden associated with the technical integration of these tools poses a formidable obstacle to many institutions in these regions.

5 Detecting AI Generated Content

Several strategies have been proposed to tackle the challenge of differentiating between human and AI content. A widely used method for this purpose is Stylometry. It entails the examination of language patterns such as vocabulary, grammar, and syntax to determine the unique style of the author of the text. By employing stylometric analysis, distinct patterns specific to individual authors can be identified, making AI-generated texts stand out more easily. Various studies have provided evidence of stylometry's effectiveness in detecting AI-generated content [28].

Another common technique is the analysis of metadata. Metadata refers to the information stored within a file or document that encompasses details about its creation, such as the device utilized, software employed, and the date and time of creation. Scrutinizing this information unveils the origin of the content [29].

However, these techniques have substantial limitations. The manipulation or removal of metadata can quickly render it useless and unreliable while language models are becoming increasingly better at mimicking human writing, including imitating the styles of specific individuals.

Current AI detectors incorporate a blend of rule-based systems and machine learning models to identify and classify the content type. Rule-based systems utilize predefined patterns, keywords, or regular expressions to pinpoint specific instances with a higher probability of being AI generated. On the other hand, machine learning models, like recurrent neural networks (RNNs) and transformers, leverage vast datasets to learn intricate patterns and semantic relationships within text.

AI content detectors leverage the probabilistic nature of language models. They analyze the likelihood of specific words or sequences appearing in a text by examining the probabilities assigned to different words, identifying patterns and anomalies.

Many of these systems make use of measures like perplexity and burstiness to uncover AI-generated content. Perplexity is instrumental in assessing text coherence and its alignment with human language patterns. When a text exhibits an unusually low perplexity score, it suggests that it might have been generated by AI. On the other hand, burstiness analysis identifies sudden bursts of repetitive or clustered words and structured phrases that are commonly associated with AI-generated content. By combining these measures, content detectors can identify suspicious text characteristics.

However, it is of utmost importance to note the concerns about their effectiveness and reliability. Many of these detectors heavily rely on specific keywords or patterns, which can result in a high false negative rate, where problematic content goes undetected [30]. Conversely, false positives are even more worrying, as they wrongly accuse individuals and perpetuate an unwarranted climate of suspicion and distrust, akin to a witch hunt. Recently Turnitin was forced to reluctantly admit that it has a much higher false positive rate than it had originally claimed [31]. Additionally, recent studies have highlighted biases in AI detectors, particularly against non-native speakers [32]. These biases not only impede accurate identification of harmful content but also unfairly impact individuals from diverse linguistic backgrounds. It is crucial to address these limitations in order to develop more inclusive and dependable AI content detection systems.

6   Conclusion

As AI and generative language models continue to evolve, it is imperative to contemplate their implications and adopt responsible measures against potential misuse. This necessitates establishing clear guidelines and regulations to ensure their ethical and responsible utilization in academic contexts. Furthermore, fostering awareness among individuals about the significance of ethical conduct while engaging with these technologies is essential to facilitate their constructive and responsible incorporation into academic research, teaching, and learning. By being mindful of the implications and implementing necessary safeguards, we can leverage their capabilities while mitigating potential risks.

In summary, the application of LLMs in higher education presents significant advantages and transformative potential. Nevertheless, it is imperative to navigate the risks linked to these technologies, specifically concerning academic misconduct. By taking proactive steps, investing in detection systems, providing education to relevant parties, and conducting regular audits, educational institutions can lessen these risks and guarantee a responsible and ethical utilization of LLMs in education. With a mindful approach that combines leveraging the benefits of LLMs with upholding principles of academic integrity, we can optimize their role in improving teaching and learning while preserving the integrity of higher education.

Whenever a novel technology emerges, it tends to induce apprehension and panic. Similar discussions concerning technology have taken place in the past, such as when advanced calculators became widely available, or the introduction of spell-checking by word processing systems. Academics bear the responsibility of maintaining an appropriate level of distrust; nonetheless, this predicament should not be seen as an unconquerable obstacle but as an integral part of our future. Leveraging AI for school or academic work does not inherently imply misconduct. Attempting to prohibit the use of AI-powered systems in the classroom would not only be ineffective, but also irresponsible. Artificial intelligence is here to stay and we must learn to work with it rather than against it.

In order to minimize the potential dangers linked with LLMs, educational establishments ought to embrace proactive actions like promoting a climate of scholarly honesty, establishing guidelines for responsible LLM utilization, improving detection mechanisms, delivering faculty training sessions, as well as conducting periodic audits on academic integrity. Moreover, continuous research efforts and collaborations with AI specialists are imperative for staying abreast of evolving LLM capabilities while improving detection techniques and crafting ethical frameworks that dictate LLM deployment in education.

References

1. Ouyang, L., et al.: Training language models to follow instructions with human feedback. Adv. Neural Inform. Process. Syst. **35**, 27730–27744 (2022)
2. Chen, M., et al.: Evaluating large language models trained on code. arXiv preprint arXiv: 2107.03374 (2021)
3. Ramesh, A., et al.: Zero-shot text-to-image generation. In: International Conference on Machine Learning, pp. 8821–8831. PMLR (2021)

4. Cao, Y., et al.: A comprehensive survey of ai-generated content (aigc): A history of generative ai from gan to chatgpt. arXiv preprint arXiv:2303.04226 (2023)

5. Stokel-Walker, C.: AI bot ChatGPT writes smart essays-should academics worry? Nature (2022)

6. Bearman, M., Luckin, R.: Preparing university assessment for a world with AI: Tasks for human intelligence. In: Bearman, M., Dawson, P., Ajjawi, R., Tai, J., Boud, D. (eds.) Re-imagining university assessment in a digital world, pp. 49–63. Springer International Publishing (2020)

7. Dawson, P.: E-Cheating, assessment security and artificial intelligence. In: Dawson, P. (ed.) Defending Assessment Security in a Digital World: Preventing E-Cheating and Supporting Academic Integrity in Higher Education, pp. 83–97. Routledge, Abingdon, Oxon; New York, NY: Routledge, 2021. (2020). https://doi.org/10.4324/9780429324178-6

8. https://academicintegrity.org/resources/fundamental-values

9. Ouyang, F., Zheng, L., Jiao, P.: Artificial intelligence in online higher education: a systematic review of empirical research from 2011 to 2020. Educ. Inform. Technol. 27(6), 7893–7925 (2022)

10. Zawacki-Richter, O., Marín, V.I., Bond, M., Gouverneur, F.: Systematic review of research on artificial intelligence applications in higher education–where are the educators? Int. J. Educ. Technol. High. Educ. 16(1), 1–27 (2019)

11. Terwiesch, C.: Would Chat GPT3 Get a Wharton MBA? A Prediction Based on Its Performance in the Operations Management Course. Mack Institute for Innovation Management at the Wharton School, University of Pennsylvania (2023)

12. Choi, J.H., Hickman, K.E., Monahan, A., Schwarcz, D.: Chatgpt goes to law school. SSRN Electron. J. (2023)

13. Blair-Stanek, A., Carstens, A.M., Goldberg, D.S., Graber, M., Gray, D.C., Stearns, M.L.: GPT-4's Law School Grades: Con Law C, Crim C-, Law & Econ C, Partnership Tax B, Property B-, Tax B. Crim C-, Law & Econ C, Partnership Tax B, Property B-, Tax B. SSRN Electron. J. (2023)

14. https://finance.yahoo.com/news/chatgpt-gained-1-million-followers-224523258.html

15. https://gvu.gatech.edu/research/projects/virtual-teaching-assistant-jill-watson

16. Harte, P., Khaleel, F.: Keep calm and carry on: ChatGPT doesn't change a thing for academic integrity (2023). https://napier-repository.worktribe.com/output/3048214/keep-calm-and-carry-on-chatgpt-doesnt-change-a-thing-for-academic-integrity

17. . O'Connor, S., ChatGPT.: Open artificial intelligence platforms in nursing education: tools for academic progress or abuse? Nurse Educ. Pract. 66, 103537 (2023). https://doi.org/10.1016/j.nepr.2022.103537

18. Aljanabi, M., Mijwil, M.: ChatGPT: Towards artificial intelligence-based cybersecurity: the practices and ChatGPT generated ways to combat cybercrime. Iraqi J. Comput. Sci. Math. 4(1), 65–70 (2023)

19. ChatGPT, Zhavoronkov, A.: Rapamycin in the context of Pascal's Wager: generative pre-trained transformer perspective. Oncoscience 9, 82–84 (2022)

20. King, M.R., chatGPT: A conversation on artificial intelligence, Chatbots, and plagiarism in higher education. Cel. Mol. Bioeng. 16, 1–2 (2023)

21. Editorials, N.: Tools such as ChatGPT threaten transparent science; here are our ground rules for their use. Nature 613(612), 10–1038 (2023)

22. Thorp, H.H.: ChatGPT is fun, but not an author. Science 379(6630), 313–313 (2023)

23. Else, H.: Abstracts written by ChatGPT fool scientists. Nature 613(7944), 423–423 (2023). https://doi.org/10.1038/d41586-023-00056-7

24. Shanahan, M.: Talking About Large Language Models. arXiv preprint arXiv:2212.03551 (2022)

25. Feng, Z., et al;: A pre-trained model for programming and natural languages (2020)
26. Sarsa, S., Denny, P., Hellas, A., Leinonen, J.: August. Automatic generation of programming exercises and code explanations using large language models. In: Proceedings of the 2022 ACM Conference on International Computing Education Research, vol. 1, pp. 27–43 (2022)
27. Destefanis, G., Bartolucci, S., Ortu, M.: A Preliminary Analysis on the Code Generation Capabilities of GPT-3.5 and Bard AI Models for Java Functions. arXiv preprint arXiv:2305. 09402 (2023)
28. Kumarage, T., Garland, J., Bhattacharjee, A., Trapeznikov, K., Ruston, S., Liu, H.: Stylometric Detection of AI-Generated Text in Twitter Timelines. arXiv preprint arXiv:2303.03697 (2023)
29. Shenkman, C., Thakur, D., Llansó, E.: Do you see what I see? Capabilities and limits of automated multimedia content analysis. arXiv preprint arXiv:2201.11105 (2021)
30. Khalil, M., Er, E.: Will ChatGPT get you caught? Rethinking of plagiarism detection. arXiv preprint arXiv:2302.04335 (2023)
31. Merod, A.: Turnitin admits there are some cases of higher false positives in AI writing detection tool. https://www.k12dive.com/news/turnitin-false-positives-AI-detector/652221/ (2023)
32. Liang, W., Yuksekgonul, M., Mao, Y., Wu, E., Zou, J.: GPT detectors are biased against non-native English writers. Patterns **4**(7), 100779 (2023). https://doi.org/10.1016/j.patter.2023. 100779

DocBot: A System for Disease Detection and Specialized Doctor Recommendation Using Patient's Speech of Symptoms

Jubayer Hossen, Md. Rishad Islam, Abir Chowdhury, Israt Jahan Ukti, and Md. Motaharul Islam[✉]

United International University, United City, Madani Avenue, Badda, Dhaka 1212, Bangladesh
{jhossen191254,mislam191134,achowdhury191255,iukti191138}@bscse.uiu.ac.bd, motaharul@cse.uiu.ac.bd

Abstract. Nowadays, Machine Learning (ML) plays a crucial role in improving healthcare by enabling researchers, doctors, and patients to explore, diagnose, and prevent diseases such as dengue, typhoid, jaundice, pneumonia, and other major ailments. Our research focuses on leveraging ML to detect various diseases from a patient's speech. The patient will describe their symptoms to the machine, akin to explaining their concerns to a doctor. The machine will then identify the disease and provide primary medication recommendations along with suggesting a specialized doctor for that particular ailment. To optimize our system's performance, we trained our machine using multiple algorithms and evaluated their results. Our evaluation revealed an accuracy of 86.59% for Naive Bayes, 83.17% for Unhyperd SVM, 98.05% for Hyperd SVM, 97.4% for Decision Tree, and the highest accuracy of 99.35% was achieved by Random Forest.

Keywords: Machine Learning · Classification · Disease Prediction

1 Introduction

Everyone has to deal with health problems occasionally. We must visit doctors or hospitals to receive treatment for any type of illness or health issue. But occasionally, for some people, finding a hospital might be a major challenge. People who reside in remote locations, in particular, are unable to visit the hospital sooner if they have any kind of health issue. Non-communicable diseases cause about 67% of fatalities [1]. If you suddenly become ill or have an illness for the time being, you should visit a doctor. When people experience different illnesses, they require quick advice and need to speak with experts. Another issue is that when individuals call or visit a hospital to receive advice from a doctor, they may encounter challenges and unfavorable suggestions for promotion because the hospital administration only wants to highlight its own physicians and facilities. People could thus encounter some serious challenges here. We have made

M. H. Miraz et al. (Eds.): iCETiC 2023, LNICST 538, pp. 71–85, 2024.
https://doi.org/10.1007/978-3-031-50215-6_6

the decision to conduct our project based on ML, and our primary goal is to identify diseases from a patient's speech and recommend primary medications and specialized doctors based on that disease.

Initially, a patient will describe his concern. The verdict will be converted to text and we will tokenize that text. We will find a higher frequency of diseases that match the tokens. The condition will then be displayed, and a primary medication will be recommended. We are aware that ML is a robust field in this time period. Many industries are currently using ML to attempt and solve their challenges. In recent times, ML has also worked in the medical industry. Clinical data management and controlling the healthcare sector are the key uses of ML techniques [2]. We will use Machine Learning to forecast diseases and recommend specialized physicians since the goals of our project are to identify the condition, provide basic therapy, and advise a specific specialist.

The problem assertions are clear from the first paragraph. Based on the issue description, a system is suggested to assist patients in remote areas or anybody in determining their ailment based on their symptoms. In addition to learning more about the illness, users may locate medical professionals that specialize in it. And they will receive some basic care or advised medications for their ailments. In other words, patients can identify their ailment and take quick treatment. A suitable ML algorithm should be trained on a dataset in order to recommend or obtain an accurate diagnosis. We have identified a wide variety of symptoms and illnesses in our dataset. On the basis of this, we will train our model, test it with further data, and then determine its correctness. The main contributions of our research are:

- We have identified Machine learning-based disease identification from patient's speech, and specialist referral.
- We have the aim to reduce improper specialized doctor choices, and facilitating proper diagnosis by specialist recommendations.
- Our framework provides primary medications for the detected disease.
- Naive Bayes, Unhypred SVM, Hypered SVM, Decision Tree, and Random Forest used for optimal system performance.
- Utilizing multiple algorithms to achieve the best accuracy for the proposed system.
- During our evaluation, we found that the Naive Bayes algorithm achieved an accuracy of 86.59%, followed by 83.17% for Unhyperd SVM, 98.05% for Hyperd SVM, and 97.4% for Decision Tree. However, the highest accuracy of 99.35% was attained by the Random Forest algorithm.

2 Related Research

In this study [3], the authors describe the construction of a disease prediction system that will use supervised learning algorithms to identify diseases based on patients' symptoms. Several algorithms will be evaluated for accuracy, including Bernoulli Naive Bayes, Decision Tree, and Support Vector Machine, with the most accurate one being used for prediction.

This survey article [4] compares several Machine Learning algorithms for the detection of various diseases like heart disease, diabetic disease, liver disease, and dengue fever as well as hepatitis disease. It draws emphasis to the Machine Learning suite. Learning algorithms and technologies are utilized in the study of illnesses and the decision-making process.

This paper [5], proposes a new approach called Ensemble of Sampled Classifier Chains (ESCC) for improving the classification of free clinical text data as a multi-label learning issue. ESCC addresses this issue by selecting relevant disease information to enhance classification performance. In experiments, ESCC outperformed other state-of-the-art multi-label algorithms in clinical text data classification.

The authors here [6] describe a disease identification method from a clinical text in Bengali that consists of a large number of diacritic characters at the sentence level. The method offers the NLP methodology for Bengali language processing and categorization. The initial diagnosis of sickness from the user's voice-to-text data is known as research, and a voice recognition system is employed to feed the sickness.

Computer Aided Diagnosis (CAD) is rapidly developing to improve the accuracy of medical diagnosis, using Machine Learning (ML). This research paper [7] examines various ML algorithms used in detecting diseases such as heart disease and diabetes. It focuses on the collection of algorithms and techniques used in ML for disease detection and decision-making processes.

In this paper [8], the authors developed a system to identify skin diseases based on input symptoms, achieving an accuracy of over 90%. Early detection is important to prevent worsening conditions and the spread of infections.

In this paper [9], the authors present a Machine Learning based system for diagnosing heart disease that uses classification algorithms and feature selection techniques to improve accuracy and reduce execution time. A novel fast conditional mutual information feature selection algorithm is proposed to address the issue of feature selection. The system's performance was evaluated using leave-one-subject-out cross-validation.

This study [10] uses notable symptoms and diseases to train a Machine Learning model to predict prevalent diseases based on real-world data. Tokenization was used to create text processing, which was integrated with other.algorithms to assess similarities and outputs. It offers advantages in the health business, such as early illness identification, faster diagnosis, and medical history for patient assessment.

NLP techniques can be used to extract lifestyle exposures from clinical texts, potentially improving the efficiency of gathering and accumulating information for AD clinical trials. The results of the proposed named-entity recognition task in this paper [11] demonstrate this potential.

The authors here [12], propose a method for automatically categorizing clinical content at the sentence level using complex convolutional neural networks, which beats many widely used approaches by 15% in a comprehensive examination.

This work here [13], created a healthcare technology that can handle a patient's medical data, including illness symptoms, emotional data, and genetic data. It includes a data warehouse that interacts with high-performance computing and cloud synchronization, and a prediction technique that predicts illness using a cloud server. They used Random Forest, Support Vector Machine (SVM), C5.0, Naive Bayes, and Artificial Neural Networks.

This paper [14] proposes a local and global cloud confederation model called FnF, which uses Fuzzy logic to make optimal selection decisions for target cloud data centers. It balances the profit of the cloud provider and user QoS and estimates resource requirements for big data processing tasks. It is superior to other approaches in meeting service level agreements, maintaining user QoS, and maximizing cloud provider profit.

The authors [15] conducted experiments using convolutional neural networks (CNNs) trained on pre-existing word vectors for sentence-level classification tasks. They found that a simple CNN with little adjustment and fixed vectors performed well, but fine-tuning the vectors for specific tasks led to even better results. A modification to the architecture allowed for both task-specific and fixed vectors.

In this paper [16], introduces a new architecture called VD-CNN for text processing, which works directly on the character level using small convolutions and pooling operations. It improves with increasing depth, surpassing the state-of-the-art in public text classification tasks by using up to 29 convolutional layers. This is the first application of very deep convolutional networks to text processing.

This study [17] proposes text classification techniques to categorize customer messages into predefined system defects. It compares five different Machine Learning classifiers and finds that SVM has the highest accuracy score in identifying defects in customer support data. This approach can help improve customer support services and customer satisfaction.

In this paper [18], proposes to combine the Bert model and Bayesian network to classify text more accurately. The Bayesian network classifies text into two categories, while the Bert model classifies text into specific categories. This combination reduces errors caused by using only one of the methods, improving text classification accuracy.

2.1 Gap Analysis

We compared the major papers and algorithms of related works in Table 1 below. There are many algorithms and work available in this platform but we are going to do some different from them.

Table 1. Gap Analysis

Autho	Voice Recognizer	Text Identification	Disease Detection	Doctor Recomendation	Primary Medication	Recommend Doctor Based on Rating	Web App
Hamsagayathri et al. (2021) [7]	✓	✓	✓	-	-	-	-
Jing Yi Leong et al. (2020) [3]	-	-	✓	✓	✓	-	-
Yoonkwon Yi et al. (2020) [11]	-	✓	✓	-	-	-	-
Songsong Liu et al. (2019) [18]	-	✓	-	-	-	-	-
Vijava Shetty et al. (2019) [10]	✓	✓	✓	-	-	-	-
Md. Ataur Rahman Bhuiyan et al. (2019) [13]	-	-	✓	-	✓	-	-
Enam Biswas et al. (2019) [6]	-	✓	✓	-	-	-	-
Our Research	✓	✓	✓	✓	✓	✓	✓

3   Methodology

In this section, we have discussed the detailed methodology and design of our system. Figure 1 shows the overview of the architecture of our system. We have got the disease dataset from Kaggle [19]. First of all, we need to clean the data. We need to remove all the duplicates and NULLs. After that, we have to train a model for the symptom extractor. For the symptom extraction, we have used Python's Flashtext package. Flashtext package is used to extract and replace keywords from a supplied text. It makes it possible to efficiently search and replace various keywords in huge amounts of text. The clean symptom dataset should be split for testing and training purposes. The test data will be used in multiple classification models and the accuracy will be evaluated. The best model will be used for the web app.

3.1   Environment Setup

As we are working on a ML model and our model will run by a Django web interface, we need to do some environmental setup:

- **WebkitSpeechRecognition:** WebkitSpeechRecognition is an API of JavaScript to convert the voice to text. It is an voice recognition tool.
- **Python:** We need to install the latest version of Python from the official Python website.
- **Virtual Environment:** We need to create a virtual environment by opening a terminal or command prompt.
- **Activating the Virtual Environment:** We need to activate the virtual environment by running the appropriate command.
- **Installing Django and Necessary Dependencies:** With the virtual environment activated, we need to install Django and other required dependencies. In our project, we need to install flashtext, pandas, numpy, scikit-learn,

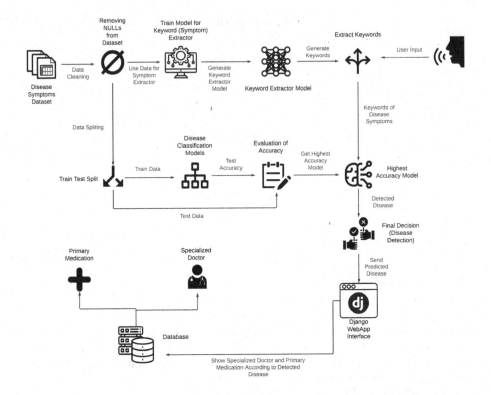

Fig. 1. System Architecture

seaborn, and matplotlib. Those dependencies are required to run the project properly.

- **Create a Django app:** We need to create a new Django app within our project using the necessary command.
- **Define models and views:** In our Django app, we needed to define the necessary models and views.
- **Import Necessary Database:** We need to start the MySQL server and import or build the necessary data in the server.
- **Prepare training data:** We need to prepare the training data required for our machine learning model.
- **Train the machine learning model:** We need to train our machine learning model using the prepared training data.
- **Save the trained model:** Once the model is trained, we need to save it to disk using a suitable format of joblib. This allows us to load the trained model later when making predictions through our Django app.

Those are the necessary steps to follow. Our system has some dependencies. Those are mentioned above. Those dependencies must be imported for our system to work smoothly.

3.2   Generate Model

For generate a ML model that can detect disease, we need to go through some layers or steps. By traversing those layers step by step we can generate our model and gain a good accuracy through our model.

Dataset: For creating our model the first thing we need is a disease dataset. We have collected our dataset from kaggle [19]. The dataset has disease symptoms and diseases in it. This dataset contains 131 symptomps and 41 disease. The description of the dataset is given below at Table 2.

Table 2. Description of Dataset

Column ->	S1	S2	S3	S4	S5	S6	S7	S8	S9
Count	4920	4920	4920	4572	3714	2934	2268	1944	1692
Unique	41	34	48	54	50	38	32	26	21
Freq	822	870	726	378	348	390	264	276	228
	S10	**S11**	**S12**	**S13**	**S14**	**S15**	**S16**	**S17**	
	1512	1194	744	504	306	240	192	72	
	22	21	18	11	8	4	3	1	
	198	120	126	72	96	144	72	72	

Here, S refers to the disease symptoms. The details of the column of the dataset are described in the dataset. The details of column count, uniqueness, and frequency are given in Table 2.

Cleaning the Dataset: The dataset has NULL values and also some unwanted spaces. These needs to be cleaned because they can put an effect on the model accuracy. Figure 2 represents the dataset before removing the NULL values and Fig. 3 represents the dataset after removing the dataset which is a straight line. That means we dont have any NULL values on the existing dataset.

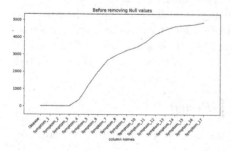

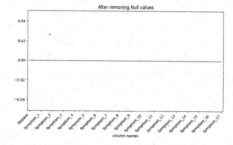

Fig. 2. Dataset before removing NULL values

Fig. 3. Dataset after removing NULL values

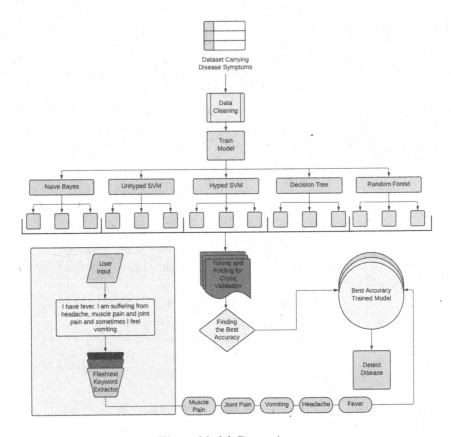

Fig. 4. Model Generation

Training the model: We have already discussed that we are using and comparing Naive Bayes, Unhypred SVM, Hypered SVM, Decision Tree, and Random Forest algorithms. As we have multiple diseases to predict, so we are using the algorithms in multi level ways. The description of those models are given below:

- **Naive Bayes:** The Naive Bayes Classifier assumes the diseases are conditionally independent given the label or category, which means that the presence or absence of a particular disease does not affect the presence or absence of any other disease. This assumption simplifies the computation of the conditional probability of the evidence given the hypothesis, which is represented by the following equation:

$$P(x|y) = \prod iP(xi|y)$$

where xi is the ith symptoms of the input sample, y is the label or category, and x is the input feature vector.

- **SVM:** A potent supervised machine learning technique used for classification tasks is called Support Vector Machines (SVM). It locates an ideal hyperplane that divides data points into various classifications. For a multi-level classification issue with K diseases, K classifiers are trained. The goal of any classifiers is to isolate one class from the others.

The class labels should be written as y ∈ 1, 2, ..., K. The following is a representation of the k-th classifier's decision function:

$$f_k(X) = W_k X + b_k$$

where b_k is the bias term particular to k diseases and w_k is the weight vector. The difference between Unhypered SVM and Hypered SVM is Hypered SVM uses the polynomial kernel. The polynomial kernel can occasionally locate a hyperplane that divides the classes by mapping the data into a higher-dimensional space.

- **Decision Tree:** Including multi-level or multi-class classification problems, decision trees are adaptable supervised machine learning techniques that are frequently employed for classification tasks. The algorithm creates a structure that resembles a tree, with each internal node standing in for a judgment call based on a feature and each leaf node standing in for a class label. A Decision Tree mathematically divides the feature space in recursive fashion in order to minimize impurity or enhance information gain. Each node's best feature and threshold for effectively separating the data are chosen using a splitting criterion.

  Based on the structure of the tree, a series of if-else statements can be used to express the decision function for categorization in a decision tree. Each decision node assesses a particular feature value starting at the root node, sending the flow through the appropriate child node until a leaf node is reached, which provides the anticipated class label. When building a decision tree, methods like ID3, C4.5, or CART are used. These algorithms use metrics like entropy, Gini impurity, or information gain to assess the quality of splits and choose the best tree structure.

  In order to anticipate a class label for multi-level classification, input symptoms are iterated through the Decision Tree while adhering to the decision rules until the relevant leaf node is reached for disease prediction.

- **Random Forest:** Multiple decision trees are used in Random Forest, an ensemble learning technique, to carry out multi-level classification tasks. To arrive at a final forecast, it combines the predictions of various decision trees. Let's refer to the input symptoms as X in mathematics and the matching class labels (diseases) as y. A set of decision trees T1, T2, ..., TN are built by Random Forest. A random portion of the training data and a subset of input symptoms are used to construct each decision tree. Each decision tree is built during training by recursively partitioning the feature space according to circumstances that maximize impurity removal or information gain.

  In order to aggregate the predictions made by the decision trees for multi-level categorization, Random Forest uses either majority voting or weighted voting. The final predicted class is decided upon using the class label with the greatest number of votes or weighted total of votes. By using a variety of decision trees and including randomness in the symptoms and data sampling processes, Random Forest offers robustness against overfitting and good predicted accuracy.

The full model generation part explained in Fig. 4. The full process with all the dependencies are demonstrated in the Fig. 4.

As we are building a Machine Learning based web app we have decided to use Django for the development of the web app. Because it is a strong web framework. It makes it possible for programmers to create intricate and scalable web applications fast and effectively. It adheres to the Model-View-Controller (MVC) architectural paradigm, which encourages concern separation and makes code simpler to extend and maintain. Developers can save a ton of time and work by utilizing the many built-in capabilities that Django offers, like an ORM, user authentication, an admin panel, and a templating engine. Because of its batteries-included design philosophy, developers are free to concentrate on coding their application logic rather than creating a new design for each project. Due to the size and activity of the Django community, there is an abundance of third-party packages, documentation, and support accessible.

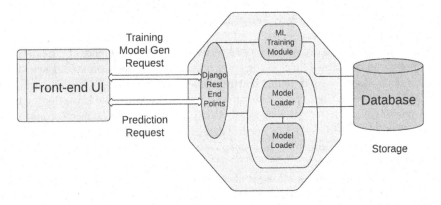

Fig. 5. ML-trained Predictive model with a Django API

Using a Django API to build a Machine Learning trained prediction model has a number of advantages. It first enables the development of an ML model that can forecast results from input data. Second, integrating the model into a web application is made simple by using a Django API. Finally, the Django framework offers an adaptable and user-friendly foundation for creating the API. Fourth, the API can be set up in the cloud and made available to users all over the world. Thirdly, automating repetitive operations with Django and ML can improve the effectiveness and efficiency of data analysis and prediction (Fig. 5).

Table 3. Comparing Multiple Algorithms

Algorithms	Precision	F1 Score	Accuracy
Unhyperd SVM	93.81%	92.56%	83.17%
Hyperd SVM	99.68%	99.65%	98.05%
Naive Bayes	88.22%	86.40%	86.59%
Decision Tree	98.08%	96.71%	97.4%
Random Forest	99.68%	99.65%	99.35%

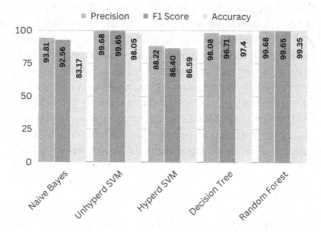

Fig. 6. Comparison of Algorithm Accuracies

4   Testing and Evaluation

In the Fig. 6 and Table 3 we are comparing the multiple algorithms. For better accuracy we have used kth-number of folds. K-fold cross-validation is a statistical modeling and machine learning approach used to evaluate a model's performance and generalizability. It aids in determining how effectively a model will function with unknown data. The initial dataset is split into k equal-sized subsets or folds for k-fold cross-validation. The model is trained and tested k times, with each evaluation utilizing the remaining folds as the training set and a different fold as the validation set. The model is trained on the training set and then examined on the validation set for each iteration. Each iteration includes a performance metric, such as accuracy or mean squared error.

We have tuned the value of K for finding the best accuracy. We have analyzed a number of algorithms. They are the Unhyperd SVM, the Hyperd SVM, Naive Bayes algorithm, Decision Tree, and the Random Forest. After comparing them, we have discovered that the Random Forest algorithm has the greatest accuracy of 99.35%. As a result, we have decided to use the Random Forest model to build our system.

5   Limitations and Future Work

Despite all the good features of our system, we have some limitations. Such as: our system works only in the English language, currently able to identify a few specific diseases, no mobile application is available right now, our system can not guarantee 100% accuracy in disease detection. We are attempting to give the primary focus on detecting the disease using an English voice recognition system, taking into account all the circumstances of our research. However, the Bangla language is also important for our research. Therefore, if only Bangla knowing person wants to use our system, our machine can easily recognize his or her voice and can also detect diseases, we will also focus on the Bengali language in the future. Besides, We are currently able to identify a few specific diseases, but our long-term objective is to identify more diseases by improving and updating the dataset currently we have and we want to build a mobile application in order to give better accessibility to the users. Also, we have a few amount of datasets. In the future, we will focus on collecting more data to get better accuracy on a large number of datasets. Besides this, we have limitations to testing our data only on a few machine learning algorithms as we have limitations on our GPU. In the future, we focus on more algorithms and come up with the best results.

6   Conclusion

We presented a concept for disease detection in this paper. This paper discussed how ML can be used to identify various diseases from a patient's speech and to get recommended specialized doctors. In many fields, ML delivers successful outcomes. This article discusses various ML techniques for diagnosing diseases. Some models, which specifically describe the characteristic, have demonstrated fantastic results. We applied some algorithms, such as Naive Bayes, Unhypred SVM, Hypered SVM, Decision Tree, and Random Forest to produce the best results. ML enables computers to process and comprehend human language. We have utilized the algorithms in the best way. As, we have used multiple algorithms we found the best accuracy for our system.

References

1. 67% of all deaths in Bangladesh due to non-communicable diseases. https://www.thedailystar.net/health/disease/news/rising-health-risk-2948321. Accessed 04 June 2023
2. What is Machine Learning in Health Care? Applications and Opportunities—Coursera. https://www.coursera.org/articles/machine-learning-in-health-care. Accessed 04 June 2023
3. Leong, J.Y.I., Booma, P.M.: Symptom-based disease prediction system using machine learning. J. Theor. Appl. Inf. Technol. 98(19) (2020)
4. Fatima, M., Pasha, M., et al.: Survey of machine learning algorithms for disease diagnostic. J. Intell. Learn. Syst. Appl. 9(01), 1 (2017)

5. Zhao, R.-W., Li, G.-Z., Liu, J.-M., Wang, X.: Clinical multi-label free text classification by exploiting disease label relation. In: 2013 IEEE International Conference on Bioinformatics and Biomedicine, pp. 311–315 (2013)
6. Biswas, E., Das, A.K.: Symptom-based disease detection system in Bengali using convolution neural network. In: 2019 7th International Conference on Smart Computing Communications (ICSCC), pp. 1–5 (2019)
7. Hamsagayathri, P., Vigneshwaran, S.: Symptoms based disease prediction using machine learning techniques. In: 2021 Third International Conference on Intelligent Communication Technologies and Virtual Mobile Networks (ICICV), pp. 747–752 (2021)
8. Kolkur, M.S., Kalbande, D.R., Kharkar, V.: Machine learning approaches to multiclass human skin disease detection. Int. J. Comput. Intell. Res. **14**(1), 29–39 (2018)
9. Li, J.P., Haq, A.U.L., Din, S.U., Khan, J., Khan, A., Saboor, A.: Heart disease identification method using machine learning classification in e-healthcare. IEEE Access **8**, 107562–107582 (2020)
10. Vijava Shetty, S., Karthik, G.A., Ashwin, M.: Symptom based health prediction using data mining. In: 2019 International Conference on Communication and Electronics Systems (ICCES), pp. 744–749 (2019)
11. Yi, Y., Shen, Z., Bompelli, A., Yu, F., Wang, Y., Zhang, R.: Natural language processing methods to extract lifestyle exposures for Alzheimer's disease from clinical notes. In: 2020 IEEE International Conference on Healthcare Informatics (ICHI), pp. 1–2 (2020)
12. Hughes, M., Li, I., Kotoulas, S., Suzumura, T.: Medical text classification using convolutional neural networks. Stud. Health Technol. Inform. **235**, 246–250 (2017). PMID: 28423791
13. Bhuiyan, M., Ullah, R., Das, A.: iHealthcare: predictive model analysis concerning big data applications for interactive healthcare systems †. Appl. Sci. **9**, 3365 (2019). https://doi.org/10.3390/app9163365
14. Das, A.K., Adhikary, T., Razzaque, M.A., et al.: Big media healthcare data processing in cloud: a collaborative resource management perspective. Cluster Comput. **20**, 1599–1614 (2017). https://doi.org/10.1007/s10586-017-0785-8
15. Chen, Y.: Convolutional neural network for sentence classification. Master's thesis, University of Waterloo (2015)
16. Conneau, A., Schwenk, H., Barrault, L., Lecun, Y.: Very deep convolutional networks for text classification, pp. 1107–1116 (2017). https://doi.org/10.18653/v1/E17-1104
17. Parmar, P.S. Biju, P.K., Shankar, M., Kadiresan, N.: Multiclass text classification and analytics for improving customer support response through different classifiers. In: 2018 International Conference on Advances in Computing, Communications and Informatics (ICACCI), Bangalore, India, pp. 538–542 (2018). https://doi.org/10.1109/ICACCI.2018.8554881
18. Liu, S., Tao, H., Feng, S.: Text classification research based on BERT model and Bayesian network. In: 2019 Chinese Automation Congress (CAC). Hangzhou, China, pp. 5842–5846 (2019). https://doi.org/10.1109/CAC48633.2019.8996183
19. https://www.kaggle.com/datasets/itachi9604/disease-symptom-description-dataset
20. Toepfner, N., et al.: Detection of human disease conditions by single-cell morphorheological phenotyping of blood. Elife **7**, e29213 (2018)

21. Roy, K., Chaudhuri, S.S., Ghosh, S., Dutta, S.K., Chakraborty, P., Sarkar, R.: Skin disease detection based on different segmentation techniques. In: 2019 International Conference on Opto-Electronics and Applied Optics (Optronix), Kolkata, India, pp. 1–5 (2019). https://doi.org/10.1109/OPTRONIX.2019.8862403

22. Kirar, A.T.: Machine learning based heart disease detection system. In: 2022 International Congress on Human-Computer Interaction, Optimization and Robotic Applications (HORA). Ankara, Turkey, pp. 1–7 (2022). https://doi.org/10.1109/HORA55278.2022.9799987

23. Dhal, P., Azad, C.: A multi-stage multi-objective GWO based feature selection approach for multi-label text classification. In: 2022 2nd International Conference on Intelligent Technologies (CONIT), Hubli, India, pp. 1–5 (2022). https://doi.org/10.1109/CONIT55038.2022.9847886

24. Fadil, R., Huether, A., Brunnemer, R., Blaber, A.P., Lou, J.-S., Tavakolian, K.: Early detection of parkinson's disease using center of pressure data and machine learning. In: 2021 43rd Annual International Conference of the IEEE Engineering in Medicine & Biology Society (EMBC), Mexico, pp. 2433–2436 (2021). https://doi.org/10.1109/EMBC46164.2021.9630451

25. Mai, W., Chen, Y., Lin, X.: Early detection of neurological degenerative diseases based on the protein chirality detection with microwaves. In: 2020 IEEE Asia-Pacific Microwave Conference (APMC), Hong Kong, pp. 965–967 (2020). https://doi.org/10.1109/APMC47863.2020.9331591

26. Dixit, S., Gaikwad, A., Vyas, V., Shindikar, M., Kamble, K.: United Neurological study of disorders: Alzheimer's disease, Parkinson's disease detection, anxiety detection, and stress detection using various machine learning algorithms. In: 2022 International Conference on Signal and Information Processing (IConSIP), Pune, India, pp. 1–6 (2022). https://doi.org/10.1109/IConSIP49665.2022.10007434

27. Bassiouny, R., Mohamed, A., Umapathy, K., Khan, N.: An interpretable object detection-based model for the diagnosis of neonatal lung diseases using ultrasound images. In: 2021 43rd Annual International Conference of the IEEE Engineering in Medicine & Biology Society (EMBC), Mexico, pp. 3029–3034 (2021). https://doi.org/10.1109/EMBC46164.2021.9630169

28. Dheer, S., Poddar, M., Pandey, A., Kalaivani, S.: Parkinson's disease detection using acoustic features from speech recordings. In: 2023 International Conference on Intelligent and Innovative Technologies in Computing, Electrical and Electronics (IITCEE), Bengaluru, India, pp. 1–4 (2023). https://doi.org/10.1109/IITCEE57236.2023.10090464

29. Sheng, T., Wu, H., Yue, Z.: An English text classification method based on TextCNN and SVM. In: 2022 3rd International Conference on Electronic Communication and Artificial Intelligence (IWECAI), Zhuhai, China, pp. 227–231 (2022). https://doi.org/10.1109/IWECAI55315.2022.00052

30. Yu, B., Deng, C., Bu, L.: Policy text classification algorithm based on BERT. In: 2022 11th International Conference of Information and Communication Technology (ICTech), Wuhan, China, pp. 488–491 (2022). https://doi.org/10.1109/ICTech55460.2022.00103

31. Hasan, S.A., et al.: Classification of multi-labeled text articles with reuters dataset using SVM. In: 2022 International Conference on Science and Technology (ICOSTECH), Batam City, Indonesia, pp. 01–05 (2022). https://doi.org/10.1109/ICOSTECH54296.2022.9829153

32. Chen, S., Kuang, Q., Yu, X., Li, S., Ding, R.: A multi-label classification algo-rithm for non-standard text. In: 2022 International Conference on Asian Language Processing (IALP), Singapore, Singapore, pp. 206–211 (2022). https://doi.org/10.1109/IALP57159.2022.9961273

33. Yao, T., Zhai, Z., Gao, B.: Text classification model based on fastText. In: 2020 IEEE International Conference on Artificial Intelligence and Information Systems (ICAIIS), Dalian, China, pp. 154–157 (2020). https://doi.org/10.1109/ICAIIS49377.2020.9194939

34. Sultana, R., Palit, R.: A survey on Bengali speech-to-text recognition techniques. In: 2014 9th International Forum on Strategic Technology (IFOST), Cox's Bazar, Bangladesh, pp. 26–29 (2014). https://doi.org/10.1109/IFOST.2014.6991064

35. Jin, G.: Application optimization of NLP system under deep learning technology in text semantics and text classification. In: 2022 International Conference on Educa-tion, Network and Information Technology (ICENIT), Liverpool, UK, pp. 279–283 (2022). https://doi.org/10.1109/ICENIT57306.2022.00068

36. Luo, W.: Research and implementation of text topic classification based on text CNN. In: 2022 3rd International Conference on Computer Vision, Image and Deep Learning & International Conference on Computer Engineering and Applications (CVIDL & ICCEA), Changchun, China, pp. 1152–1155 (2022). https://doi.org/10.1109/CVIDLICCEA56201.2022.9824532

37. Muthu, B.A., et al.: IOT based wearable sensor for diseases prediction and symp-tom analysis in healthcare sector. Peer-to-peer Netw. Appl. **13**, 2123–2134 (2020)

38. Health care costs: Gallup survey finds Americans borrowed $88 billion. https://www.usatoday.com/story/news/health/2019/04/02/health-care-costs-gallup-survey-americans-borrowed-88-billion/3333864002/. Accessed 04 June 2023

Digitalisation Transformation in High Schools: Analysis of the COVID-19 Pandemic's Accelerating Impact

Majlinda Fetaji[1] (ID), Maaruf Ali[2,3] (ID), Bekim Fetaji[4(✉)] (ID), and Mirlinda Ebibi[4] (ID)

[1] Faculty of Contemporary Science and Technology, South East European University, Tetovë, North Macedonia
M.Fetaji@seeu.edu.mk

[2] Faculty of Computer Science and IT, Universiteti Metropolitan Tiranë (UMT), Tirana, Albania
Maaruf.Ali@umt.edu.al

[3] The Doctoral College, University of Wales Trinity St. David, Lampeter, Wales, UK

[4] Faculty of Informatics, Mother Teresa University, Shkup (Skopje), North Macedonia
{Bekim.Fetaji,Mirlinda.Ebibi}@unt.edu.mk

Abstract. How COVID-19 has impacted digitalisation in high schools is presented. The scale of the utilisation of Information Systems (ISs) is presented as statistical study which addresses a notable gap in the published literature. The study focussed on the impact of the adoption of LMS (Learning Management System) and other related variables in digitalisation in higher education with a comparison made before and after the pandemic. The research also sought to understand the level of LMS usage by the administration during the pandemic. The research methodology employed was a triangulation technique, which combined qualitative and quantitative methods. This approach allowed for a comprehensive investigation of the research questions. The quantitative method involved the use of questionnaires to acquire data from a large number of participants, whilst the qualitative method involved the use of focus groups to gain more in-depth insights into the experiences and perceptions of the participants. The study used statistical data analyses: ANOVA; one sample t-test; crosstab comparison; Bayesian factor and estimates – to analyse the data collected. These analyses provided valuable insights into the impact of the pandemic on the digitalisation process in high schools. These being to provide recommendations for enhancing the digitalisation process in high schools such as guiding educators, school administrators and policymakers in their efforts to improve the digital learning experience for high school students in the context of the ongoing pandemic and beyond. The study concluded that the digitalisation process has improved after the pandemic.

Keywords: Education 4.0 · COVID-19 Pandemic · Technology Adoption · E-learning Efficacy · Digital Pedagogy

M. H. Miraz et al. (Eds.): iCETiC 2023, LNICST 538, pp. 86–102, 2024.
https://doi.org/10.1007/978-3-031-50215-6_7

1 Introduction

1.1 General Introduction

The pandemic has necessitated a shift towards digital learning platforms [1]. This study aims to assess the current situation and investigate the level of use of Information Systems [2] in education. The focus is on the work of the teacher and the management of the teacher's activities, as these are key areas that have been significantly affected by the shift to online learning.

While there has been some studies on this on education in general, there is a lack of focused studies on the specific context of high schools and the digitalisation process within this context. The study investigates the impact and assesses several variables related to the digitalisation process. These variables include the use of digital Learning Management System (LMS) platforms [3], the perceived benefits of digital social platforms in learning, the use of digital exam apps or platforms in classes and the perceived improvement in the digitalisation process compared to before the pandemic.

The insights from this study are discussed and augmented, providing a clear understanding of the current state of high school digitalisation and the impact of the pandemic.

The principle of equity and inclusion is crucial in the situation of internet use in indigent [4] and affluent countries. The pandemic has highlighted the disparities in internet access, with 19% internet use in indigent countries compared to 87% in affluent countries. This disparity has significant implications for the high school digitalisation.

The pandemic of COVID-19 [5] has brought about unprecedented changes in various sectors, including education. The sudden shift from traditional classroom learning to online platforms has highlighted the importance of digitalisation in high schools. However, this transition has not been uniform, neither across different regions nor in socio-economic groups, leading to a discussion on the principle of equity and inclusion.

The introduction of this research study begins by highlighting the stark contrast in internet usage between high-income and low-income countries. The data shows that only 19% of the population in low-income countries have access to the internet, compared to 87% in high-income countries. This disparity in internet access has significant implications for the digitalisation process in high schools, as it directly affects the ability of students to participate in online learning.

The study then delves into the main research questions, which revolve around the preferences and experiences of students and teachers in the new digital learning environment. These questions include whether students prefer online learning or physical presence in lectures, whether they believe online learning could be improved if professors were more active and engaged and whether they find synchronous (everyone attending online lectures at the same time) or asynchronous (accessing recorded videos at their own pace) online teaching more effective.

The research also investigates the use of digital Learning Management System (LMS) platforms in classes, the perceived benefits of digital social platforms in learning and the use of digital exam apps or platforms for assessment. It also seeks to understand the perceived improvement in the digitalisation process compared to before the pandemic and whether the administration uses any electronic software system during the pandemic.

The introduction is followed by the research methodology, data collection and analysis, statistical data analyses and the conclusions and recommendations based on the findings of the research. The goal is to ascertain the current status of high school digitalisaion and the effect of COVID-19.

1.2 Literature Review

Five very specific papers were selected covering the period 2020–2022 relevant to this study.

"A Resilient ICT4D Approach to ECO Countries' Education Response During COVID-19 Pandemic" [6]
This paper discusses the pandemic's impact and identifies gaps in the implementation of ICTs in secondary and primary education levels in the Economic Cooperation Organization (ECO) [7] member states. The study highlights the impact of various factors such as internet connectivity, access to digital devices and other infrastructural factors on distance learning. The paper proposes a robust ICT-for-Development (ICT4D) structure to study the endurance, coping, and return to pre-COVID existence in the education systems. The novelty of this research lies in its comparative approach and the comprehensive analysis of various factors affecting education during the pandemic. The paper suggests future work on addressing the identified challenges to improve crisis management in the education sector.

"The Impact of Knowledge of the Issue of Identification and Authentication on the Information Security of Adolescents in the Virtual Space" [8]
This research investigates the security of information in high school students in the virtual space during the pandemic of COVID-19. This research identifies a gap in the knowledge of high school students regarding information security in the virtual space. The authors propose additional education in the field of information security as a solution. The contribution of this paper lies in its analysis of student behaviours that compromise their information security. The novelty of the research is in its focus on the issue of identification and authentication. The authors suggest designing a framework for the level assessment of adolescent digital literacy and conducting further research in the field of juvenile information literacy.

"School Closures and Educational Path: How the Covid-19 Pandemic Affected Transitions to College" [9]
This study investigates the pandemic's impact on the change between college and high school in Brazil. The authors find that the pandemic increased enrolment for students in high-quality schools at the detriment of students from poorer quality schools. The paper contributes to the comprehension of the effects of the pandemic on education and suggests that the pandemic has stalled the educational paths of underprivileged students. The novelty of this research lies in its use of microdata from students that applied to a

selective university. The authors suggest future work on mitigating the negative effects of the pandemic on education.

"SARS-CoV-2 Impact on Online Teaching Methodologies and the Ed-Tech Sector: Smile and Learn Platform Case Study" [10]

This paper analyses the rank of online methodologies and the usage of the Learn and Smile platform during the COVID-19 pandemic. The authors identify a gap in the availability of resources for families and teachers to continue their teaching practice during the pandemic. The paper contributes to the understanding of the impact of the pandemic on the digitalisation of pedagogy. The novelty of this study lies in its focus on the Learn and Smile platform. The authors suggest future work on analysing the outcomes on education.

"Driving Innovation Through Project-Based Learning: A Pre-University STEAM for Social Good Initiative" [11]

This study presents the experiences of pre-university Indian students participating in a STEAM for Social Good innovation challenge during the pandemic. The authors identify a gap in imparting education to children on critical future-oriented issues. The paper proposes a constructionist approach where children ideate and reflect upon their community problems. The novelty of this research lies in its university-school partnership model and the use of "Engineering Design Thinking" [12]. The authors recommend more research into how to assist kids in their management of social problems more effectively and also to teach them to see social challenges as chances to improve their lives and the lives of those around them.

2   Research Methodology

The study poses several research questions, including preferences for online learning or physical presence in lectures, the potential for improved online learning if professors were more active and engaged, the comparison between synchronous and asynchronous online teaching [13], and the pandemic's level of impact on students, teachers, administration and parents. The research methodology used is a triangulation technique [14], combining qualitative methods (focus groups) and quantitative methods (questionnaires). This approach was chosen to provide a comprehensive and multi-faceted understanding of the impact of COVID-19 on high school digitalisation.

The quantitative method involved the use of questionnaires. These questionnaires were designed to gather data on a range of variables related to the digitalisation process.

The qualitative method involved the use of focus groups. These focus groups were designed to provide more in-depth insights into the experiences and perceptions of the participants. The focus groups allowed the researchers to delve deeper into the nuances of the digitalisation process and the impact of the pandemic on various stakeholders, including students, teachers, administration and parents. The research questions were designed to provide a comprehensive understanding of the digitalisation process in high schools and the impact of COVID-19. To gain significant insights and conclusions, the replies to these questions were then assessed utilizing statistical data analysis, such as:

ANOVA (Analysis of Variance) [15], One Sample t-Test [16], Bayesian Factor [17] and Estimates, and Crosstab Comparison [18].

2.1 Data Collection and Analysis

The data was collected through questionnaires and focus groups. The data included preferences for physical presence or online learning, the use of digital exam apps or platforms for assessment and the perceived impact of the pandemic on various stakeholders. The data was then analysed using various statistical methods.

The data collection and analysis process in this research study was designed to provide a comprehensive understanding of the effect of the pandemic on high school digitalisation. This process was guided by the main research questions and involved both quantitative and qualitative methods.

The quantitative data was obtained through a questionnaire, that was designed to gather information on a range of variables related to the digitalisation process.

The qualitative data was collected through focus groups, which allowed for more in-depth insights into the experiences and perceptions of the participants. These focus groups provided valuable qualitative data that complemented the quantitative data collected through the questionnaire.

Once the data was collected, it was subjected to rigorous statistical analyses. These analyses included ANOVA, One sample t-test, Bayesian factor and estimates, and crosstab comparison. For instance, the One-Sample t-Test was used to compare the means of different variables, such as the perceived improvement in the digitalisation process compared to that before the pandemic, the potential for better online learning if professors were more active and engaged, the comparison between synchronous and asynchronous online teaching, and the pandemic's level of impact on students.

The results of these analyses provided valuable insights into the impact of COVID-19 on the digitalisation process in high schools. For example, based on the crosstab comparison of the frequency between the variable "online learning or physical presence" and the dependent variable "digitalisation process has been improved compared before the pandemic", it was concluded that a high percentage (90.9%) of participants assessed a positive value for the improvement in the digitalisation process since the pandemic.

This comprehensive data collection and analysis process allowed for a thorough investigation of the research questions, providing valuable high school pedagogical digitalisation insights into the effect of COVID-19. The insights derived from this process contributed to the conclusions and recommendations of the study, which aimed to enhance high school digitalisation.

2.2 Strategy and Approach to Assess Digitalization During Covid-19

Our approach to asses digital learning during covid was multifaced and not only through survey but also through comparing observed student engagement with digital learning across instructional activities and interviews; focus groups with IT staff; administrators; instructors and students.

Our trained research team conducted structured observations of classes to document real-time engagement with digital tools across core instructional activities like: online lectures, discussions, assessments and project collaboration. Detailed observational data was collected on participation levels, tool usage, teaching practices, technical issues and accommodations.

Additionally, one-on-one interviews were conducted with school IT staff, administrators, instructors and students. Experts provided perspectives on technology infrastructure, training, policies and best practices. The students offered lived experiences of challenges, benefits and preferences related to digital learning.

Finally, the focus groups allowed less vocal students to open up about their shared experiences and desires for the future. Quotes and narratives from these discussions added important context.

This multifaceted data collection approach, triangulating rigorous quantitative surveys with rich qualitative insights from observations, expert interviews and student focus groups, strengthened our study's comprehensiveness, validity and strategic value. The blended methods provide a well-rounded assessment of the nuances, successes, growing pains and potential of the digital transformation of high school education during an unprecedented pandemic disruption.

Comparing Observed Student Engagement with Digital Learning Across Instructional Activities.

Table 1 shows the number of students for each type of instructional activity and the type of digital tool utilised.

Table 1. №. of students for each type of instructional activity and the type of digital tool utilised.

Instructional Activity	Digital Tool	№. of Students
I. Lectures	Online video lectures	121
II. Discussions	Online discussion boards	115
III. Quizzes	Online quizzes	120
IV. Projects	Online project management tools	120
V. Assessments	Online exams	120

Table 2, shows how the particular digital tool was integrated with the type of instructional activity and how it complemented the counterpart non-digital activity.

As Table 2 shows, the digital tools have been integrated into a variety of instructional activities to enhance student engagement. By using digital tools in a thoughtful and intentional way, instructors created learning experiences that are more engaging, effective and inclusive.

Table 2. Comparing observed student engagement with digital learning across instructional activities.

Instructional Activity	Digital Tool	How the Digital Tool was Integrated	How the Digital Tool Complemented Non-Digital Activities
I. Lectures	Online video lectures	Lectures were recorded and made available to students online. This allowed students to watch the lectures at their own pace and review them as needed	Online lectures allowed students to access the same information as their classmates, regardless of their location or time zone. This helped to create a more inclusive learning environment
II. Discussions	Online discussion boards	Students were able to participate in discussions with their classmates and the instructor on an online discussion board. This allowed students to share their thoughts and ideas with others, and to get feedback on their work	Online discussions provided a space for students to collaborate and learn from each other. This helped to promote deeper learning and engagement
III. Quizzes	Online quizzes	Quizzes were administered online, allowing students to take them at their own convenience. This was a convenient way for students to assess their understanding of the material	Online quizzes helped students to stay on track with their learning. They also provided the instructor with feedback on how well students were understanding the material
IV. Projects	Online project management tools	Students were able to use online project management tools to collaborate with their classmates on projects. This allowed students to share files, track progress and communicate with each other	Online project management tools helped students to stay organized and on track with their projects. They also provided a space for students to collaborate and learn from each other
V. Assessments	Online exams	Exams were administered online, allowing students to take them at their own convenience. This was a convenient way for students to take exams, especially if they were unable to attend a scheduled exam	Online exams provided the instructor with a way to assess student learning without having to collect paper exams. This saved the instructor time and resources

3   Results

Table 3, show the analysis of the proportions of students engaged in the various instructional activities.

Table 4 show the average time spent by each student for each particular instructional activity (I–V). Table 4, clearly shows that the majority of the time was spent conducting project work using online project management digital tools.

Table 3. Analyses of proportions of students engaged in the various instructional activities.

Instructional Activity	Digital Tool	Proportion of Students (%)
I. Lectures	Online video lectures	50
II. Discussions	Online discussion boards	37.5
III. Quizzes	Online quizzes	25
IV. Projects	Online project management tools	12.5
V. Assessments	Online exams	5

Table 4. Average Time spent on instructional activities.

Instructional Activity	Digital Tool	Average Time spent (minutes)
I. Lectures	Online video lectures	42.5
II. Discussions	Online discussion boards	23
III. Quizzes	Online quizzes	21
IV. Projects	Online project management tools	245
V. Assessments	Online exams	90

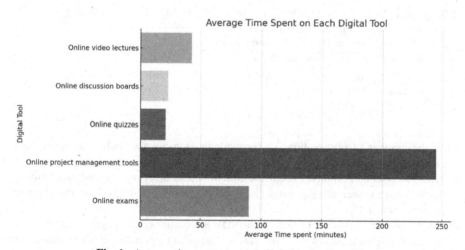

Fig. 1. Average time spent on each digital tool per student.

Representing information from Table 4, graphically as a bar chart in Fig. 1, shows that students surprisingly did not spend substantial time online regarding the video lectures but preferred to spend more time doing their collaborative project work online. The results show the importance of having a good and effective online project management tool for effective online group collaboration.

The One-Sample statistics, as shown in Table 5, provided a summary of the data collected through the questionnaire. Table 1 presents the average, standard deviation and standard error mean for the variables:

- Q. 6: "How much, in your opinion, has the digitalisation process advanced since the pandemic?";
- Q. 3: "Do you believe that online learning could be significantly improved if professors were more involved and active?";
- Q. 4: "Is synchronous (where everyone logs in at the same time) online teaching superior than asynchronous (where people watch recorded videos at their own leisure) online education?" and
- Q. 8: "How much of an influence, in your opinion, has the pandemic had on students?".

Table 5. One-sample Statistics

$N = 121$	Mean	Std. Deviation	Std. Error Mean
6. How much, in your opinion, has the digitalization process advanced since the pandemic?	4.45	0.688	0.0625
3. Do you believe that online learning could be significantly improved if professors were more involved and active?	4.00	0.775	0.0705
4. Is synchronous (where everyone logs in at the same time) online teaching superior than asynchronous (where people watch recorded videos at their own leisure) online education?	4.00	0.775	0.0705
8. How much of an influence, in your opinion, has the pandemic had on students?	4.45	0.688	0.0625

- N: the number of observations or respondents (sample size) who answered each question. Here, each question was answered by 121 respondents.
- Mean: the average response to each question by adding up every response and dividing by the total number of responses. For example, for the first question, the average response was 4.45.
- Std. Deviation (Standard Deviation, or SD): a measure of the degree of variety or spread amongst the answers. A low SD indicates that responses are often within one SD of the mean, whereas a high SD indicates that responses are dispersed across a wider range. For example, for the first question, the standard deviation was 0.688, indicating a relatively low level of dispersion in the responses.
- Std. Error Mean (Standard Error of the Mean): this gauges how widely sample means vary from the population mean. It is calculated by dividing the SD by the sample size square root. The sample mean's likelihood of deviating from the actual population mean is indicated by the standard error. The standard error of the mean, for instance, for question six was 0.0625. The data in Table 1, provides a summary of the responses

to each of the four survey questions. The mean values suggest that on average, respondents gave high ratings or agreed with the statements in the survey questions. The standard deviations and standard errors of the mean provide information about the variability and reliability of these mean values.

The One-Sample t-Test, as shown in Table 6, was used to compare the means of these same four variables. The test value was set to 0 and the significance was 2-tailed. The mean difference and 95% confidence interval of the difference were calculated for each variable. The outcome of the One-Sample t-Test provided valuable insights into the participants' perceptions of the digitalisation process and the impact of the pandemic.

Table 6. One-sample t-Test.

Test Value = 0	t	df	Sig. (2-tailed)	Mean Diff.	95% Confidence Interval of Diff.
6. How much, in your opinion, has the digitalization process advanced since the pandemic?	21.488	10	0.000	4.455	3.99
3. Do you believe that online learning could be significantly improved if professors were more involved and active?	12.111	10	0.000	4.000	3.26
4. Is synchronous (where everyone logs in at the same time) online teaching superior than asynchronous (where people watch recorded videos at their own leisure) online education?	17.127	10	0.000	4.000	3.48
8. How much of an influence, in your opinion, has the pandemic had on students?	21.488	10	0.000	4.455	3.99

- Test Value = 0: the value that the sample mean is being compared to, which is 0 in this case.
- *t*: the t statistic, which measures the deviation from the sample mean. It is used to determine whether the sample mean is significantly different from the test value.
- *df* (Degrees of Freedom): the total number of independent data points used to get the estimate. It is frequently described as the sum of all observations less all essential relations between those observations. In this case, it is 10.
- Sig. (2-tailed): this is the *p*-value. If the *p*-value is less than or equal to the significance level (usually 0.05), the null hypothesis is rejected. In this case, the *p*-value is 0.000, indicating a statistically significant difference from the test value of 0.
- Mean Difference: the difference between the sample mean and the test value (0 in this case).
- 95% Confidence Interval of the Difference: this is an interval estimate of the mean difference. In 95% of the calculated confidence intervals, the actual population mean difference would be contained if the method were to be done numerous times.

The results suggest that for all four questions, the mean response is significantly different from 0, as indicated by the *p*-values of 0.000. This means that the respondents' perceptions on all four aspects – digitalisation process, professors' engagement, synchronous vs asynchronous teaching and pandemic's impact on students – are significantly different from neutrality (assuming the scale used was the Likert [19]: either 1–5 or 1–7, where 0 would represent a neutral or non-response).

The crosstab comparison of the frequency between the most important indirect variable "online learning or physical presence" and the dependent variable "digitalization process has been improved compared before the pandemic" revealed that 90.9% of participants assessed a positive value for the improvement in the digitalisation process since the pandemic.

Table 7, below, is part of an Analysis of Variance (ANOVA) test, specifically focusing on Question 6.: "What percentage do you think the digitalization process has advanced since the pandemic?".

Table 7. Results of the Anova Test Analysis.

6. What percentage do you think the digitalization process has advanced since the pandemic?	Sum of Squares	*df*	Mean Square	*F*	Sig.
Between Groups	1.907	21	0.953	0.422	0.670
Within Groups	18.073	89	2.259	0.135	0.287
Total	19.979	100	3.212	0.557	0.957

- Sum of Squares: this represents all of the data's variation. It is determined by adding the squared deviations between each observation and the mean value as a whole. The variation between groups is divided into the sum of squares. (1.907) and the variation within groups (18.073).

- *df* (Degrees of Freedom): the total number of independent data points used to get the estimate. It is often defined as the number of observations minus the number of necessary relations among those observations. For the "Between Groups" variation, *df* is 21 and for the "Within Groups" variation, *df* is 89.
- Mean Square: is the average variation. It is calculated by multiplying the degrees of freedom by the total of the squares. For the "Between Groups" variation, the mean square is 0.953 and for the "Within Groups" variation, the mean square is 2.259.
- *F*: When an ANOVA test or a regression analysis is performed to see whether the means of two populations differ significantly, a result known as the F statistic will be obtained. To calculate it, divide the mean square of the variation "Between Groups" by the mean square of the variation "Within Groups". In this case, the *F* value is 0.422.
- Sig. (Significance): this is the *p*-value. If the significance threshold must be less than or equal to the *p*-value (usually 0.05), the null hypothesis will be rejected. In this case, the *p*-value is 0.670, which is greater than 0.05, suggesting that the null hypothesis is not rejected. This means that the difference in the means between the groups is not statistically significant.
- In the context of the question "How much do you consider that the digitalization process has been improved compared before the pandemic?", the ANOVA results suggest that there is not a statistically significant difference in responses between different groups.

The Bayes Factor statistical analysis is given in Table 8, below.

Table 8. Statistical Data Analyses.

6. What percentage do you think the digitalization process has advanced since the pandemic?	Bayes Factor [a]
Between Groups	1.147
Within Groups	1.697
Total	2.844

- **Bayes Factor[a]**: The Bayes Factor is a statistic used in Bayesian statistics to quantify the evidence for a hypothesis. It is the ratio of the probabilities of the observed data under two competing hypotheses. In this case, the Bayes Factor is 0.111 for the "Between Groups" variation. The Bayes Factor can be interpreted as the strength of evidence in favour of one hypothesis over the other. A Bayes Factor close to 1 indicates that the data are equally likely under both hypotheses. A Bayes Factor much less than 1 (as in this case) indicates strong evidence for the second hypothesis (usually the null hypothesis), while a Bayes Factor much greater than 1 indicates strong evidence for the first hypothesis.

- **Between Groups**: This is the variation that is due to the interaction between the groups. In this case, the "Between Groups" variation is 0.111.
- **Within Groups**: This is the variation that is due to differences within individual groups. In this case, the "Within Groups" variation is 1.697.
- **Total**: This is the total variation in the data. In this case, the total variation is not provided in Table 4.

Table 4, also includes a note about the Bayes Factor, explaining that it shows the likelihood of an event given enough repeats of it at a given relative frequency. In contrast, probabilities are reinterpreted as a level of belief for an outcome under the Bayesian statistics paradigm. The degree for the outcome "digitalization process has been improved" has been shown as significant level.

These statistical data analyses provided a thorough understanding of the impact of COVID-19 on the digitalisation process in high schools. The insights derived from these analyses contributed to the conclusions and recommendations of the study, which aimed to enhance high school digitalisation. Already technology is being utilised to both deliver education and personalise it beyond the traditional classroom with the new emerging field of Education 4.0 [20].

3.1 Discussion of Results and Insight

To analyse student engagement across instructional activities, we documented the number of students utilizing different digital tools for common learning tasks as shown in Table 2.

Online video lectures for delivering core content reached the broadest number of students at 121 out of 121 total. Online exams and project collaboration tools also saw widespread adoption at 120 students each. Online quizzes and discussion boards engaged slightly fewer students, but still maintained high usage.

Building on this data, Table 3 shows the proportional breakdown of student usage across the digital learning activities. Online lectures made up 50% of usage, indicating it was the most prevalent instructional application. Exams and projects followed at 25% and 12.5% respectively. Online quizzes and discussions accounted for the remaining 12.5% each.

Finally, Table 4 provides statistics on the average time students spent actively engaged with each digital learning activity. Online video lectures averaged 42.5 min of logged viewing time per student. Exams unsurprisingly required the longest average engagement at 90 min. Collaboration tools were used extensively as well with 245 average minutes per student. Online discussions and quizzes required less time on average, at 23 and 21 min respectively.

Taken together, these data points provide tangible insights into how fully and actively students have adopted digital tools across core instructional activities. While online lectures are the gateway into digital learning, students demonstrate substantial engagement across asynchronous discussions, practice quizzes, collaborative projects and high-stakes assessments. This underscores how integrated technology has become across the in-class to out-of-class learning experience.

Here are the statistical data analyses, shown in Table 9, for the number of students using each digital tool (Table 2) and the average time spent on each digital tool (Table 4). Note, the number of observations (nobs) was five.

Table 9. Statistical Analyses of instructional activity of students using educational digital tools.

Statistical Measures	Values for №. of Students	Values for Time (minutes)
Minimum Value (min)	115	21
Maximum Value (max)	121	245
Mean (mean)	119.2	84.3
Variance (variance)	5.7	8842.2
Skewness (skewness)	−1.37	1.21
Kurtosis (kurtosis)	0.11	−0.20

Here are explanations of the statistical measures:

- Number of observations (nobs): The number of data points in the dataset.
- Minimum Value (min): The smallest value in the dataset.
- Maximum Value (max): The largest value in the dataset.
- Mean (mean): The average value of the dataset.
- Variance (variance): A measure of the spread of the data points in the dataset.
- Skewness (skewness): A measure of the asymmetry of the probability distribution of a real-valued random variable about its mean.
- Kurtosis (kurtosis): A measure of the "tailedness" of the probability distribution of a real-valued random variable.

Note: Skewness and kurtosis are less interpretable in this context due to the small number of observations in our dataset. For skewness, a value close to 0 implies that the data is fairly symmetrical. For kurtosis, a value close to 0 means that the tails of the distribution are similar to a normal distribution, while a negative value means the distribution has lighter tails and a flat peak and a positive value means the distribution has heavier tails and a sharp peak.

3.2 The Bias Related with this Approach to Asses Digital Learning during Covid 19

There are several potential sources of bias that should be considered with the approach of using classroom observations and self-reports to assess digital learning during COVID-19:

Selection bias: The classrooms and schools observed may not be representative of all high schools if they are not randomly sampled. Schools that are struggling with technology integration may be less likely to volunteer for observations.

Reporting bias: Survey and interview responses from students, teachers and administrators may be subject to social desirability bias if participants feel inclined to overstate the effectiveness of digital learning tools. They may also suffer from recall bias when comparing current practices to pre-pandemic times.

Here are some ways our research study worked to address and minimize potential biases:

- We used random sampling to select a diverse and representative subset of schools and classrooms for observation. This reduced selection bias.
- Surveys were anonymous to encourage honest self-reports from students and teachers without fear of judgement.
- Classrooms were observed by multiple researchers independently and compared to reduce individual observer bias.
- Our observation rubric and survey questions went through multiple iterations of refinement and pilot testing to remove ambiguous, leading or narrow wording.
- We actively recruited schools with known technology access limitations to participate in the study to avoid only observing tech-savvy classrooms.
- Interviews were conducted with disengaged and low-performing students to include their voices and experiences in the data.
- Data was collected at three time points over the school year to track evolution and reduce recall bias.
- We used mixed methods to allow qualitative data to provide context to counter misinterpretations of quantitative results.
- Limitations of the convenience sampling and potential biases were disclosed in the study methodology.
- Conclusions were conservatively stated based only on the data at hand to avoid overstating conclusions.

4 Conclusions

The study concludes that the digitalisation process has improved compared to before the pandemic. The research contributed to the understanding of the benefits of digitalisation and the current state of software information systems used by schools. It also determined the level of impact that online learning had on students. The study recommends further research and practice in this area to enhance the digitalisation process in high schools.

Through its analysis of the conceptualized digitization as a process, this work advances both research and practice. The primary goal of the research project was to examine how the COVID19 epidemic affected the high school digitalisation process and what the major influencing elements were.

The initial contribution of this research study sought was to examine and show the advantages of digitalisation and current condition, with the goal of understanding the changes occurring both globally and locally. The epidemic has a significant negative influence on society, particularly in the area of education, which is one of the society's cornerstones and a foundation for future growth. The second contribution it made was to assess the level of impact that online learning had on students and the state of the software information systems now in use by the schools. The research study focused and contributed with an analysis of the following:

1. Assessed and analysed the most important factors of digitalisation in education with focus in high schools.
2. Analysed graphicly using charts the respondents' inputs on the most important factors that are assessed.
3. Described the correlation between the different variables focusing especially on the dependent variable and its crosstab analyses with indirect variables.
4. Statistically investigated and assessed the insights and results from the questionnaire.

According to the results and feedback from the respondents the digitalisation process in education and especially in high schools has shown quite high improvement and is in direct correlation with the independent variables.

While biases can never be fully eliminated in classroom research, leveraging thoughtful sampling, measurement design, diverse data sources, transparency and cautious interpretation helped strengthen the reliability and validity of this study's findings on the impacts of digital transformation. We aim to continue refining our methods to produce high-quality unbiased research on this important topic.

For future work, the study suggests further research to enhance the digitalisation process in high schools. This could include investigating the long-term impacts of the pandemic on digital learning, exploring the effectiveness of different digital learning platforms and tools and examining the role of teachers and school administrators in facilitating digital learning. Education 4.0 is already here with the application of technology.

References

1. Brown, S.: Digital education platforms and how they're helping schools. Blog DfE Digital, Data and Technology, 12 Feb 2021. https://dfedigital.blog.gov.uk/2021/02/12/digital-education-platforms/. Last accessed: 17 July 2023
2. Department of Education (UK): Choosing a school management information system (MIS), 13th July 2022. https://www.gov.uk/government/publications/choosing-a-school-management-information-system-mis. Last accessed 17 July 2023
3. Ali, M., Miraz, M.H.: Assessment of delivery platforms and online pedagogy requirements. In: 2020 International Conference on Computing, Electronics & Communications Engineering (iCCECE), Southend, United Kingdom, 17–18 Aug 2020, pp. 176–181. Electronic ISBN: 978-1-7281-6330-7. USB ISBN: 978-1-7281-6329-1. (PoD). ISBN: 978-1-7281-6331-4. https://doi.org/10.1109/iCCECE49321.2020.9231220
4. Gani, M.A., Molvi, S.A., Ali, M., Hussein, A.H.: Impact of e-learning on child education and development in rural areas of India. In: Ali, M., Miraz, M.H., Hari Kunasekaran, K.K. (eds.) BCS Proceedings of the International Conference on eBusiness, eCommerce, eManagement, eLearning and eGovernance (IC5E 2014). University of Greenwich, London, UK, Published by ASDF, 30–31 July 2014, , pp. 77–82. (2014). https://www.academia.edu/7877969/Impact_of_E_learning_on_Child_Education_and_Development_in_Rural_Areas_of_India. Last accessed 17 July 2023
5. European Centre for Disease Prevention and Control: Surveillance Report Weekly Communicable Disease Threats Report, week 39, Week 28, 9–15 Jul 2023, pp. 5–6. https://www.ecdc.europa.eu/sites/default/files/documents/communicable-disease-threats-report-week-28-2023.pdf. Last accessed 17 Jul 2023

6. Akbari, A.: A Resilient ICT4D Approach to ECO Countries' Education Response During COVID-19 Pandemic. http://arxiv.org/abs/2108.09742v1. Last accessed 17 Jul 2023
7. Pomfret, R.: The economic cooperation organization: current status and future prospects. Eur. Asia Stud. **49**(4), 657–667 (1997). https://doi.org/10.1080/09668139708412465
8. Luic, L., Svelec-Juricic, D., Misevic, P.: The impact of knowledge of the issue of identification and authentication on the information security of adolescents in the virtual space. WSEAS Trans. Syst. Control **16**(49), 527–533 (2021). https://doi.org/10.37394/23203.202. http://arxiv.org/abs/2111.00460v1
9. Estevan, F., Finamor, L.: School closures and educational path: how the Covid-19 pandemic affected transitions to college. 30 Sep 2022. http://arxiv.org/abs/2210.00138v1
10. Nieto-Márquez, N.L., Baldominos, A., Petronila, A.G.: SARS-CoV-2 Impact on Online Teaching Methodologies and the Ed-Tech Sector: Smile and Learn Platform Case Study, 15 Jul 2020. http://arxiv.org/abs/2007.07587v1
11. Manikutty, G., Sasidharan, S., Rao, B.: Driving innovation through project-based learning: a pre-university STEAM for Social Good initiative. In: IEEE Frontiers in Education Conference (FIE), Uppsala, Sweden, 8–11 Oct 2022, pp. 1–8. https://doi.org/10.1109/FIE56618.2022.996 2420. http://arxiv.org/abs/2211.01998v1
12. Lammi, M., Becker, K.: Engineering design thinking. J. Technol. Educ. **24**(2), 55–77 (2013). https://files.eric.ed.gov/fulltext/EJ1005688.pdf. Last accessed 17 July 2023
13. Szoke, J.: Hybrid? Blended? Synchronous or asynchronous? How do you take your online teaching? Cambridge Blog, 5 Mar 2021. https://www.cambridge.org/elt/blog/2021/03/05/hyb rid-blended-synchronous-asynchronous-how-do-take-your-online-teaching/. Last accessed 17 July 2023
14. Heale, R., Forbes, D.: Understanding triangulation in research. Evid. Based Nurs. **16**(4), 98 (2013). https://doi.org/10.1136/eb-2013-101494
15. Simkus, J.: What Is An ANOVA Test In Statistics: Analysis of Variance, Simply Psychology, 21 June 2023. https://www.simplypsychology.org/anova.html. Last accessed 17 July 2023
16. Prabhakaran, S.: One Sample T Test – Clearly Explained with Examples ¦ ML+, machine learning+ (2023). https://www.machinelearningplus.com/statistics/one-sample-t-test/. Last accessed 17 July 2023
17. van Doorn, J., et al.: The JASP guidelines for conducting and reporting a Bayesian analysis. Psychon. Bull. Rev. **28**, 813–826 (2021). https://doi.org/10.3758/s13423-020-01798-5
18. Qualtrics.com: Cross tabulation analysis for researchers. https://www.qualtrics.com/uk/exp erience-management/research/cross-tabulation/?rid=ip&prevsite=en&newsite=uk&geo= AL&geomatch=uk (2023). Last accessed 17 July 2023
19. Bernstein, I.H.: Likert scale analysis. In: Kimberly, K.-L. (ed.) Encyclopedia of Social Measurement, pp. 497–504, Elsevier (2005). ISBN 9780123693983. https://doi.org/10.1016/B0-12-369398-5/00104-3
20. Mukul, E., Büyüközkan, G.: Digital transformation in education: a systematic review of education 4.0. Technol. Forecast. Soc. Change **194**, 122664 (2023). https://doi.org/10.1016/j.techfore.2023.122664

Information and Network Security

Cube Attacks on Round-Reduced Grain-128AEAD

Wil Liam Teng, Iftekhar Salam$^{(\boxtimes)}$ ⓘ, Wei-Chuen Yau ⓘ, and Jia Yew Teh

School of Computing and Data Science, Xiamen University Malaysia, 43900 Sepang,
Malaysia
{cst1709690,iftekhar.salam,wcyau,jiayew.teh}@xmu.edu.my

Abstract. Lightweight cryptography aims to design secure and efficient cryptographic algorithms for resource-constrained devices. Traditional cryptographic algorithms may not be readily usable in resource-
constrained environments. To standardise cryptographic solutions tailored for such resource-constraint environments, the National Institute
of Standards and Technology (NIST) launched the Lightweight Cryptography (LWC) project. Grain-128AEAD is a stream cipher-based finalist
in the NIST LWC project. In this work, we examine the security of the
initial version of Grain-128AEAD against cube attacks. We present distinguishing attacks on a reduced-round version of the cipher, assuming
that the keystream can be observed immediately after the reduced-round
initialisation of the pre-output generator. We obtained various cubes of
sizes 25 to 45 for reduced-round Grain-128AEAD. The best cube reported
in this work can distinguish the output of a 165-round initialisation of
Grain-128AEAD with a cube size of 35. The complexity of the distinguishing attack is $\mathcal{O}(2^{35})$. The results are confirmed experimentally. We
conclude that even with fewer rounds of initialisation for the first version
of Grain-128AEAD, the cipher still has a good security margin against
cube attacks.

Keywords: Cube attack · Cube tester · Grain-128AEAD ·
Authenticated encryption · Stream cipher · NIST LWC

1 Introduction

The growing utilisation of Internet-of-Things (IoT) applications, particularly
in industries such as manufacturing and healthcare, has led to a significant
increase in the presence of electronic devices, such as sensors and actuators.
As a result, there is a growing demand to enhance the security of data communication for these electronic devices. However, as most of the cryptographic
algorithms are intended for the environments of desktops and servers, implementing the standard cryptographic algorithms on such electronic devices, which are

© ICST Institute for Computer Sciences, Social Informatics and Telecommunications Engineering 2024
Published by Springer Nature Switzerland AG 2024. All Rights Reserved
M. H. Miraz et al. (Eds.): iCETiC 2023, LNICST 538, pp. 105–126, 2024.
https://doi.org/10.1007/978-3-031-50215-6_8

usually lightweight in terms of computing resources and operate in a resource-constrained environment, may cause performance degradation in the IoT electronic devices [1]. To overcome this, a new sub-branch of cryptography has emerged that researches designs of cryptographic algorithms tailored for IoT devices with low computing hardware.

The Lightweight Cryptography (LWC) Standardisation [2] was initiated in 2013 by the United States Department of Commerce's National Institute of Standards and Technology (NIST) to provide an evaluation of the current state of lightweight cryptography and standardise a cryptographic algorithm for lightweight devices. The ten finalist candidates for the LWC Project were announced in 2021 [3], and ASCON was announced as the winner of the LWC Project in early 2023. Third-party analyses provide a crucial service in identifying the weaknesses and strengths of the designs. It also helps to assess the security claims of the designs against known cryptanalysis techniques. This work contributes to the independent third-party analysis of one of the NIST LWC finalists, Grain-128AEAD. We applied cube attacks to Grain-128AEAD to investigate its security against the attack.

Grain-128AEAD [4] is an authenticated encryption stream cipher. It has two versions, the initial version was released in March 2019, and the second version, Grain-128AEADv2 [5], was released in May 2021 with minor modifications of the original version. Our attacks are mainly applied to the initial version of Grain-128AEAD. The cubes identified in this paper may not be readily applicable to Grain-128AEADv2 due to the re-introduction of the secret key in the last 128 rounds of initialisation of the pre-output generator. However, they may be used to estimate the level of diffusion of the key and nonce bits during the initialisation process of Grain-128AEADv2. The term "Grain-128AEAD" used throughout the rest of the paper refers to the initial version of the cipher unless explicitly mentioned otherwise. Grain-128AEAD and its predecessors are still well-recognised and widely adopted for the construction of new designs, although it was not selected to be standardised by NIST. Therefore, the results presented in this paper will be useful in evaluating the security of Grain-128AEAD while using it for inventing or improving new and existing designs.

1.1 Cube Attacks Against Stream Cipher-Based AEAD Designs

Cube attack is a cryptanalytic technique that was first introduced by Dinur and Shamir [6]. It extends the concepts of the algebraic IV differential attack (AIDA) [7] and higher-order differential cryptanalysis [8]. Dinur and Shamir showed that the output polynomials of many ciphers might not possess a high degree of randomness as most of the output polynomials are derivations of a master polynomial obtained by setting the values of tweakable variables, thus the term "tweakable polynomials" shown in the title of their paper. In AEAD stream ciphers, the tweakable variables may refer to either one of the public information or the input to the ciphers. These include the public initialisation vector/nonce, the associated data, and the plaintext. By this observation, the attacker can set the values of the tweakable variables to the attacker's need so as to acquire the derived output polynomial equations whose terms consist of the secret variables and the tweakable variables. Nonetheless, the output polynomials of a properly designed cryptosystem would have a high polynomial degree of its variables. For a well-constructed cipher, it is computationally infeasible to trace the symbolic expressions of its output polynomial programmatically or manually. Thus, cube attack treats the output polynomial as a black-box polynomial that the attacker interacts with.

In the attack, the output $\mathcal{P}$ is considered a black box polynomial and evaluated for all combinations of a selected set of tweakable variables. The goal is to lower the degree of the polynomial $\mathcal{P}$. The chosen set of tweakable variables is referred to as a cube $\mathcal{C}$ and is identified exclusively by a specified group of input indices I. The polynomial obtained after summing $\mathcal{P}$ over $\mathcal{C}$ is referred to as a superpoly $\mathcal{P}_{S(I)}$. The cube attack was first applied to the stream cipher Trivium in 2009 [6]. Since then, it has been widely used for analysing various symmetric primitives, especially stream ciphers, see references [9–21], for some examples of cube attacks on symmetric ciphers.

Cube attack can be applied to various phases of an AEAD stream cipher, including initialisation, associated data processing, encryption, decryption and verification. The underlying assumptions vary depending on the operational phase to which the attack is applied. The attacks applied in this paper are mainly during the initialisation phase of Grain-128AEAD. More specifically, we applied cube attacks at the initialisation phase of the pre-output generator of the cipher. During the initialisation phase of Grain-128AEAD, the secret key is loaded into its internal state with a public variable called the nonce. Therefore, cubes in our attack are selected from the nonce variables. The aim of the attacks is to recover the secret key of the cipher, or to differentiate the cipher output from a random output.

1.2 Our Contributions

The attacks reported in this paper are applied to the reduced round initialisation of Grain-128AEAD. We have tested cube attacks on the initialisation of the pre-output generator of Grain-128AEAD for five different parameters of the experiment. All cubes were chosen from the 96 bits of the nonce, i.e., $\mathcal{C} \in \{v_0, \cdots, v_{95}\}$. Table 1 summarises our results from the application of cube attacks to Grain-128AEAD. The best result reported in this work is a distinguisher up to 165-round initialisation of Grain-128AEAD for a cube size of 35.

We note that there are a few existing works on the security analysis of Grain-128AEAD. These include applications of differential fault attacks to recover the initial internal state [22] and key recovery attacks from known internal state [23]. We also acknowledge that the work reported by Hao, Leander, Meier, Todo and Wang [17] is currently the first and best result of the cube attack on Grain-128AEAD using three-subset division property without unknown subset. Based on the division property, they have demonstrated a cube-based key recovery for 190 rounds and distinguishers for 189 rounds of Grain-128AEAD with a complexity of 2^{123} and 2^{96}, respectively. However, due to their large complexities

Table 1. Summary of the cube testers obtained for Grain-128AEAD.

Cube size	Reduced initialisation rounds
25	158
30	160
35	165
40	163
45	161

of 2^{96} for the distinguishing attacks and 2^{123} for the key recovery attack, the obtained results in the study are not experimentally verifiable. To the best of our knowledge, the results reported in this paper are the first third-party analysis of Grain-128AEAD against cube attacks that produce experimentally verifiable results. The results presented in this paper provide some insights into the application of traditional cube attacks against Grain-128AEAD.

2   Overview of Cube Attack

The output of any symmetric cipher can be expressed as a Boolean polynomial over a set of secret and public variables. To apply cube attack, it is assumed that an adversary can compute the Boolean polynomial over a set of public variables to reduce the output polynomial's degree. These public variables for AEAD designs are typically comprised of bits from the initialisation vector and associated data; plaintext bits could also be considered as the public variables under the chosen plaintext attack (CPA) model. The adversary is assumed to be capable of manipulating these public variables arbitrarily. In contrast to algebraic attacks, the cube attack treats the keystream polynomial as a black box.

Consider a scenario where an adversary can observe a cipher's keystream polynomial defined over the Galois field with two elements, i.e., $GF(2)$. The keystream polynomial $\mathcal{P}$ is constructed over the i secret-key variables $K = \{k_0, \cdots, k_{i-1}\}$ and j public variables $V = \{v_0, \cdots, v_{j-1}\}$. Let the degree of the polynomial is denoted as deg. A maxterm t_I of the output polynomial $\mathcal{P}$ is defined to consist of the public variables with their indices specified by an arbitrary subset $I \subseteq \{0, \cdots, j-1\}$. The set of variables that are indexed by the subset I is called a cube, $\mathcal{C}$. Thus, we can write the output polynomial $\mathcal{P}$ as

$$\mathcal{P}(k_0, \cdots, k_{i-1}, v_0, \cdots, v_{j-1}) \equiv t_I . \mathcal{P}_{S(I)} + q(k_0, \cdots, k_{i-1}, v_0, \cdots, v_{j-1}), \quad (1)$$

where each term of $q(k_0, \cdots, k_{i-1}, v_0, \cdots, v_{j-1})$ misses one or more public variable(s) that are present in the maxterm t_I. The polynomial $\mathcal{P}_{S(I)}$ is known as a superpoly of the corresponding index subset I in the output polynomial $\mathcal{P}$ if it does not have any shared variable with the maxterm t_I. To differentiate the notation used for the cardinality of I and the cube size, we used $|I|$ to refer to the cardinality of I and ℓ_c to denote the cube size. Observe that the value of $|I| = \ell_c$.

A linear superpoly $\mathcal{P}_{S(I)}$ is guaranteed to be constructed in the particular case where $|I| = deg - 1$.

To execute cube attacks, a polynomial $\mathcal{P}$ is evaluated by summing its values for all combinations of Boolean values of the cube variables indexed by I. By using a sufficiently large cube, for example, $\ell_c = deg - 1$, we can reduce the degree of the polynomial $\mathcal{P}$ to one. Consequently, the sum results in a linear superpoly $\mathcal{P}_{S(I)}$. By repeating this process, we can identify a set of unique cubes that produce a set of linear equations over the secret variables. Once we have enough equations, we can solve the equations to deduce the secret variables. Generally, the cube attack consists of two phases: pre-processing and online.

2.1 Pre-processing Phase

In this phase, we assume that the description of the cipher is public, and both public and secret variables can be accessed and manipulated by the adversary. The aim is to find appropriate cubes that yield linear superpolies involving the secret variables. Since the form of the keystream polynomial $\mathcal{P}(K, V)$ is unknown, we must estimate its degree to determine which cube sizes may produce a linear superpoly. To begin, we randomly select small cubes. We randomly choose a subset of indices I_c from $\{0, \cdots, vlen - 1\}$ to select a random cube $\mathcal{C}$ of size ℓ_c, where $vlen$ refers to the size of the initialisation vector V, and $\ell_c = |I_c|$. We then compute $\mathcal{P}_{\mathcal{C}}(K, V)$ as the sum of the master polynomial $\mathcal{P}(K, V)$ over 2^{ℓ_c} cube summations, i.e., sum over all possible Boolean values of the random cube $\mathcal{C}$. If we have selected the right cube, we expect that the resultant superpoly $\mathcal{P}_{\mathcal{C}}(K, V) = \mathcal{P}_{S(I)}$ is linear over the secret key variables $\{k_0, \cdots, k_{klen-1}\}$, where $klen$ denotes the size of the secret key K. On the other hand, it is possible that the resulting superpoly $\mathcal{P}_{\mathcal{C}}(K, V) = \mathcal{P}_{S(I)}$ is a constant instead of a linear equation over the secret-key variables, in which case it can only be used to perform a distinguishing attack. A linearity test for the resultant polynomial $\mathcal{P}_{\mathcal{C}}(K, V)$ is necessary to determine the useful cube.

We use the BLR test [24] to identify if the cube summation $\mathcal{P}_{\mathcal{C}}(K, V)$ resulted in a linear superpoly. The BLR test checks the below relation:

$$\mathcal{P}_{\mathcal{C}}(K_0, V) + \mathcal{P}_{\mathcal{C}}(K_1, V) + \mathcal{P}_{\mathcal{C}}(K_2, V) \stackrel{?}{=} \mathcal{P}_{\mathcal{C}}(K_1 + K_2, V), \qquad (2)$$

where $K_0 = \{0\}^{klen}$ and K_1, K_2 are chosen at random. We infer that the resultant superpoly, $\mathcal{P}_{S(I)}$, is linear with a probability of $(1 - 2^{-n})$, if a random cube $\mathcal{C}$ passes n number of BLR linearity tests. If we select a sufficiently large value of n, for instance, $n = 100$, we can ensure that the resulting superpoly is linear with a high degree of certainty, specifically a probability of $(1 - 2^{-100})$. The algebraic normal form (ANF) of the linear superpoly $\mathcal{P}_{\mathcal{C}}(K, V) = \mathcal{P}_{S(I)}$ can be expressed as follows

$$\mathcal{P}_{S(I)}(K) = \alpha_{-1} + \alpha_0 k_0 + \alpha_1 k_1 + \cdots + \alpha_{klen-1} k_{klen-1}, \qquad (3)$$

where the public initialisation vector bits from $V \backslash \mathcal{C}$ are set to zero. We have the ANF representation as shown above, but the binary coefficients α_i; $i =$

$-1, 0, \ldots, klen - 1$ are unknown. We can determine these binary coefficients by conducting $klen + 1$ trials of cube summations. We compute the constant $\alpha_{-1} \in \{0, 1\}$ in the ANF of the superpoly $\mathcal{P}_{S(I)}$ by determining the cube summation where the secret key variables are all zeroes, i.e., computing $\mathcal{P}_C(K_0, V) = \mathcal{P}_{S(I)}(K_0, V)$. For all the other coefficients $\alpha_i \in \{0, 1\}$ for $i = 0, \ldots, klen - 1$, we run $klen$ cube experiments to compute $\mathcal{P}_C(K_i, V) + \alpha_{-1} = \mathcal{P}_{S(I)}(K_i, V) + \alpha_{-1}$, with all the key bits set to zero except k_i. If there are no key bits present in a superpoly, $\mathcal{P}_{S(I)}$, then the superpoly is known as a distinguisher. Cubes that yield distinguishers are known as cube testers [9]. Clearly, if a superpoly, $\mathcal{P}_{S(I)}$, is a distinguisher for some cube tester, C, with an index subset, I, that is, a constant of either the value of one or zero, then only the constant α_{-1} of the ANF can be retrieved and the secret variables extraction procedure could not proceed. However, the distinguisher can be used in determining non-randomness and/or degree of diffusions of the variables of the underlying polynomial, $\mathcal{P}(K, V)$.

2.2   Online Phase

The online phase of the cube attack procedure involves two stages: the stage of generating the values of the superpolies using a random key and the stage of solving the system of polynomials or checking the value of the distinguisher of the online phase with the one that is obtained in the pre-processing phase. We assume that the adversary has access to the cipher's output but does not have knowledge of the secret variables. We also assume that the adversary has completed the pre-processing phase and found $klen + 1$ superpolies $\mathcal{P}_{S(I_j)}$ that are linearly independent and correspond to its respective cubes C_j. Based on this, the adversary can create an equation system as follows:

$$\mathcal{P}_{S(I_j)}(K) = \alpha_{-1,j} + \alpha_{0,j} k_0 + \alpha_{1,j} k_1 + \cdots + \alpha_{klen-1,j} k_{klen-1}, \qquad (4)$$

where $j = 1, \ldots, klen + 1$. The value for each superpoly $P_{S(I_j)}(K)$ is generated by using the output value of the corresponding cube summation $\mathcal{P}_{C_j}(K, V)$, for a random key K. After obtaining the values for each linear superpoly $\mathcal{P}_{S(I_j)}$, the equation system can now be formed where the left-hand side of equations lists the superpolies computed in the pre-processing phase, whereas the right-hand side of the equations lists the values of the superpolies generated from the online phase. The adversary can use Gaussian elimination to solve the equation system from Eq. (4). Solving these equations shall recover the underlying secret variables if sufficient independent linear superpolies are obtained. For superpolies that only consist of the constant α_{-1}, known as distinguishers, the value of the superpoly $\mathcal{P}_{S(I_j)}$ calculated in the online phase is checked with its constant value from the pre-processing phase to distinguish the output of the cipher from a random output.

3   Overview of Grain-128AEAD

Grain-128AEAD is the latest addition to the Grain family of stream ciphers [4]. It is one of the ten finalists of the LWC Project, and a second tweaked version of Grain-128AEAD, named Grain-128AEADv2 [5], was submitted in May 2021. The difference between Grain-128AEAD and its predecessor Grain-128a is that in Grain-128AEAD, the authentication aspect is no longer optional, and the size of MAC increases from 32 bits to 64 bits. Additionally, the key in Grain-128AEAD is reintroduced in the last 128 rounds of the initialisation phase, as compared to Grain-128a. Unless explicitly specified, the below general description is based on the first version of Grain-128AEAD.

3.1   Specification of Grain-128AEAD

The components used in Grain-128AEAD are similar to its predecessor Grain-128a. Grain-128AEAD uses a 128-bit secret key $K = \{k_0, k_1, \cdots, k_{127}\}$ and a 96-bit initialisation vector $V = \{v_0, \cdots, v_{95}\}$, which is regarded as a nonce in the cipher. The internal state of Grain-128AEAD comprises of two major components, namely, a pre-output generator and an authentication generator. The pre-output generator of Grain-128AEAD consists of a 128-bit Linear Feedback Shift Register (LFSR), $S_t = \{s_0^t, s_1^t, \cdots, s_{127}^t\}$, and a 128-bit Non-linear Feedback Shift Register (NFSR), $B_t = \{b_0^t, b_1^t, \cdots, b_{127}^t\}$, at time instance t. In contrast, the authentication generator of Grain-128AEAD at time instance i, which differs from the time instance t due to the steps in the initialisation phase, consists of a 64-bit accumulator $A_i = \{a_0^i, a_1^i, \cdots, a_{63}^i\}$ and a 64-bit shift register $R_i = \{r_0^i, r_1^i, \cdots, r_{63}^i\}$.

3.2   Grain-128AEAD State Update Function

The primitive LFSR feedback polynomial, $f(x)$, and the nonlinear NFSR feedback polynomial, $g(x)$, are both defined over Galois Field with two elements, $GF(2)$, and are shown in Eq. (5) and Eq. (6), respectively.

$$f(x) = 1 + x^{32} + x^{47} + x^{58} + x^{90} + x^{121} + x^{128} \tag{5}$$

$$g(x) = 1 + x^{32} + x^{37} + x^{72} + x^{102} + x^{128} + x^{44}x^{60} + x^{61}x^{125} + x^{63}x^{67} + x^{69}x^{101}$$
$$+ x^{80}x^{88} + x^{110}x^{111} + x^{115}x^{117} + x^{46}x^{50}x^{58} + x^{103}x^{104}x^{106} + x^{33}x^{35}x^{36}x^{40} \tag{6}$$

Based on the feedback polynomials, the corresponding functions for updating the last bit of the LFSR, s_{127}^{t+1}, and the last bit of the NFSR, b_{127}^{t+1}, for the next time instance $t + 1$ are shown in the Eq. (7) and Eq. (8), respectively.

$$s_{127}^{t+1} = s_0^t + s_7^t + s_{38}^t + s_{70}^t + s_{81}^t + s_{96}^t$$
$$= \mathcal{L}(S_t) \tag{7}$$

$$b_{127}^{t+1} = s_0^t + b_0^t + b_{26}^t + b_{56}^t + b_{96}^t + b_3^t b_{67}^t + b_{11}^t b_{13}^t + b_{17}^t b_{18}^t + b_{27}^t b_{59}^t$$
$$+ b_{40}^t b_{48}^t + b_{61}^t b_{65}^t + b_{68}^t b_{84}^t + b_{22}^t b_{24}^t b_{25}^t + b_{70}^t b_{78}^t b_{83}^t + b_{88}^t b_{92}^t b_{93}^t b_{95}^t \tag{8}$$
$$= s_0^t + \mathcal{F}(B_t)$$

The filter function $h(x)$, also defined over $GF(2)$, takes in a total of nine variables as inputs: two of them from the NFSR and the remaining seven from the LFSR, to produce a single-bit output. This is shown in Eq. (9) and the variables $\{x_0, x_1, x_2, x_3, x_4, x_5, x_6, x_7, x_8\}$ correspond to the variables of the LFSR and the NFSR, i.e., $\{b_{12}^t, s_8^t, s_{13}^t, s_{20}^t, b_{95}^t, s_{42}^t, s_{60}^t, s_{79}^t, s_{94}^t\}$.

$$h(x) = x_0 x_1 + x_2 x_3 + x_4 x_5 + x_6 x_7 + x_0 x_4 x_8 \tag{9}$$

The filter function $h(x)$ is then used in computing the one-bit output at time instance t of the pre-output function, y_t, illustrated in Eq. (10). This is done together with one state bit of the LFSR, s_{93}^t, and seven state bits of the NFSR with indices of $\mathcal{A} = \{2, 15, 36, 45, 64, 73, 89\}$.

$$y_t = h(x) + s_{93}^t + \sum_{j \in \mathcal{A}} b_j^t \tag{10}$$

3.3   Operation Phases of Grain-128AEAD

Grain-128AEAD has four phases: initialisation, associated data processing, and interleaved encryption and plaintext authentication. For decryption, it follows the same initialisation and associated data processing steps as it does for encryption. The subsequent steps involve decryption and tag verification. Our implementation of cube attacks is applied only to the initialisation phase of Grain-128AEAD, so we briefly discuss the initialisation phase. Interested readers are referred to the original description of Grain-128AEAD for more details on the other operation phases following the initialisation phase.

Initialisation Phase. Algorithm 1 shows the working process of the initialisation phase of Grain-128AEAD. In the beginning, the 96-bit nonce and the 128-bit secret key are loaded into the pre-output generator of the cipher. Specifically, the nonce, $V = \{v_0, v_1, \cdots, v_{95}\}$, is loaded into the LFSR, $S_0 = \{s_0^0, s_1^0, \cdots, s_{95}^0\}$, and the remaining 32 LFSR bits, $\{s_{96}^0, s_{97}^0, \cdots, s_{127}^0\}$, are filled with a constant 0xFFFFFFFE. Meanwhile, the key, $K = \{k_0, k_1, \cdots, k_{127}\}$, is loaded into the NFSR, $B_0 = \{b_0^0, b_1^0, \cdots, b_{127}^0\}$. The loaded pre-output generator is then initialised by going through 256 rounds of updates, during which the pre-output keystream y_t is XOR-ed with specific state bits to produce the feedback bits of the LFSR and the NFSR.

The initialisation of the authentication generator follows the initialisation of the pre-output generator. Following the 256 clocks of the pre-output generator, time instances $t = 256$ to $t = 319$ are used to first fill the accumulator, $A_0 = \{a_0^0, a_1^0, \cdots, a_{63}^0\}$, with the pre-output keystreams in each clock. Then, another additional 64 clocks, i.e., from $t = 320$ to $t = 383$, are used to similarly fill the shift register $R_0 = \{r_0^0, r_1^0, \cdots, r_{63}^0\}$ with the pre-output keystreams in each clock. During these last 128 clocks, i.e., $t = 256$ to $t = 383$, the NFSR and the LFSR are concurrently updated, with the key being shifted into the LFSR. This

---

Algorithm 1 Initialisation Phase of Grain-128AEAD

Input: $(b_0^0, b_1^0, ..., b_{127}^0) \leftarrow (k_0, k_1, ..., k_{127})$

Input: $(s_0^0, s_1^0, ..., s_{95}^0, s_{96}^0, s_{97}^0, ...s_{126}^0, s_{127}^0) \leftarrow (v_0, v_1, ..., v_{95}, 1, 1, ..., 1, 0)$

1: **for** $i = 0$ to 255 **do**

2:     $s_{127}^{t+1} \leftarrow \mathcal{L}(S_t) + y_t$

3:     $b_{127}^{t+1} \leftarrow s_0^t + \mathcal{F}(B_t) + y_t$

4: **end for**

5: **for** $j = 0$ to 63 **do**

6:     $a_j^0 = y_{256+j}$

7:     $s_{127}^{256+j+1} \leftarrow \mathcal{L}(S_{256+j}) + k_j$

8:     $b_{127}^{256+j+1} \leftarrow s_0^{256+j} + \mathcal{F}(B_{256+j})$

9: **end for**

10: **for** $j = 0$ to 63 **do**

11:     $r_j^0 = y_{320+j}$

12:     $s_{127}^{320+j+1} \leftarrow \mathcal{L}(S_{320+j}) + k_{64+j}$

13:     $b_{127}^{320+j+1} \leftarrow s_0^{320+j} + \mathcal{F}(B_{320+j})$

14: **end for**

---

gives the initialisation phase of Grain-128AEAD a total of 384 clocks. In Grain-128AEADv2, the number of initialisation rounds of the pre-output generator is increased from 256 clocks to 384 clocks, where the key is reintroduced into the internal state during the additional 128 rounds of updates. Including the initialisation of the authenticator generator, Grain-128AEADv2 has a total of 512 rounds of initialisation.

4   Cube Attack Against Grain-128AEAD

Observe that the key and the nonce are only input in the initialisation phase, particularly before the initialisation of the pre-output generator. Clearly, the designers of the cipher intended to decrease the reliance on introducing the key in every state update. Instead, with the large degree of the feedback polynomial of the pre-output generator, the security of the cipher comes from the large algebraic degree of the variables, i.e., the degree of diffusion of the variables.

4.1   Description of the Attack

According to the specification of the first version of Grain-128AEAD, the cipher goes through 384 rounds of the initialisation phase and additional rounds in the associated data processing phase before the keystream is observable. However, the pre-output keystream bits y_t can be expressed purely in terms of the key bits and the nonce bits if we assume that these bits are immediately accessible

---

Algorithm 2 Pre-output Computation of Grain-128AEAD for Reduced-round r

---

Input: Beginning state S, B
Input: Cube chosen randomly from $v_0, v_1, \cdots, v_{95}$
1: **function** Grain128AEADInitImp(K, IV, r)
2:      $(b_0^0, b_1^0, ..., b_{127}^0) \leftarrow (k_0, k_1, ..., k_{127})$
3:      $(s_0^0, s_1^0, ..., s_{95}^0, s_{96}^0, s_{97}^0, ...s_{126}^0, s_{127}^0) \leftarrow (v_0, v_1, ..., v_{95}, 1, 1, ..., 1, 0)$
4:      **for** $i = 0$ to $r - 1$ **do**
5:          Compute y_t
6:          $s_{127}^{t+1} \leftarrow \mathcal{L}(S_t) + y_t$
7:          $b_{127}^{t+1} \leftarrow s_0^t + \mathcal{F}(B_t) + y_t$
8:      **end for**
9:      **return** y_t
10: **end function**

---

after the initialisation of the pre-output generator. In other words, if the cipher does not go through the associated data processing phase and the interleaving encryption and the plaintext authentication phase, then we can theoretically obtain superpolies in terms of the key bits.

With this setup in mind, we implement and investigate cube attacks against Grain-128AEAD. Specifically, we assume that the starting state of the LFSR and the NFSR is at clock $t = 0$, i.e., S_0 and B_0. As such, the pre-output keystream bits are defined over the key bits and the nonce bits. Thus, the cubes are chosen only from all 96 bits of the nonce. It is assumed that the implementation, which imitates an attacker, can only modify the nonce bits and have neither the knowledge nor the means to modify the key bits. Using the pre-output keystream bits, we intend to find cube testers or cubes whose superpolies are linearly dependent on some key bits. Note that due to the large algebraic degree of the pre-output generator function, our attack is applied to the round-reduced variants of Grain-128AEAD. The implementation assumes that the pre-output keystream generated immediately after the reduced version of clocks, r, can be observed. Algorithm 2 shows the implemented function that returns the pre-output keystream computed after the reduced initialisation rounds.

Parameters of the Implementation. The complexity of the pre-processing phase of cube attack is mainly reliant on the cube size ℓ_c and the number of the BLR tests n conducted on each cube. Thus, for each cube to be selected as a candidate to generate its corresponding superpoly requires $n \times 2^{\ell_c}$ cube summations to pass the n BLR tests. This gives a complexity of the order $\mathcal{O}(2^{\ell_c + \log_2 n})$. If the cubes are chosen from the nonce, and all cubes from the 96 bits of nonce space are tested for each cube size ℓ_c in the pre-processing phase, the total number of cube summations will be calculated as $\binom{96}{\ell_c} \times n \times 2^{\ell_c}$ and the order of complexity is then $\mathcal{O}(2^{\ell_c + \log_2(n\binom{96}{\ell_c})})$. For a reasonable number of BLR tests and cube size ℓ_c, the complexity goes beyond practical limits as the cube size increases. Note also that the above complexity does not account for the cube summations in generating the coefficients of the ANF of the superpolies. If the part of the coefficient generation in the pre-processing phase is considered, then the complexity will be even higher for exhaustive cube searches.

That is, an exhaustive cube search would have an adverse impact on the feasibility of the experiments of the implementations. Thus, a maximum number of cubes, $cmax$, is chosen to limit the number of random cubes tested in an instance of the experiment. In our experiments, the values of $cmax$ are set between 5000 to 100,000, depending on the cube size ℓ_c. On top of that, the degree of the output of the pre-output generator for a full version of the initialisation phase is estimated to be high, which will require a large number of cube sizes to reduce the degree of the output to one. Thus, the initialisation phase of the pre-output generator in Grain-128AEAD with reduced r clocks is used to test the cubes in the implementations. Lastly, the other two parameters that are set in the experiments are the sizes of the random cubes, ℓ_c, and the n number of BLR linearity tests to test the linearity of the superpolies.

Pre-processing Phase of the Implementation. With the parameters set for the implementation, in the pre-processing phase of the implementation, experiments are run to obtain cubes that will either generate linear superpolies or distinguishers. The generic implementation of the pre-processing phase of the cube attack is described in Algorithm 3, which aims to detect cube testers or cubes with linear superpolies. Since the degree of the output polynomial is unknown, we need to identify the cube dimensions experimentally. We try out various cube sizes ℓ_c and check the resulting superpolies for linearity.

As outlined in Algorithm 3, the pre-processing phase of the implementation starts by first generating a random cube C with an index subset I and a size of ℓ_c. For each random cube, we conducted n number of BLR tests. Using this approach on Grain-128AEAD, the output of the initialisation of the pre-output generator, y_t, is treated as a keystream z used in the cube summations in the BLR tests and the coefficient generation phase. In each BLR test, the 2^{ℓ_c} outputs over the possible values of the random cube C are summed using random keys and the criteria of the BLR test are verified. Once the random cube C passes all the n BLR tests, the coefficients in the ANF of the superpoly, $\mathcal{P}_{S(I)}$, of the random cube C are generated, and the presence of each key bit is checked. Following this, the random cube C with or without the presence of key bits in the superpoly $\mathcal{P}_{S(I)}$ is recorded.

Online Phase of the Implementation. The results obtained from the pre-processing stage show that only distinguishers are obtained from the cube attack experiments on Grain-128AEAD. Even though a key recovery could not be performed using the cube testers, the online phase of the implementation can check for potential non-randomness of the cipher. Algorithm 4 shows the steps of the online phase of implementing a cube attack on Grain-128AEAD using the cube testers. According to Algorithm 4, the online phase starts by first generating

---

Algorithm 3 Pre-processing Phase of Cube Attack against Grain-128AEAD

Input: Cube size ℓ_c, No. of tested cubes $cmax$ for each cube size, No. of BLR linearity tests n, Reduced initialisation round r

1: **for** 1 to $cmax$ **do**
2:     Choose a cube $\mathcal{C}$ of size ℓ_c at random
3:     $success \leftarrow 0$
4:     **for** 1 to n **do**
5:         $K_0 \leftarrow 0^{128}$
6:         $K_1 \leftarrow rand\{0,1\}^{128}$
7:         $K_2 \leftarrow rand\{0,1\}^{128}$
8:         $K_3 \leftarrow rand\{0,1\}^{128}$
9:         Re-initialise the state
10:        **for** $i = 0$ to 3 **do**
11:            Compute $\mathcal{P}_\mathcal{C}(K_i, V)$ using y_t compute from `Grain128AEADInitImp`
12:        **end for**
13:        **if** $\mathcal{P}_\mathcal{C}(K_0, V) + \mathcal{P}_\mathcal{C}(K_1, V) + \mathcal{P}_\mathcal{C}(K_2, V) = \mathcal{P}_\mathcal{C}(K_1 + K_2, V)$ **then**
14:            $\mathcal{P}_{S(I)}$ passes the respective BLR test
15:            $success \leftarrow success + 1$
16:        **else**
17:            **break**
18:        **end if**
19:     **end for**
20:     **if** $success = n$ **then**
21:         Construct coefficients in the ANF of $\mathcal{P}_{S(I)}$
22:         $\alpha_{-1} \leftarrow \mathcal{P}_{S(I)}(K = (0, \ldots, 0))$
23:         $\alpha_i \leftarrow \mathcal{P}_{S(I)}(K = (0, \ldots, \underbrace{1}_{i\text{-th}}, 0, \ldots, 0)) + \alpha_{-1}$ for $i = 0, \ldots, 127$
24:         $\mathcal{P}_{S(I)}(K) \leftarrow \alpha_{-1} + \alpha_0 k_0 + \alpha_1 k_1 + \cdots + \alpha_{127} k_{127}$
25:         Record $\mathcal{C}$, reduced round r, and $\mathcal{P}_{S(I)}$
26:     **end if**
27: **end for**

---

an arbitrary key K. Next, a cube summation over 2^{ℓ_c} possible values of a cube tester (obtained from the pre-processing stage) is computed using the arbitrary key. The output after the initialisation of the pre-output generator of Grain-128AEAD can be differentiated from a random output if the distinguisher value of a cube tester obtained from the pre-processing phase has the same value as the result of the cube summation. All the cubes reported in this work have been experimentally verified using the online phase of the attack for 100 random keys.

4.2   Experimental Results for Cube Attack on Grain-128AEAD

We have implemented the pre-processing phase of the experiments using Algorithm 3, and the online phase of the experiments using Algorithm 4. The implementations for the cube attack of Grain-128AEAD have been optimised during the experimentation to give 32 values of the reduced clock r instead of only one value of the reduced clock r for each random cube C with an index subset I.

Algorithm 4 Online Phase of Cube Attack against Grain-128AEAD

Input: A set of cubes C for a reduced round r obtained from the pre-processing phase
1: Create a random key K
2: **for** each cube C from the pre-processing phase **do**
3:   Compute $\sum_{v \in C} P(K, V)$ using `Grain128AEADInitImp`
4:   **if** $\mathcal{P}_{S(I)} = \sum_{v \in C} P(K, V)$ **then**
5:     Cube C is verified to distinguish the output of Grain-128AEAD from random
6:   **else**
7:     The cube C is determined as a false cube
8:   **end if**
9: **end for**

This is possible due to the parallelisability of Grain-128AEAD, where only the last bit of the NFSR and the LFSR is updated with the feedback. With the native 32-bit arrangement of the bits in the C++ implementation, 32 bits of the output after the initialisation of the pre-output generator can be computed at a time. For the case of the cube attack implementation on Grain-128AEAD, this optimisation enables the experiments to generate 32 rounds of superpoly output for each random cube and optimally saves experimental time. Nevertheless, the experiments that are conducted based on the implementations yield only cube testers and their corresponding distinguishers.

We first tested the experiments using a cube size of $\ell_c = 25$ and for reduced clock values r ranging in between $r = 129$ to $r = 160$ that are verified with $n = 50$ BLR linearity tests. This produces 34 cube testers that pass for a maximum reduced clock of $r = 158$. We list a sample of six of these cube testers in Table 2. A complete list is attached in Appendix 5. The table details: a set of cube indices (first column), a set of the clock values r that the cube tester has passed (second column).

Using the same 32 reduced clocks r ranging in between $r = 129$ to $r = 160$, we have found twelve cube testers of size $\ell_c = 30$ that passed $n = 50$ BLR linearity tests. All twelve cube testers with size $\ell_c = 30$ are tabulated in Table 3. For the first four cube testers in Table 3, we have obtained them by checking for the 32 reduced clocks at a time (using the optimised implementation of cube attack). The other eight cube testers of size $\ell_c = 30$ are obtained using the implementations before the optimised version, which only calculates the superpoly output for one reduced clock r at a time for each random cube. Although the remaining eight cube testers of size $\ell_c = 30$ in Table 3 are only listed with $r = 160$, this does not mean they do not pass the linearity tests for other reduced clock values between $r = 129$ and $r = 160$. This is because we have only tested those cubes with a single r reduced clock value.

We extended the experiments to test higher values of reduced clocks r and a larger cube size ℓ_c. The parameters for one of such experiments are set to test random cubes of size $\ell_c = 35$ for reduced clocks r ranging between $r = 161$ to $r = 192$ with $n = 50$ of BLR linearity tests. In this experiment, only three cube testers are obtained that passed a maximum reduced clock value of $r = 165$, and these cube testers are shown in Table 4.

Table 2. Examples of cube testers found of size $\ell_c = 25$.

Cube (Nonce) Indices, I	Reduced Clocks, r
0, 3, 4, 6, 7, 12, 14, 28, 31, 32, 36, 38, 40, 43, 45, 46, 51, 53, 54, 57, 65, 69, 70, 71, 75	129, 130, 131, 132, 133, 134, 135, 136, 137, 138, 139, 140, 141, 142, 143, 144, 145, 146, 147, 148, 149, 150, 151, 152, 153, 154, 155, 156, 157, 158
5, 11, 17, 18, 19, 20, 23, 25, 27, 34, 35, 36, 40, 42, 44, 48, 49, 53, 58, 65, 71, 72, 78, 88, 95	129, 130, 131, 132, 133, 134, 135, 136, 137, 138, 139, 140, 141, 142, 143, 144, 145, 146, 147, 148, 149, 150, 151
0, 2, 5, 10, 12, 13, 16, 21, 27, 28, 34, 35, 42, 44, 51, 58, 59, 61, 65, 66, 70, 72, 75, 80, 89	129, 130, 131, 132, 133, 134, 135, 136, 137, 138, 139, 140, 141, 142, 143, 144, 145
1, 2, 7, 9, 23, 29, 31, 32, 40, 41, 42, 43, 49, 50, 55, 56, 60, 77, 80, 81, 84, 86, 88, 89, 95	129, 130, 131, 132, 133, 134, 135, 136, 137, 138, 139, 140, 141, 142, 143, 144, 145, 146, 147, 148, 149, 150, 151, 152, 153, 154, 155
0, 2, 9, 13, 14, 16, 17, 24, 26, 27, 30, 31, 34, 41, 54, 55, 62, 66, 73, 74, 81, 82, 83, 86, 91	129, 130, 131, 132, 133, 134, 135, 136, 137, 138, 139, 140, 141, 142, 143, 144, 145, 146, 147, 148, 149, 150
5, 8, 17, 18, 23, 24, 27, 32, 35, 43, 48, 51, 52, 59, 60, 61, 62, 69, 81, 86, 88, 89, 90, 94, 95	129, 130, 131, 132, 133, 134, 135, 136, 137, 138, 139, 140, 141, 142, 143, 144, 145, 146, 147, 148, 149, 150, 151

With the same reduced clocks r ranging in between $r = 161$ to $r = 192$, we have tested random cubes with cube sizes of $\ell_c = 40$ and $\ell_c = 45$ with $n = 50$ BLR linearity tests. For a cube size of $\ell_c = 40$, we have found only three cube testers for a maximum value of reduced clock $r = 163$ which are presented in Table 5. As for cube size of $\ell_c = 45$, we have found only one cube tester for reduced clocks r in the range of $r = 161$ and $r = 192$ that passes a maximum value of reduced clock $r = 161$ with $n = 50$ BLR linearity tests. For comparison purposes, we have also recorded this cube tester in Table 6.

Attack Complexity. The sizes of the cube testers that we have obtained with $n = 50$ BLR linearity tests vary from $\ell_c = 25$ to $\ell_c = 45$ for values of reduced clocks r ranging from $r = 129$ to a maximum of $r = 165$. The total complexity of the pre-processing phase for obtaining a grand sum of 53 cube testers is then calculated as $\mathcal{O}(50 \times (34 \times 2^{25} + 12 \times 2^{30} + 3 \times 2^{35} + 3 \times 2^{40} + 2^{45})) = \Theta(2^{50.78})$, ignoring the complexity of testing the random cubes that fail any one of the $n = 50$ BLR linearity tests. From the results, it is clear that this implies a key recovery attack is not possible based on the acquired results. Nevertheless, we have verified the gathered cube testers in the online phase, and they indeed

Table 3. Examples of cube testers found of size $\ell_c = 30$.

Cube (Nonce) Indices, I	Reduced Clocks, r
1, 2, 4, 5, 7, 18, 19, 23, 25, 27, 30, 39, 40, 44, 50, 52, 54, 61, 63, 64, 66, 67, 70, 72, 77, 78, 84, 91, 94, 95	129, 130, 131, 132, 133, 134, 135, 136, 137, 138, 139, 140, 141, 142, 143, 144, 145, 146, 147, 148, 149, 150, 151, 152, 153, 154, 155, 156, 157, 158, 159
11, 12, 14, 15, 19, 21, 25, 26, 30, 32, 33, 36, 37, 39, 40, 41, 44, 48, 52, 55, 58, 62, 63, 64, 66, 70, 71, 80, 82, 83	129, 130, 131, 132, 133, 134, 135, 136, 137, 138, 139, 140, 141, 142, 143, 144, 145, 146, 147, 148, 149, 150
6, 8, 11, 13, 14, 18, 19, 20, 22, 29, 31, 32, 34, 42, 46, 49, 57, 58, 59, 61, 73, 74, 76, 77, 81, 82, 83, 89, 90, 95	129, 130, 131, 132, 133, 134, 135, 136, 137, 138, 139, 140, 141, 142, 143, 144, 145, 146, 147, 148, 149, 150, 151, 152, 153, 154, 155
12, 18, 20, 22, 32, 34, 37, 38, 40, 43, 48, 54, 55, 56, 57, 59, 61, 62, 64, 67, 68, 74, 78, 80, 84, 85, 87, 90, 94, 95	129, 130, 131, 132, 133, 134, 135, 136, 137, 138, 139, 140, 141, 142, 143, 144, 145, 146, 147, 148, 149, 150, 151, 152, 153, 154, 155, 156, 157, 158, 159
0, 2, 7, 10, 11, 14, 19, 22, 23, 25, 36, 37, 39, 47, 49, 51, 54, 57, 61, 68, 70, 74, 77, 80, 85, 86, 89, 91, 92, 93	160
0, 5, 7, 14, 16, 21, 22, 23, 31, 32, 35, 36, 37, 43, 45, 51, 55, 56, 59, 60, 65, 66, 69, 72, 74, 77, 81, 90, 91, 92	160
1, 3, 4, 5, 6, 8, 10, 14, 24, 27, 34, 37, 45, 46, 47, 50, 55, 56, 57, 60, 67, 68, 71, 72, 75, 79, 82, 83, 84, 92	160
2, 4, 6, 8, 9, 10, 11, 16, 22, 23, 24, 35, 36, 37, 41, 48, 51, 52, 55, 56, 57, 63, 66, 71, 73, 74, 76, 79, 82, 93	160
1, 10, 11, 14, 17, 19, 21, 22, 25, 27, 33, 35, 38, 39, 43, 45, 46, 48, 60, 61, 62, 63, 65, 69, 75, 77, 78, 86, 89, 95	160
0, 1, 7, 8, 9, 13, 19, 21, 23, 24, 29, 37, 41, 42, 46, 49, 51, 54, 58, 61, 64, 81, 83, 84, 87, 89, 92, 93, 94, 95	160
0, 2, 3, 6, 16, 19, 20, 23, 29, 33, 35, 39, 43, 48, 49, 52, 54, 55, 60, 65, 66, 67, 68, 70, 75, 83, 87, 91, 93, 95	160
3, 4, 6, 8, 9, 10, 13, 14, 19, 20, 26, 28, 31, 32, 34, 36, 37, 40, 42, 48, 50, 51, 56, 62, 73, 76, 78, 84, 88, 93	160

Table 4. Examples of cube testers found of size $\ell_c = 35$.

Cube (Nonce) Indices, I	Reduced Clocks, r
2, 5, 8, 18, 19, 27, 34, 35, 37, 39, 42, 45, 49, 51, 53, 54, 58, 59, 62, 65, 66, 71, 72, 73, 74, 79, 82, 83, 84, 85, 86, 88, 89, 91, 93	161
0, 1, 2, 4, 5, 7, 8, 18, 20, 25, 30, 31, 40, 45, 47, 52, 53, 55, 56, 57, 63, 69, 70, 71, 72, 73, 74, 75, 78, 80, 81, 82, 86, 92, 93	162
1, 2, 3, 4, 6, 9, 11, 12, 15, 17, 18, 20, 23, 28, 36, 40, 41, 44, 45, 49, 57, 60, 61, 65, 69, 70, 71, 73, 75, 79, 80, 82, 83, 90, 94	161, 162, 163, 165

Table 5. Examples of cube testers found of size $\ell_c = 40$.

Cube (Nonce) Indices, I	Reduced Clocks, r
0, 1, 3, 5, 11, 12, 16, 17, 20, 25, 29, 30, 33, 35, 39, 44, 46, 47, 48, 51, 53, 57, 61, 62, 63, 65, 72, 74, 75, 76, 77, 79, 80, 81, 85, 91, 92, 93, 94, 95	161
0, 5, 6, 9, 13, 14, 15, 22, 23, 24, 28, 33, 34, 36, 38, 39, 42, 44, 47, 48, 50, 51, 53, 54, 55, 59, 61, 65, 66, 67, 71, 72, 78, 79, 82, 85, 86, 89, 94, 95	161, 162, 163
1, 3, 4, 6, 7, 11, 14, 16, 17, 19, 32, 33, 35, 36, 37, 41, 42, 45, 47, 49, 51, 52, 54, 55, 57, 58, 59, 62, 63, 67, 69, 75, 77, 78, 79, 80, 82, 86, 87, 93	163

Table 6. Examples of cube testers found of size $\ell_c = 45$.

Cube (Nonce) Indices, I	Reduced Clocks, r
0, 1, 3, 4, 11, 15, 16, 21, 22, 23, 24, 27, 35, 39, 40, 44, 47, 48, 49, 51, 52, 53, 56, 57, 58, 59, 60, 61, 62, 67, 70, 71, 72, 73, 75, 77, 82, 83, 84, 86, 88, 89, 91, 92, 94	161

indicate potential non-randomness in the initialisation phase of the pre-output generator in Grain-128AEAD for at least $r = 165$ reduced clocks. However, through this study, it is inconclusive if the degree of the output immediately after the initialisation phase of the pre-output generator beyond the reduced clock of $r = 165$ is larger than 45 as the number of cube testers obtained in our investigation is negligible compared to the number of cubes that are tested in an exhaustive cube search.

Judging from the current state of existing cryptanalyses on Grain-128AEAD, the full version of 384 clocks in the initialisation phase of the cipher is secure against cube attacks, and the best-reduced clock value r to date using cube attack on Grain-128AEAD is $r = 190$, using a white-box approach of cube attack with division property [17]. Hence, the full version of Grain-128AEAD is expected to have high security against cube attacks, and Grain-128AEADv2 will have an even high-security margin due to the additional rounds in the initialisation phase according to its specification. Although the results obtained by Hao, Leander, Meier, Todo and Wang [17] are the first and currently the best results for cube attack on Grain-128AEAD, due to the large complexities of 2^{96} for the distinguishing attacks and 2^{123} for the key recovery attack, the results are not practically verifiable. As of the time of this writing, it is to the best of our knowledge that our results are the first experimentally verifiable results using a black-box polynomial approach for the cube attack on Grain-128AEAD. The cube testers obtained in our experiments can be used directly for distinguishing attacks. The attacks require a complexity ranging from $\mathcal{O}(2^{25})$ and $\mathcal{O}(2^{30})$ for reduced clocks of $r = 129$ to $r = 160$, and a complexity ranging from $\mathcal{O}(2^{35})$ to $\mathcal{O}(2^{45})$ for reduced clocks of $r = 161$ to a maximum of $r = 165$. The best result obtained in this work requires a complexity of $\mathcal{O}(2^{35})$ to break $r = 165$ rounds of Grain-128AEAD. These results provide insights into the number of initialisation rounds up to which a practical cube attack might apply to Grain-128AEAD.

5   Conclusion

In this paper, we analysed the security margin of Grain-128AEAD against cube attacks. We have demonstrated distinguishing attacks on the reduced-round initialisation phase of the pre-output generator of Grain-128AEAD. Our distinguishing attacks are tested over different cube sizes of 25, 30, 35, 40, and 45. The implementation of the attack has been optimised to output 32 results of superpolies for each random cube. From the cube experiments, we obtained 53 cube testers. Out of the 53 cube testers, our best result is a cube tester of size $\ell_c = 35$ for reduced initialisation clocks of $r = 165$. These results indicate that there exists some non-randomness in Grain-128AEAD for at least 165 rounds in its initialisation phase. The results presented in this paper are the first cryptanalysis results using cube attack on Grain-128AEAD that are experimentally verifiable and can directly be used in distinguishing attacks. Our findings do not pose a threat to the security claim of Grain-128AEAD. We expect that the cubes reported in this paper will help to have a better comprehension of the cipher's security margin.

Future works could investigate the application of cube attacks against Grain-128AEAD with BLR quadraticity tests. Furthermore, state recovery attacks can also be a direction for future work pertaining to cube attacks on Grain-128AEAD. This can be further investigated by first defining the output polynomial in terms of the state bits at a chosen time instance and by selecting cubes from the variables that are input to the state update function at the chosen time instance.

Acknowledgements. This work is supported by the Ministry of Higher Education Malaysia through the Fundamental Research Grant Scheme (FRGS), project no. FRGS/1/2021/ICT07/XMU/02/1, as well as the Xiamen University Malaysia Research Fund under Grants XMUMRF/2019-C3/IECE/0005 and XMUMRF/2022-C9/IECE/0032.

Appendix A Additional Results for Cube Size $\ell_c = 25$

A list of other cube testers obtained for a cube size of $\ell_c = 25$ for reduced rounds r in between 129 to 160 are shown in Table 7.

Table 7. Additional cube testers of size $\ell_c = 25$ for $r = 129$ to 160.

Cube (Nonce) Indices, I	Reduced Clocks, r
1, 5, 6, 14, 19, 26, 28, 37, 40, 43, 44, 45, 47, 52, 56, 60, 61, 62, 63, 68, 75, 86, 88, 92, 93	129, 130, 131, 132, 133, 134, 135, 136, 137, 138, 139, 140, 141, 142, 143, 144, 145, 146, 147, 148, 149, 150, 151, 152, 153
3, 5, 8, 9, 10, 12, 19, 20, 25, 33, 37, 39, 48, 54, 56, 58, 65, 67, 68, 80, 82, 83, 85, 89, 93	129, 130, 131, 132, 133, 134, 135, 136, 137, 138, 139, 140, 141, 142, 143, 144, 145, 146, 147, 148, 149, 150, 151, 152, 155
0, 2, 4, 8, 10, 12, 14, 17, 23, 27, 31, 33, 44, 54, 60, 64, 67, 72, 74, 75, 77, 83, 85, 88, 89	129, 130, 131, 132, 133, 134, 135, 136, 137, 138, 139, 140, 141, 142, 143, 144, 145, 146, 147, 148, 149, 150, 151, 152, 153, 154, 155
0, 1, 5, 7, 15, 16, 17, 26, 35, 43, 44, 48, 54, 55, 59, 60, 61, 63, 65, 67, 68, 69, 79, 81, 88	129, 130, 131, 132, 133, 134, 135, 136, 137, 138, 139, 140, 141, 142, 143, 144, 145, 146, 147, 148, 149, 150, 153
0, 3, 5, 6, 8, 15, 16, 21, 26, 31, 34, 38, 41, 42, 43, 52, 53, 57, 59, 68, 77, 79, 80, 84, 85	129, 130, 131, 132, 133, 134, 135, 136, 137, 138, 139, 140, 141, 142, 143, 144, 145, 146, 147, 148, 149, 150, 151, 152
3, 7, 12, 14, 17, 20, 24, 26, 28, 32, 36, 38, 43, 51, 52, 53, 54, 64, 68, 73, 80, 81, 86, 88, 89	129, 130, 131, 132, 133, 134, 135, 136, 137, 138, 139, 140, 141, 142, 143, 144, 145, 146, 147, 148, 149, 150, 151, 152, 153, 154, 155, 156
8, 16, 19, 22, 24, 26, 28, 30, 31, 32, 35, 37, 38, 42, 54, 60, 61, 77, 78, 83, 86, 87, 88, 92, 95	129, 130, 131, 132, 133, 134, 135, 136, 137, 138, 139, 140, 141, 142, 143, 144, 145, 146, 147, 148, 149, 150
2, 6, 7, 8, 13, 17, 20, 21, 30, 35, 39, 41, 44, 47, 48, 58, 63, 66, 68, 75, 76, 84, 85, 86, 89	129, 130, 131, 132, 133, 134, 135, 136, 137, 138, 139, 140, 141, 142, 143, 144, 145, 146, 147, 148, 149, 150, 151, 152, 153, 154, 155

(*continued*)

Table 7. (*continued*)

Cube (Nonce) Indices, I	Reduced Clocks, r
6, 8, 9, 10, 11, 16, 18, 23, 42, 43, 45, 52, 65, 67, 69, 72, 74, 76, 78, 81, 85, 86, 89, 91, 93	129, 130, 131, 132, 133, 134, 135, 136, 137, 138, 139, 140, 141, 142, 143
1, 2, 13, 14, 17, 18, 19, 22, 24, 33, 34, 35, 36, 40, 42, 45, 57, 63, 66, 69, 72, 86, 87, 91, 95	129, 130, 131, 132, 133, 134, 135, 136, 137, 138, 139, 140, 141, 142, 143, 144, 145, 146, 147, 148, 149, 150, 151, 152, 153, 156
3, 5, 6, 12, 19, 23, 26, 27, 31, 32, 34, 35, 37, 43, 47, 51, 67, 69, 73, 80, 81, 90, 92, 94, 95	129, 130, 131, 132, 133, 134, 135, 136, 137, 138, 139, 140, 141, 142, 143, 144, 145, 146, 147, 148, 149, 150, 151, 152, 153, 154, 156, 157, 158
0, 1, 2, 5, 6, 10, 21, 22, 24, 25, 28, 40, 42, 48, 57, 59, 69, 72, 76, 83, 86, 87, 88, 91, 94	129, 130, 131, 132, 133, 134, 135, 136, 137, 138, 139, 140, 141, 142, 143, 144, 145, 146, 147, 148, 149, 150
2, 4, 8, 14, 23, 25, 26, 30, 37, 38, 41, 49, 50, 55, 56, 63, 68, 69, 76, 77, 82, 88, 89, 91, 94	129, 130, 131, 132, 133, 134, 135, 136, 137, 138, 139, 140, 141, 142, 143, 144, 146, 147, 148, 149
0, 1, 4, 5, 15, 16, 18, 27, 28, 31, 32, 34, 36, 43, 46, 49, 57, 65, 68, 70, 71, 75, 77, 84, 92	129, 130, 131, 132, 133, 134, 135, 136, 137, 138, 139, 140, 141, 142, 143, 144, 145, 146, 147, 148, 149, 150, 151, 152, 153, 154, 156
3, 11, 14, 25, 28, 36, 38, 39, 40, 42, 43, 46, 48, 49, 51, 52, 55, 56, 71, 76, 80, 82, 83, 86, 94	129, 130, 131, 132, 133, 134, 135, 136, 137, 138, 139, 140, 141, 142, 143, 144, 145, 146, 147, 148, 149, 150, 151
5, 10, 13, 18, 26, 30, 31, 33, 34, 41, 48, 49, 50, 51, 57, 58, 62, 64, 66, 82, 84, 85, 93, 94, 95	129, 130, 131, 132, 133, 134, 135, 136, 137, 138, 139, 140, 141, 142, 143, 144, 146, 147, 149, 150, 152, 153
8, 10, 11, 30, 34, 35, 38, 39, 40, 46, 48, 50, 52, 53, 54, 59, 62, 65, 75, 79, 80, 81, 84, 87, 90	129, 130, 131, 132, 133, 134, 135, 136, 137, 138, 139, 140, 141, 142, 143, 144, 145, 146, 148, 149, 150, 151, 152
0, 1, 4, 5, 7, 29, 31, 35, 40, 42, 43, 47, 50, 53, 63, 66, 70, 71, 76, 78, 81, 86, 89, 90, 94	129, 130, 131, 132, 133, 134, 135, 136, 137, 138, 139, 140, 141, 142, 143, 144, 145, 146, 147, 148, 149, 150, 151, 152, 153, 155
13, 15, 21, 22, 23, 25, 27, 29, 47, 50, 51, 52, 57, 60, 67, 71, 75, 76, 80, 81, 84, 87, 89, 91, 93	129, 130, 131, 132, 133, 134, 135, 136, 137, 138, 139, 140, 141, 142, 143, 144, 145, 146, 147, 148, 149, 150
1, 4, 10, 11, 12, 15, 20, 28, 32, 34, 35, 48, 51, 52, 53, 57, 61, 65, 66, 67, 70, 73, 75, 82, 84	129, 130, 131, 132, 133, 134, 135, 136, 137, 138, 139, 140, 141, 142, 143, 144, 145, 146, 147, 148, 149, 150, 151, 153, 154, 155

(*continued*)

Table 7. (*continued*)

Cube (Nonce) Indices, I	Reduced Clocks, r
1, 9, 11, 13, 14, 17, 29, 31, 34, 43, 45, 46, 51, 53, 57, 59, 64, 67, 70, 74, 80, 81, 86, 88, 92	129, 130, 131, 132, 133, 134, 135, 136, 137, 138, 139, 140, 141, 142, 143, 144, 145, 146, 147, 148, 149, 150, 151, 153, 154, 155
6, 7, 14, 19, 20, 29, 30, 32, 36, 49, 51, 54, 57, 60, 64, 70, 73, 74, 76, 78, 79, 84, 86, 93, 94	129, 130, 131, 132, 133, 134, 135, 136, 137, 138, 139, 140, 141, 142, 143, 144, 145, 146, 147, 153, 155
3, 7, 8, 9, 12, 14, 17, 18, 23, 24, 32, 33, 46, 50, 54, 59, 61, 63, 67, 68, 71, 81, 84, 86, 91	129, 130, 131, 132, 133, 134, 135, 136, 137, 138, 139, 140, 141, 142, 143, 144, 145, 146, 147, 148, 151, 155
0, 3, 7, 14, 22, 23, 25, 38, 41, 46, 51, 58, 60, 63, 64, 67, 68, 70, 73, 82, 83, 84, 88, 91, 92	129, 130, 131, 132, 133, 134, 135, 136, 137, 138, 139, 140, 141, 142, 143, 144, 145, 146, 147, 148, 149, 150
5, 12, 15, 17, 21, 25, 28, 30, 32, 36, 46, 56, 57, 60, 61, 63, 66, 68, 76, 77, 81, 84, 86, 91, 95	129, 130, 131, 132, 133, 134, 135, 136, 137, 138, 139, 140, 141, 142, 143, 144, 145, 146, 147, 148, 149, 150, 154
7, 11, 13, 24, 28, 29, 33, 35, 36, 38, 39, 41, 44, 55, 57, 60, 61, 65, 66, 67, 72, 78, 79, 84, 89	129, 130, 131, 132, 133, 134, 135, 136, 137, 138, 139, 140, 141, 142, 143, 144, 145, 146, 147, 148, 149, 150, 151, 152, 154, 155
1, 5, 9, 10, 16, 18, 23, 29, 34, 36, 38, 41, 46, 48, 51, 56, 59, 63, 68, 70, 80, 81, 82, 84, 92	129, 130, 131, 132, 133, 134, 135, 136, 137, 138, 139, 140, 141, 142, 143, 144, 145, 146, 147, 148, 149
0, 4, 6, 7, 9, 15, 16, 24, 26, 27, 33, 38, 39, 45, 49, 52, 59, 60, 64, 68, 72, 77, 78, 83, 90	129, 130, 131, 132, 133, 134, 135, 136, 137, 138, 139, 140, 141, 142, 143, 144, 145, 146, 147, 148, 149, 150, 151, 152, 153, 154
0, 3, 4, 6, 7, 12, 14, 28, 31, 32, 36, 38, 40, 43, 45, 46, 51, 53, 54, 57, 65, 69, 70, 71, 75	129, 130, 131, 132, 133, 134, 135, 136, 137, 138, 139, 140, 141, 142, 143, 144, 145, 146, 147, 148, 149, 150, 151, 152, 153, 154, 155, 156, 157, 158
5, 11, 17, 18, 19, 20, 23, 25, 27, 34, 35, 36, 40, 42, 44, 48, 49, 53, 58, 65, 71, 72, 78, 88, 95	129, 130, 131, 132, 133, 134, 135, 136, 137, 138, 139, 140, 141, 142, 143, 144, 145, 146, 147, 148, 149, 150, 151
0, 2, 5, 10, 12, 13, 16, 21, 27, 28, 34, 35, 42, 44, 51, 58, 59, 61, 65, 66, 70, 72, 75, 80, 89	129, 130, 131, 132, 133, 134, 135, 136, 137, 138, 139, 140, 141, 142, 143, 144, 145
1, 2, 7, 9, 23, 29, 31, 32, 40, 41, 42, 43, 49, 50, 55, 56, 60, 77, 80, 81, 84, 86, 88, 89, 95	129, 130, 131, 132, 133, 134, 135, 136, 137, 138, 139, 140, 141, 142, 143, 144, 145, 146, 147, 148, 149, 150, 151, 152, 153, 154, 155

(*continued*)

Table 7. (*continued*)

Cube (Nonce) Indices, I	Reduced Clocks, r
0, 2, 9, 13, 14, 16, 17, 24, 26, 27, 30, 31, 34, 41, 54, 55, 62, 66, 73, 74, 81, 82, 83, 86, 91	129, 130, 131, 132, 133, 134, 135, 136, 137, 138, 139, 140, 141, 142, 143, 144, 145, 146, 147, 148, 149, 150
5, 8, 17, 18, 23, 24, 27, 32, 35, 43, 48, 51, 52, 59, 60, 61, 62, 69, 81, 86, 88, 89, 90, 94, 95	129, 130, 131, 132, 133, 134, 135, 136, 137, 138, 139, 140, 141, 142, 143, 144, 145, 146, 147, 148, 149, 150, 151

References

1. Mouha, N.: The design space of lightweight cryptography. In: NIST Lightweight Cryptography Workshop (2015). https://csrc.nist.gov/csrc/media/events/lightweight-cryptography-workshop-2015/documents/papers/session5-mouha-paper.pdf. Accessed 10 May 2023
2. NIST: Lightweight cryptography. https://csrc.nist.gov/projects/lightweight-cryptography. Accessed 10 May 2023
3. Turan, M.S., et al.: Status report on the second round of the NIST lightweight cryptography standardization process. National Institute of Standards and Technology Interagency or Internal Report 8369 (2021). https://doi.org/10.6028/NIST.IR.8369. Accessed 10 May 2023
4. Hell, M., Johansson, T., Meier, W., Sönnerup, J., Yoshida, H.: Grain-128AEAD - a lightweight AEAD stream cipher. https://csrc.nist.gov/CSRC/media/Projects/lightweight-cryptography/documents/finalist-round/updated-spec-doc/grain-128aead-spec-final.pdf. Accessed 10 May 2023
5. Hell, M., Johansson, T., Maximov, A., Meier, W., Sönnerup, J., Yoshida, H.: Grain-128AEADv2 - a lightweight AEAD stream cipher (2021). https://csrc.nist.gov/CSRC/media/Projects/lightweight-cryptography/documents/finalist-round/updated-spec-doc/grain-128aead-spec-final.pdf. Accessed 10 May 2023
6. Dinur, I., Shamir, A.: Cube attacks on tweakable black box polynomials. In: Joux, A. (ed.) EUROCRYPT 2009. LNCS, vol. 5479, pp. 278–299. Springer, Heidelberg (2009). https://doi.org/10.1007/978-3-642-01001-9_16
7. Vielhaber, M.: Breaking ONE.FIVIUM by AIDA an algebraic IV differential attack. IACR Cryptology ePrint Archive (2007). https://eprint.iacr.org/2007/413.pdf. Accessed 10 May 2023
8. Lai, X.: Higher order derivatives and differential cryptanalysis. In: Blahut, R.E., Costello, D.J., Maurer, U., Mittelholzer, T. (eds.) Communications and Cryptography. The Springer International Series in Engineering and Computer Science, vol. 276, pp. 227–233. Springer, Boston (1994). https://doi.org/10.1007/978-1-4615-2694-0_23
9. Aumasson, J.-P., Dinur, I., Meier, W., Shamir, A.: Cube testers and key recovery attacks on reduced-round MD6 and trivium. In: Dunkelman, O. (ed.) FSE 2009. LNCS, vol. 5665, pp. 1–22. Springer, Heidelberg (2009). https://doi.org/10.1007/978-3-642-03317-9_1
10. Dinur, I., Shamir, A.: Breaking grain-128 with dynamic cube attacks. In: Joux, A. (ed.) FSE 2011. LNCS, vol. 6733, pp. 167–187. Springer, Heidelberg (2011). https://doi.org/10.1007/978-3-642-21702-9_10

11. Dinur, I., Shamir, A.: Applying cube attacks to stream ciphers in realistic scenarios. Cryptogr. Commun. **4**, 217–232 (2012). https://doi.org/10.1007/s12095-012-0068-4

12. Knellwolf, S., Meier, W.: High order differential attacks on stream ciphers. Cryptogr. Commun. **4**, 203–215 (2012). https://doi.org/10.1007/s12095-012-0071-9

13. Salam, M.I., Bartlett, H., Dawson, E., Pieprzyk, J., Simpson, L., Wong, K.K.-H.: Investigating cube attacks on the authenticated encryption stream cipher ACORN. In: Batten, L., Li, G. (eds.) ATIS 2016. CCIS, vol. 651, pp. 15–26. Springer, Singapore (2016). https://doi.org/10.1007/978-981-10-2741-3_2

14. Banik, S.: Conditional differential cryptanalysis of 105 round Grain v1. Cryptogr. Commun. **8**, 113–137 (2016). https://doi.org/10.1007/s12095-015-0146-5

15. Salam, I., Simpson, L., Bartlett, H., Dawson, E., Pieprzyk, J., Wong, K.KH.: Investigating cube attacks on the authenticated encryption stream cipher MORUS. In: 2017 IEEE Trustcom/BigDataSE/ICESS, pp. 961–966. IEEE (2017). https://doi.org/10.1109/Trustcom/BigDataSE/ICESS.2017.337

16. Todo, Y., Isobe, T., Hao, Y., Meier, W.: Cube attacks on non-blackbox polynomials. IEEE Trans. Comput. **67**(12), 1720–1736 (2018). https://doi.org/10.1109/TC.2018.2835480

17. Hao, Y., Leander, G., Meier, W., Todo, Y., Wang, Q.: Modeling for three-subset division property without unknown subset. In: Canteaut, A., Ishai, Y. (eds.) EUROCRYPT 2020. LNCS, vol. 12105, pp. 466–495. Springer, Cham (2020). https://doi.org/10.1007/978-3-030-45721-1_17

18. He, Y., Wang, G., Li, W., Ren, Y.: Improved cube attacks on some authenticated encryption ciphers and stream ciphers in the internet of things. IEEE Access **8**, 20920–20930 (2020). https://doi.org/10.1109/ACCESS.2020.2967070

19. Teng, W.L., Salam, I., Yau, W.-C., Pieprzyk, J., Phan, R.C.-W.: Cube attacks on round-reduced TinyJAMBU. Sci. Rep. **12**, 5317 (2022). https://doi.org/10.1038/s41598-022-09004-3

20. Cianfriglia, M., Onofri, E., Onofri, S., Pedicini, M.: Fourteen years of cube attacks. Appl. Algebra Eng. Commun. Comput. (2023). https://doi.org/10.1007/s00200-023-00602-w

21. Che, C., Tian, T.: A new correlation cube attack based on division property. In: Simpson, L., Rezazadeh Baee, M.A. (eds.) ACISP 2023. LNCS, vol. 13915, pp. 53–71. Springer, Cham (2023). https://doi.org/10.1007/978-3-031-35486-1_3

22. Salam, I., Ooi, T.H., Xue, L., Yau, W.-C., Pieprzyk, J., Phan, R.C.-W.: Random differential fault attacks on the lightweight authenticated encryption stream cipher Grain-128AEAD. IEEE Access **9**, 72568–72586 (2021). https://doi.org/10.1109/ACCESS.2021.3078845

23. Chang, D., Turan, M. S. Recovering the key from the internal state of Grain-128AEAD. IACR Cryptology ePrint Archive (2021). https://eprint.iacr.org/2021/439.pdf. Accessed 30 July 2023

24. Blum, M., Luby, M., Rubinfield, R.: Self-testing/correcting with applications to numerical problems. J. Comput. Syst. Sci. **47**(3), 549–595 (1993). https://doi.org/10.1016/0022-0000(93)90044-W

A Literature Review of Various Analysis Methods and Classification techniques of Malware

Vaishnavi Madhekar[1]([⊠]) and Sakshi Mandke[2]

[1] Northeastern University, Boston, MA, USA
madhekarvaishnavi@gmail.com
[2] Cummins College of Engineering, Pune, MH, India
sakshi.mandke@cumminscollege.in

Abstract. Malware disrupts the natural behaviour of computer systems, hinders performance, and may cause a significant loss to the computer system owner. The growth or advancement in the number of malware variants has necessitated the requirement of advanced techniques for the detection, identification, and classification of malware. The hybrid approach is predominantly employed since static and dynamic analysis methods have drawbacks and are time-consuming. Moreover, recent malware variants use obfuscation techniques and exhibit polymorphic and metamorphic behaviour. It was noticed that even though classical machine learning methods gave better performance and quicker classification, they suffered from the problem of misclassification. Newer approaches such as image processing techniques and deep learning architectures are thus employed. The paper focuses on the survey of various detection, identification, and classification methods of malware and is an effort to put forward the best approach.

Keywords: Malware classification methods · static analysis · dynamic analysis · image processing · machine learning algorithms · sandbox · binary · PEheaders · CNN · Random Forest

1 Introduction

Malware is sometimes viewed as being trivial due to greater threats. However, the rise in computer systems with virus infections is noticeable as a result of the Internet's recent expansion. Malware attacks on computer systems dramatically increased in 2021 and 2022. However, each malware infection has its own attack methods, making it difficult to detect. Malware is software created to hinder computer systems' functioning or damage the computers [1]. Ransomware was the biggest threat to enterprises in 2021 [2], emphasizing the significance of malware detection, identification, and classification. The detection of malware is painstaking because the developers of malware apply profuse concealment strategies to make it difficult to detect and further classify. Malware mitigation is now a developing problem in the field of cyber security [7] since it is difficult to classify malware into a specific family [3]. The remaining paper is structured as

© ICST Institute for Computer Sciences, Social Informatics and Telecommunications Engineering 2024
Published by Springer Nature Switzerland AG 2024. All Rights Reserved
M. H. Miraz et al. (Eds.): iCETiC 2023, LNICST 538, pp. 127–142, 2024.
https://doi.org/10.1007/978-3-031-50215-6_9

follows: In section two, we briefly discuss the types of malwares, section three involves a detailed overview of different detection techniques, and section four and five will dive deep into various analysis methodologies and classification models used for classifying the malware.

2   Types of Malwares

Action-based malware, concealment strategy-based malware, and detection evasion-based malware are the three basic categories of malware [1]. Adware, Ransomware, Spyware, Rootkit, Trojan, Backdoors, Rogue security software, and browser hijackers are examples of action-based and concealment strategy malware.

2.1   Action-Based and Concealment Strategy Based

Adware is used as a revenue-generating tool. The developers of adware capture any advertising-supported software or website, and adware is distributed mainly through pop-up ads. Ransomware was developed to hold captive files or computer software in return for a ransom amount. Spyware is used for passive attacks to spy on user activity. It monitors computer activity, collects keystrokes, and does data harvesting. A rootkit is very hard to detect. As a consequence of its effects on the boot sector, it becomes one of the first programs to start when the machine turns on. Trojan, is a class of malware that impersonates genuine software while harming the system and exploiting security measures. The backdoor creates an entry point in the system (creates an open port) and makes the system vulnerable to remote access without authentication. Rogue security software imitates the actual anti-virus software. It turns off the real anti-virus and impersonates a real one by tricking the user into buying them for a lesser amount. A Browser Hijacker modifies the settings of the web browser by injecting an unwanted form of software without the user's permission.

2.2   Detection Evasion-Based

The polymorphic virus, encrypted virus, oligomorphic virus, and metamorphic virus all belong to the type of detection evasion techniques. The polymorphic virus uses obfuscation techniques or mutates while persisting the original algorithm. The metamorphic virus is of significant concern since it is one of the hardest to detect. Every time it is run, the code mutates. To avoid signature detection, it uses a mutation engine and obfuscation techniques. The only difference between the former and latter is that polymorphic changes its codes when it mutates, and metamorphic rewrites the entire code. The encrypted virus works intending to make detection difficult. It encrypts the payload or the critical part to hide the signature of the malware file. The Oligomorphic virus is an advanced version of an encrypted virus. It produces multiple detectors and selects one at random. However, it can be easily discovered, because the antivirus software simply places multiple entries in the database with multiple signatures.

3 Detection Methods of Malware

The three techniques for malware detection discussed in the [7] are Signature, Behavioural, and Heuristic-based. Out of these techniques the oldest and primary technique is the signature-based method. This technique detects the existence of malware by performing a comparative search and simultaneously looking for a match within the malware definition database. To account for new variants, the malware definition database, is updated on a timely basis. In order to search the solution space and determine where it is most likely to find a match, it uses a heuristic search strategy. However, this technique requires extensive domain knowledge and faces code obfuscation problems [6]. The behavioural method executes in three steps. First, is the data collection phase. In this phase, the data collector collects the information about the executable. Second, is the interpreter phase. In this phase, the interpreter converts or transforms the information present in raw form into intermediate transformations. The matcher phase is the final step. The matcher compares malware behaviour during this stage. As a result, a behavioural-based malware detection method examines what malware actually does rather than what it hypothesizes. The last malware detection method employs different heuristics to detect malware. Therefore, it uses the above methods to learn the behaviour of malware and execute feature engineering (Fig. 1).

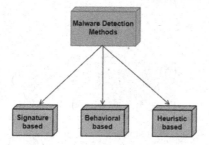

Fig. 1. Malware Detection Methods

4 Analysis Methods and Classification Models of Malware

The analysis of malware is crucial as it helps in extracting essential information regarding the malware. Moreover, malware analysis since helps in determining the nature, motive, capability, and scalability of malware programs that infect the computer system. The methodologies for malware analysis are divided into two categories in current literature surveys: static analysis and dynamic analysis. The primary distinction between the two approaches is that the static analysis approach extracts feature from the malware file rather than executing it. The signature-based detection methods form a core part of static analysis [1]. On the flip side, dynamic analysis executes the file in isolated environment or a sandboxed environment to monitor the behaviour of malware. The dynamic analysis method generally yields better results and performance than static analysis but is costlier with respect to the static analysis method. In [5] N. Poonguzhali et al., employed machine learning algorithms in the static analysis and in imaging processing techniques and for dynamic analysis used sandboxed environments and API calls to detect malware.

This literature survey will explore different malware detection methods, analysis methods, and classification models and comparison on the different approaches. Throughout the paper, several datasets will be referred to for analysis of different approaches. The dataset used for PE files static analysis has the following structure (Fig. 2):

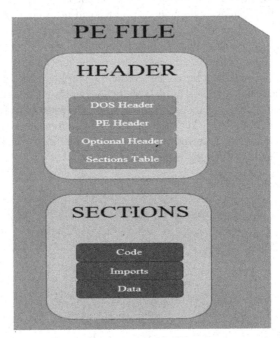

Fig. 2 Header and Section of the PE File

The most commonly used dataset for the image processing techniques is the Malimg dataset [18]. The dataset contains image representations of malware files. It can be extended by converting any executable file into its image file. Table 1 shows the sample of Maling dataset with the malware families[21]. SARVAM is collection of malware files openly available for image processing and machine learning techniques. The database of malware contains MD5 sum for analyzed malware and new variants similar Regin are added to update the database [4].

Table 1. Detailed description of Malimg dataset with the malware families [21]

	Family/Class	Type
0	Adialer.C	Dialer
1	Agent.FYI	Backdoor
2	Allaple.A	Worm
3	Allaple.L	Worm
4	Alueron.gen!J	Worm
5	Autorun.K	Worm:AutoIT
6	C2LOP.P	Trojan
7	C2LOP.gen!g	Trojan
8	Dialplatform.B	Dialer
9	Dontovo.A	Trojan Downloader
10	Fakerean	Rogue
11	Instantaccess	Dialer
12	Lolyda.AA1	PWS
13	Lolyda.AA2	PWS
14	Lolyda.AA3	PWS
15	Lolyda.AT	PWS
16	Malex.gen!J	Trojan
17	Obfuscator.AD	Trojan Downloader
18	Rbot!gen	Backdoor
19	Skintrim.N	Trojan
20	Swizzor.gen!E	Trojan Downloader
21	Swizzor.gen!l	Trojan Downloader
22	VB.AT	Worm
23	Wintrim.BX	Trojan Downloader
24	Yuner.A	Worm

4.1 Analysis Methods

There are many different ways for detecting malware, and each one uses either static analysis, dynamic analysis, or hybrid analysis.

4.1.1 Static Analysis

As mentioned above, static analysis is the method that analyses without executing the program. It usually detects the patterns, hence known as static analysis. The patterns detected in the static analysis are N-grams, Opcodes, Strings, byte sequence frequency information, the unpacked structure of malware, or deconstructed programs. This method requires the malicious program or malware file to be unpacked or decrypted in sequences for analysis. The recent and common approach is the analysis of PE files (Portable executables) using domain-level knowledge. The other commonly used techniques are n-grams and strings, which do not require domain knowledge. These methods are computationally extensive, face obfuscation problems, and exhibit poor performance, and since these two techniques do not use domain-level knowledge, it becomes difficult to extract features. Therefore, the former approach of using PE files is more effective than the latter. The former approach combined with machine and deep learning approaches yields better results. Ijaz et al. [8] used machine learning algorithms on the PE dataset, with features obtained from PE files.

N-grams. In this approach, N-grams are used to describe the malware file. N-gram is a substring of a string that is N characters long. A malware file's N-grams are a continuous series of N hexadecimal values. Depending on the context of the n-gram, there are two primary n-gram approaches. The first is the byte code n-grams, and the second is the opcode n-grams.

The first pioneer of using the N-grams approach for malware analysis was the IBM research group in the 1990s. In N-grams, each element in the sequence can be one of the 257 different values, which includes the 256-byte range and an additional special ('??') character in the symbol list. The n-gram approach is to have a collection of n-grams of malicious programs or frequent or common sequences of n-grams in bytes or opcode to compare and classify the malware files.

Abou-Assaleh [9] used the approach as extracted the most common n-gram bytes from the malicious files. The approach used a labelled set of malicious programs and a non-labelled set of malicious programs. The features are extracted and then fed to the KNN model used to classify the new programs or new instances.

I. Satos [10] stated that unknown variants are effectively detected using the N-grams technique. This was accomplished by extracting the features, code, or text fragments from a group of malicious programs or files, that were run under controlled conditions. In [10] used the opcode n-grams due to the semantics. The operation to be carried out is specified by an opcode, which is a constituent of the machine-level language. This approach of employing opcode as a feature for malware identification is carried out by calculating the similarity between opcode sequences or measuring the frequency of appearance of specific sequences. This approach of N-grams is computationally heavy and is difficult to apply to domain knowledge.

Strings. Strings serve as a great source of information. The strings extracted from the malicious program provide information that helps in identifying the malware. These typically include URLs, error messages, or any comments. Hence sometimes, the strings in executable files, provides information such as the Ip address of the command-and-control server.

Websites. A recent widely used approach of static analysis is scanning the malware file on a website. This is performed for preliminary research. These type of websites acts as online scanner. The file to be checked is uploaded, and the online scanner will look for suspicious malware such as worms, trojans, and viruses. One of the examples of such websites is VirusTotal.

PE Files. PE or Portable executable is a format of files that are executables, DLLs, and object codes. PE files are commonly used in the windows operating system. In [Ijaz et al. (209)], static features were extracted from the PE files using the PEFILE library of python. This approach does not execute the file in a controlled environment. This method of static analysis involved extracting the necessary features of PE files. The two main sub-parts are the Header and Sections. The header sub-part consists of information such as header, optional header, DOS header, and Sections table. The sections' sub-part consists of code, imports, and data.

Ijaz et al. [8], extracted more than ninety-two features. Subsequently, machine learning techniques are applied to those features. Anderson and Roth [11], acquired the features by analysing information from portable executable files and further applied machine learning algorithms to those features. The approach also included methods followed in [Saxe and Berlin (2015)], such as byte entropy histogram, formatting of raw byte histogram, and additional employment of string extraction.

An SVM-based approach using PE files is used by Wang et al. [13]. In this paper Wang used structure static analysis to extract the features of the portable executable files and then fed them as input to the SVM classifier. Subsequently, when enough data is trained, the PE files are classified as either benign or malicious. One prominent architecture is the MalConv, proposed by Raff et al. [14]. It compared the deep learning approach on PE files with machine learning algorithms. However, this method has limitations because of the packed nature of malware.

4.1.2 Dynamic Analysis

In dynamic analysis the malicious program is run in controlled environment to monitor the malicious program behaviour. The dynamic analysis does not need the hexadecimal bits of the malware file to be unpacked or decoded [1]. This comprises of methods, in which malware is executed in a sandbox setting. By running the malware in a sandboxed environment, different features can be extracted from it which can then be used for classification malware. The features extracted mainly include windows API calls, stack contents and actual function parameters. In [8] Ijaz et al., performed dynamic analysis of malware using cuckoo sandbox. It is software which provides a controlled environment. The cuckoo sandbox primarily consists of three parts, first is the host, second is the virtual environment and the last is the agent. In [8] Ijaz et al., preferred Cuckoo box due to the logging functionality it offered. The information acquired through Cuckoo sandbox analysis involve registry keys, API calls, IP address and DNS queries, access URLs and summary information about the files. The other tools which can be used are Wireshark, Capture BAT, Process Monitor, Process explorer.

API Calls. An application programming interface, is used to connect or establish communication between two software components or between software and hardware components. A function call or a collection of automated subroutines can be used to get the necessary information. Dynamic analysis is done by extracting the API calls that the binary file makes while it is executed. The sequence of API calls is of utmost importance since the similarity of API sequence calls helps in the categorization of malicious files into distinct families. By comparing and collecting the signatures of API call sequences, malware files can be classified into malicious and benign categories. In [15] Tobiyama et al. used features extracted from API calls of five minutes and then passed it to a classification model such as CNN. In [16] Huang et al. collected samples of benign and harmful malware files. Subsequently, the feature sets of API calls were fed to a shallow feed-forward network. Even though this approach gave better results than the approach followed in [15] by Tobiyama et al., it is not suitable for real-time analysis as it lacks the speed needed for evaluation.

Registry Keys. The registry is a database that contains information, configuration settings, options, and preferences of hardware and software installed on computers. A registry key is used to identify the associated registry value and is created when hardware, software, or adapter gets installed.

If a harmful malware file changes the registry, the applications might not start, utilities might not work, or worse computer might not boot. In [8] Ijaz et al. used the Cuckoo sandbox to perform dynamic analysis. The cuckoo sandbox maintains information about the registry changes, such as when the registry is accessed, written, opened, read, or deleted. This is an effective way of detecting malware because malware can make changes to multiple registry entries. Malware will make the changes to multiple entries, to break into a computer system and bypass the firewall security and windows security. All the registry changes are captured, and the new registry matrix is used for comparison to detect new malware. Often keeping a backup of the registry, online or outside of the computer helps in recovering the computer system.

The other information generated by tools is IPS and DNS queries, summary information, and information on files created, accessed, deleted, and opened. The other tools, such as a process monitor, observe the processes registry and events, and the process explorer monitors the run-time behaviour of malware and the memory. One prominent used and a famous tool is Wireshark which does network monitoring by traffic fingerprinting to determine if any malicious payloads exist.

However, a major drawback of dynamic analysis methods is the different behaviours exposed by malware within a controlled environment. This can occur because specific malicious files are only triggered under specific conditions when a specific command, consequence, system date, or action takes place. Hence making malware detection difficult in a virtualized environment or a controlled environment as malware may behave normally.

4.1.3 Hybrid Analysis

Dynamic analysis is expensive but obtains better results than static analysis. With technological advances, dynamic analysis has been proven to be beatable. Dynamic analysis takes a significant amount of time, exhibits guileful behavior, and produces false positives. But static analysis is not powerful as well, due to code obfuscation and zero-day malware. Hence, dynamic analysis complemented with static analysis is the ideal approach for identifying malware.

In [17] Shijo et al. applied dynamic and static analysis to the dataset containing malicious and benign files. Shijo et al. [17], using static analysis extracted the PSI features and using dynamic analysis extracted the API call sequence. The API calls are based on the n-grams. Since both n-grams and API calls are combined, the method is known as API-call-grams. In [6] Vinayakumar followed a hybrid approach by integrating multiple approaches and proposed a model known as ScalMalNet. The proposed approach in [6], combined static analysis, dynamic analysis, and deep learning architectures. It is comprised of WSBD, WDBD, and DIMD, which are Windows-Static-Brain-Droid, Windows-Dynamic-Brain-Droid, and Deep-Image-Mal-Detect respectively. This approach is an effective method for the visual detection of malware since it uses the Malimg dataset (a visual representation of malware files). It is a highly scalable and novel image processing technique. For real-time analysis, it is combined with DNN architectures. It is effective against zero-day malware and is highly scalable, hence can be applied as a hybrid method in a big data environment.

Figure 3 summarizes the above analysis methods.

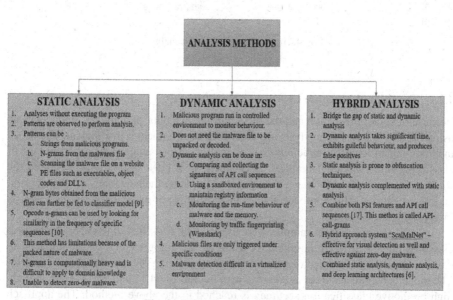

Fig. 3. Different analysis methods

4.2 Classification Models Using Image Processing Techniques, Machine Learning Models and Deep Learning Architectures on Malwares Represented as Images

In the preceding section, various analysis methodologies were explored. The use of machine learning and deep learning techniques on PE files, data gathered through dynamic tools, or hybrid approaches were also described in the previous section. However, in this section, we will look at a specific approach, which involves visualizing malware as grey-scale images and then applying various techniques to the dataset.

Methods for converting malware binaries into vectors of zeros and ones and subsequently into images are of great importance. In [18] Nataraj et al., found a novel approach for classifying and analysing malware. According to the methodology, any malware executable or binary can be represented as a continuous string of 0 s and 1 s. Therefore, a vector containing zeros and ones is reshaped into a matrix. Subsequently, this matrix is converted to a grey-scale image. Figure 4 describes these steps. Using the technique described, a striking visual similarity in the image texture of malware binaries from the same families was noticed.

A reason for the same visual texture could be that new variants have code that is, frequently reused. Consequently, the issue of malware classification has evolved into a problem of image classification. This method is resilient to obfuscation techniques and other encryption sections.

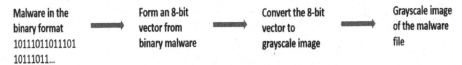

Fig. 4. Image Visualisation of malware

4.2.1 Traditional Machine Learning Algorithms

Because of code obfuscation and the metamorphic behavior of malware, static analysis using PE files or dynamic analysis in a controlled environment is insufficient. The above methods fail to identify malicious files as malignant or benign, let far be the task of classifying into individual families. Subsequently, in [19], Garcia et al. operated the Random Forest method for categorizing and segregating the new malware binaries into various categories. This approach abodes the advantage of malware files represented as images of feature vectors.

In [19], Malimg dataset samples were used, which consisted of 9,342 examples preclassified into 25 different families. By using the sampling method on the imbalanced dataset, Garcia et al. avoided overfitting and generalization of typical malware families. The model's overall accuracy is 94.64%, with bounds of 94.11 and 95.14. Even though, high predictive classification accuracy is reached in the above method. The approach still suffers from the misclassification problem of malware files that are visually similar [19]. Hence, the future work for traditional machine learning algorithms could be the extraction of features using image processing techniques. This results in additional insights and better predictive models.

4.2.2 Analysis Using Image Processing Techniques and Machine Learning Algorithms

The most used method with the Malimg dataset is to use gist descriptors and follow the image processing technique for detection. In [18], Nataraj et al. employed a supervised learning algorithm KNN or K-Nearest Neighbor with Euclidean distance for classification on the Malimg dataset. The features were computed using GIST descriptors. The gist descriptors have demonstrated substantial accuracy in object classification and scene classification. The dimension of the GIST feature used in [18] is 320. The dataset was split into k-sets using a k-fold cross-validation procedure by Nataraj et al. in [18] and the number of selected were 10. At each iteration of k, a confusion matrix is computed. For each iteration, a random subset is used for training and testing. In each subspace, ten percent set is the test set, and the rest ninety is the train set. The confusion matrices formed are 10 in total. The final confusion matrix is the average of all confusion matrices. The KNN employed in [18] used the optimal cluster k = 3 and operated tenfold cross-validation for classification. The classification rate achieved was 0.9818. The model was then tested on additional datasets, including the Malheur and Anubis datasets.

To solve the problem of feature selection [22], performed feature reduction experiments based on linear support vector classification which is an improved form of the well-known support vector machine technique is SVC, or Support vector Classification. The SVC technique is a multi-class classification algorithm. The feature reduction is performed for obtaining better results, and to obtain an equivalent feature set. In [22], Yajamanam et al. applied RFE to the Malicia dataset for eliminating the features. The SVC is then applied twice. In the first turn linear SVC is applied to eliminate the feature with lowest weight. [22]. In the second turn, SVC is applied on the reduced set. This is done until only the strongest feature exists. The results were "nearly-optimal" with reduced feature set.

Yajamanam et al. [22] also employed UFS, in which SVC is applied for each feature separately, and accuracies are used to rank the features. Finally, an accuracy of 92% was acquired, by considering only the 60 highest ranked features, which account for 1% of the total 320 features. Yajamanam et al. subsequently applied the salting technique to degrade the score of gist-based scores. This made clear that a highly effective strategy against gist-based score detection exists.

The GIST + SVM method followed in [23] by Kalash et al., used two datasets, the Malimg and Microsoft Malware dataset. The classification accuracy achieved for the Malimg dataset was 93.23%, and for the Microsoft Malware it was 88.74%

Furthermore, [20] applied clustering techniques to malware images, collected a corpus of malware files, and computed the compact features. Later the mean shift clustering was applied to cluster samples having the same families.

4.2.3 Deep Learning Techniques

The deep learning architectures are required due to scalability problems of with earlier approaches. Moreover, neural networks have proven to bridge many of the image processing technique's problems.

In [21], the Malimg dataset from [18] was used with the CNN model. The CNN model was built using Keras. Two convolutional layers make up the model's structure, and each convolutional layer is linked to a max pooling layer. Next in the architecture are the dropout, flatten, dense dropout, and finally two consecutive dense layers. However, since the Malimg dataset is unbalanced, a lower weight is assigned to the higher majority class and a higher weight to the lower majority class. The accuracy of the above model achieved was 0.9514632.

Kalash et al. performed extensive experiments on both Malimg and Microsoft datasets and achieved an accuracy of 98.52% and 99.97%, respectively. The approach proposed in [23] by Kalash et al. is generic and not tailored toward any specific dataset. Kalash et al. in [23] trained a model known as, M-CNN or Convolutional Neural Network for Malware classification. The M-CNN model is based on VGG-16. The experiment conducted on the Microsoft malware dataset was performed in two settings. Setting A performed a random split, with ninety percent of the dataset for the train and ten percent for the test, and achieved an accuracy of 98.99%. Setting B used the train-test split instructed by Microsoft and achieved an accuracy of 99.97%.

In [22], Yajamanam et al. used SoftMax regression and deep learning instead of gist descriptors for malware classification on the image-based dataset. Therefore in [22], the gist descriptors are not used to extract the features, but raw bytes from the malware file represented as images, are used as features. The above approach was used to ensure that the results were as accurate as the gist descriptors. SoftMax regression is a generalized logistic regression and yielded only 57% accuracy with five malware families. This strategy is therefore proven to be less effective than the GIST descriptors. Later, Yajamanam et al. utilized TensorFlow to conduct deep learning experiments. The model used in [22] depends on transfer learning. The model was pre-trained on another set of images from ImageNet. Subsequently, the existing model was re-traained on the malware binaries for the classification problem. This was done to make the model work faster. Yajamanam et al. observed that by applying deep learning directly to raw image files, it is possible to obtain a test accuracy of 98%.

In [5], Poonguzhali et al. used convolutional neural networks for mapping the raw image pixels to their respective class scores. Poonguzhali et al. used SVM to separate the boundaries defined in the classes. The limits were determined using the decision planes or hyperplanes of SVM, and the ultimate result was 68 different malware families classified using the SVM. The dataset considered was a zipped NumPy array, which is converted to a NumPy array, and that NumPy array serves as the input for the data set. This NumPy array is transformed into a grey-scale image using CNN. For feature extraction and reduction of the number of parameters, Poonguzhali et al. applied multiple convolutional and padding layers. Subsequently, the dataset was divided into train and test by employing a bio-inspired technique known as the BAT algorithm. After the split, this dataset was given as input to the Support vector machine. The dataset used during the experiments was unbalanced therefore the bat algorithm was used to eliminate the imbalances and to avoid overfitting or underfitting that may occur due to data. The classification accuracy achieved by the model was 94.01%.

The relevance of deep convolution neural networks in malware classification is discussed in the paper [24], as well as approaches for using machine learning to identify and categorise malware families via transfer learning. In the transfer learning approach, data is gathered from real-world images or objects and apply it to the static malware detection target domain. As a result, deep neural network training times are sped up while maintaining strong classification performance.

Zilin et al. [25] proposed method that visualises malware binary files as colour images, produces the necessary image size directly, and enhances the algorithm's performance with data-gathering techniques. Improved CNN method is applied. This technique can directly extract sample features without the need for reverse analysis.

In the Table 2 summarization of all the methods is mentioned.

Table 2. Summarization of literature

Sr. No.	Paper	Approach	Methods	Remarks
1.	Random Forest for Malware Classification (2016)	Traditional Machine Learning Algorithm	Random Forest method for categorizing and segregating the new malware binaries into various categories	This approach suffers from the misclassification problem of malware files that are visually similar
2.	Malware Images: Visualization and Automatic Classification (2011)	Image Processing techniques and machine learning algorithms	Employed a supervised learning algorithm KNN. The features were computed using GIST descriptors	Counter measures can be taken to beat the system
3.	Malware Classification with Deep Convolutional Neural Networks (2018)	Image Processing techniques and machine learning algorithms	Followed a GIST + SVM method on two datasets	Achieved an accuracy of 93.23% and 88.74% on the two datasets
4.	Deep Learning versus Gist Descriptors for Image-based Malware Classification (2018)	Image Processing and machine learning algorithms	Followed feature reduction by applying linear SVC Also employed UFS to highest rank 60 features out 320 features	Nearly-optimal results with reduced feature set. A highly effective strategy against gist-based score detection exists
5.	Article on TwardsDataScience (2020)	Deep Learning techniques	CNN model using Keras was applies on the Malimg dataset	The Malimg dataset is unbalanced, a lower weight is assigned to the higher majority class and a higher weight to the lower majority class. The accuracy of the model achieved was 0.9514632

(continued)

Table 2. (*continued*)

Sr. No.	Paper	Approach	Methods	Remarks
6.	Malware Classification with Deep Convolutional Neural Networks (2018)	Deep Learning techniques	Trained a model known as, M-CNN. The M-CNN model is based on VGG-16	Consisted of two settings and applied CNN on two different datasets. Achieved an accuracy of 98.99% on setting A and 99.97 on setting B
7.	Deep Learning versus Gist Descriptors for Image-based Malware Classification (2018)	Deep Learning techniques	Transfer learning	By applying deep learning directly to raw image files, it is possible to obtain a test accuracy of 98%
8.	Identification of malware using CNN and bioinspired technique (2019)	Deep Learning techniques	Used SVM to separate boundaries and CNN for feature for feature extraction	Due to unstable dataset, BAT algorithm was used to eliminate imbalances. An accuracy of 94.01% was achieved

There are some recent trends in trends in malware detection and analysis methods.

1. AI and Machine Learning Approch:These techniques use sophisticated algorithms and vast datasets to find patterns and behaviours that point to the existence of malware. In order to increase detection accuracy and adapt to new malware types, machine learning models can be trained on enormous amounts of labelled data.

2. Behavior based analysis: In behavior-based analysis; behavior of programs and processes is observe to identify suspicious activities. This approach significantly detect previously unknown malware variants and zero-day attacks.

3. Sandboxing: Sandboxing is the process of running potentially harmful files or programmes in segregated settings to watch how they behave. It aids analysts in comprehending the operations carried out by malware, including file modifications, network communications, or alterations to system-level settings. Sandboxing offers a controlled setting for malware investigation without jeopardizing the security of the host system.

4. Threat Intelligence Sharing: Information is shared between businesses and the security communities regarding new malware variants, attack methods, and indications of compromise (IOCs). The security landscape's detection and response capabilities are enhanced by this collective knowledge.

5. Automated malware analysis: It is necessary because manual analysis cannot keep up with the growing number of malware samples. Static analysis, dynamic analysis, and machine learning are some of the methodologies that automated malware analysis systems combine to automatically analyse and categorise malware samples. These systems are capable of quickly processing huge numbers of samples, extracting pertinent data, and producing reports for additional research.

6. Big Data Analytics: Malware analysis systems generates complex, huge volume of data. This data can be processed and analysed using big data analytics techniques to identify trends, correlations, and anomalies connected to malware activity.

7. Threat hunting: It is proactive process that searches indications of network breach or malicious activity rather than merely relying on automated detection techniques. To find hidden hazards and reduce potential risks, threat hunters combine manual analysis, data correlation, and intelligence-driven procedures.

These are some recent trends in the malaware detection. Organizations can combine various methods that increases their resistance to deal with malwares.

5 Conclusion

This paper is an effort to summarize the different ways to analyze, detect and classify malware files using various methods mentioned in the literature. It can be concluded that the signature-based method takes less time but does not detect zero-day malware and is prone to obfuscation. The static analysis has a faster turnaround time and lesser risk but is prone to code obfuscation and data location obfuscation. The dynamic analysis, even though more robust and harder to defeat than the static analysis, takes a lot of time. However dynamic analysis, is not suitable for real-time since it produces many false positives, and not insurmountably resistant. Considering these factors, a hybrid approach emerges as a promising middle ground and more effective analysis method. Regarding classification methods, deep learning architectures have shown to be highly efficient. Deep learning models offer superior performance due to their ability to automatically learn and extract intricate features from malware samples. However, a balanced dataset must be used to avoid overfitting or underfitting of the model. In summary, while each malware analysis and classification method have its advantages and limitations, a hybrid approach incorporating various techniques can provide more effective results. Additionally, employing deep learning architectures for classification tasks can yield improved performance, provided that the training dataset is carefully balanced to ensure optimal model performance.

References

1. Selvin, V.R.S.: Malware Scores Based on Image Processing. Master's Projects, San Jose State University (2017). https://scholarworks.sjsu.edu/cgi/viewcontent.cgi?article=1546&context=etd_projects
2. Threat Hunter Team: The Ransomware Threat Landscape; What to Expect in 2022. Threat Intelligence 08 Mar 2022. https://symantec-enterprise-blogs.security.com/blogs/threat-intelligence/ransomware-threat-landscape-what-expect-2022
3. Supervised Classification with k-fold Cross Validation on a Multi Family Malware Dataset. 09 Aug 2014. https://sarvamblog.blogspot.com/2014/08/supervised-classification-with-k-fold.html
4. Sarvam Blog. http://sarvam.ece.ucsb.edu/ (2013). https://sarvamblog.blogspot.com/
5. Poonguzhali, N., Rajakamalam, T., Uma, S., Manju, R.: Identification of malware using CNN and bio-inspired technique. In: IEEE International Conference on System, Computation, Automation and Networking (ICSCAN), pp. 1–5 (2019)
6. Vinayakumar, R., Alazab, M., Soman, K.P., Poornachandran, P., Venkatraman, S.: Robust intelligent malware detection using deep learning. IEEE Access **7**, 46717–46738 (2019). https://doi.org/10.1109/ACCESS.2019.2906934

7. Bazrafshan, Z., Hashemi, H., Fard, S.M.H., Hamzeh, A.: A Survey on heuristic Malware detection Techniques. Presented at the 5th Conference on Information and Knowledge Technology (IKT) (2013)

8. Ijaz, M.,Durad, M.H., Ismail, M.: Static and Dynamic Malware Analysis Using Machine Learning. Presented at the 16th International Bhurban Conference on Applied Sciences and Technology (IBCAST) (2019)

9. Abou-Assaleh, T., Cercone, N., Keselj, V., Sweidan, R.: Detection of new malicious code using n-grams signatures. In: Second Annual Conference on Privacy, Security and Trust, pp. 193–196 (2004)

10. Santos, I., Cercone, N., Keselj, V., Bringas, P.G.: N-grams-based File Signatures for Malware Detection. In: International Conference on Enterprise Information Systems, pp. 317–320 (2009)

11. Anderson, H.S., Roth, P.: EMBER: An Open Dataset for Training Static PE Malware Machine Learning Models. ArXiv, vol. abs/1804.04637 (2018)

12. Saxe, J., Berlin, K.: Deep neural network based malware detection using two dimensional binary program features. In: 10th International Conference on Malicious and Unwanted Software (MALWARE). IEEE (2015)

13. Wang, T.-Y., Wu, C.-H., Hsieh, C.-C.: Detecting unknown malicious executables using portable executable headers. In: Fifth International Joint Conference on INC, IMS and IDC. IEEE (2009)

14. Raff, E., Barker, J., Sylvester, J., Brandon, R., Catanzaro, B., Nicholas, C.: Malware detection by eating a whole EXE (2017). arXiv:1710.09435

15. Tobiyama, S., Yamaguchi, Y., Shimada, H., Ikuse, T., Yagi, T.: Malware detection with deep neural network using process behavior. In: IEEE 40th Annual Computer Software and Applications Conference (COMPSAC), pp. 577–582. IEEE (2016)

16. Huang, W., Stokes, J.W.: MtNet: a multi-task neural network for dynamic malware classification. In: Caballero, J., Zurutuza, U., Rodríguez, R.J. (eds.) DIMVA 2016. LNCS, vol. 9721, pp. 399–418. Springer, Cham (2016). https://doi.org/10.1007/978-3-319-40667-1_20

17. Shijo, P.V., Salim, A.: Integrated static and dynamic analysis for malware detection. Procedia Comput. Sci. **46**, 804–811 (2015). https://doi.org/10.1016/j.procs.2015.02.149

18. Nataraj, L., Karthikeyan, S., Jacob, G., Manjunath, B.S.: Malware images: visualization and automatic classification. In: Proceedings of the 8th International Symposium on Visualization for Cyber Security - VizSec'11 (2011). https://doi.org/10.1145/2016904.2016908.

19. Garcia, F.C.C., Muga, F.P.: Random Forest for Malware Classification. ArXiv, vol. abs/1609.07770 (2016)

20. Nataraj, L.:Clustering a Malware Corpus (2013). https://sarvamblog.blogspot.com/2013/04/clustering-malware-corpus.html

21. Mallet, H.: Malware Classification using Convolutional Neural Networks — Step by Step Tutorial. Medium, 28 May 2020. https://towardsdatascience.com/malware-classification-using-convolutional-neural-networks-step-by-step-tutorial-a3e8d97122f

22. Yajamanam, S., Selvin, V.R.S., Di Troia, F., Stamp, M.: Deep learning versus gist descriptors for image-based malware classification. In: Proceedings of the 4th International Conference on Information Systems Security and Privacy (2018). https://doi.org/10.5220/0006685805530561

23. Kalash, M., Rochan, M., Mohammed, N., Bruce, N.D.B.,. Wang, Y, Iqbal, F.: Malware Classification With Deep Convolutional Neural Networks. In: IEEE Xplore, 1 Feb 2018. https://ieeexplore.ieee.org/document/8328749

24. AlGarni, M.D., AlRoobaea, R., Almotiri, J., Ullah, S.S., Hussain, S., Umar, F.: An efficient convolutional neural network with transfer learning for malware classification. Wirel. Commun. Mobile Comput. **2022**, 1–8 (2022). https://doi.org/10.1155/2022/4841741

Exploring Data Encryption Standard (DES) Through CrypTool Implementation: A Comprehensive Examination and Historical Perspective

Alba Meça[✉]

Epoka University, Tirana, Albania
ameca18@epoka.edu.al

Abstract. DES has been serving as the official federal standard for data encryption since the 70s, until it was replaced in 2001 by the Advanced Encryption Standard (AES). This paper thoroughly examines the encryption and decryption procedure, describing in detail and illustrating each step of the process. Additionally, we showcase the practical implementation of DES using the CrypTool platform, addressing the lack of a comprehensive and user-friendly tutorial on DES within this context. The paper endeavors to address this gap, enhancing the readers' understanding of the DES operation by delving into its internal mechanism and the transformations the plaintext undergoes to become ciphertext. In addition, we engage in a critical examination of CrypTool's implementation of DES and the platform's utility as an educational resource, highlighting both its strengths and shortcomings. The review of CrypTool as a learning tool not only provides insights into the practical implementation of DES but also emphasizes the significance of hands-on learning in modern cryptography. Moreover, we present a historical analysis of attempts at breaking the DES cipher, from its approval as a standard until more recent developments, and assess its relevance in today's cryptographic landscape. Ultimately, this paper aspires to serve as a valuable teaching resource for cryptography students and educators, bridging the gap between theoretical knowledge and practical application.

Keywords: Data Encryption Standard · Block Cipher · Feistel scheme · Substitution Permutation Network

1 Introduction

The block-cipher cryptographic algorithm nowadays known as the Data Encryption Standard (DES) was first developed in the early 1970s, based on Horst Feistel's Lucifer cipher. After undergoing serious scrutiny and some minor modifications made by the National Security Agency (NSA), it was adopted as a federal standard by the U.S. National Bureau of Standards, now known as the National Institute of Standards and Technology (NIST), in November 1976, and published as official encryption standard

© ICST Institute for Computer Sciences, Social Informatics and Telecommunications Engineering 2024
Published by Springer Nature Switzerland AG 2024. All Rights Reserved
M. H. Miraz et al. (Eds.): iCETiC 2023, LNICST 538, pp. 143–160, 2024.
https://doi.org/10.1007/978-3-031-50215-6_10

in January 1977 [1]. In the subsequent years, DES continued to be reaffirmed as a standard. Despite the growing concerns regarding the security of this algorithm and several successful attempts at breaking it, DES was reaffirmed as a standard in 1983, 1988 and again in 1999, before AES was finally adopted as its replacement in 2002.

DES, like any other algorithm based on the Feistel scheme, is a conventional symmetric algorithm: using the same single key, shared by secure means between the sender and the receiver, for both encryption and decryption, and relying on the key being kept secret at all times. While it may have started out as a propriety algorithm when first created by IBM, the inner workings and implementations of DES soon became public knowledge, but that was no detriment to its security, which depends on keeping secret the key and not the algorithm itself.

DES functions as a block-cipher, which means that it processes a complete block of bits simultaneously, rather than one at a time. During encryption, the plaintext input is processed in fixed-sized blocks of 64 bit, and a ciphertext block of the same size is generated for each inputted block of plaintext. The key size is the same as the block size, 64 bits, however eight of these bits are used for parity and only 56 serve as an effective part of the key. The input goes through 16 identical stages of processing, with each stage having its own unique 48 bit subkey, generated from the 56 bits of the original main key through a key scheduling algorithm. Later, when decrypting the message on the receiver side, we use the exact same subkeys, only this time in reverse order, with subkey number 16 being used during the first iteration, followed by subkey nr.15 on the second iteration and so on, all the way to subkey nr.1 which is used in the 16th and final iteration. This is due to the fact that DES was created based on a Feistel Network.

2   Encryption – Decryption Procedure

2.1   Feistel Structure

A Feistel cipher, also known as a Feistel network, named after the German cryptographer and physicist Horst Feistel, is a cryptographic symmetric structure which has served as the backbone of many modern block ciphers. It has n rounds of processing, where a single round consists of a round function F, which takes as input a block of data (half of the original block size) and a round key, and returns a data block of the same size, the result of which is XOR-ed with the other half of the current round's input. Michael Luby and Charles Rackoff have proved that given a cryptographically secure invertible permutation generator (what we refer to as the round function in DES), three rounds of processing suffice for the cipher to be a pseudorandom permutation, while four rounds would turn it into a "super" (meaning strong) pseudorandom permutation [2].

A major advantage of Feistel ciphers is that the whole process is guaranteed to be invertible. Furthermore, the encryption and decryption procedures are very similar, allowing us to use the same construction (hardware and software) for both, without needing to change anything other than applying the subkeys in reverse order. This greatly simplifies implementation and lowers its cost, because we are practically reducing the size of code and circuit components required for the cipher's construction by almost half.

2.2 Data Encryption Standard

The DES algorithm starts with the 64 bit of plaintext input going through an Initial Permutation (IP) which simply changes the position of the bits, outputting the same 64 bits in a new order. At the end of the 16 rounds, as the last layer, we have the Inverse Initial Permutation (IP-1) which returns each bit to the original position. IP and IP-1 do not appear to have any real cryptographic significance.

After the Initial Permutation, we split the block of data into two 32 bit parts (the left part and the right part). The right part and the round key are inputted into the F function, whose result is then used to encrypt the left part through an Exclusive-OR operation. The parts are then exchanged, with the result of the aforementioned encryption of the left part becoming the right part for the next round, and the right part of the current round being forwarded unaltered to become the new left part. This procedure is repeated for all 16 rounds. The only exception being that in the last and 16th round we no longer perform the exchange, but following the encryption of the left part, both parts are reunited into a 64 bit block which is forwarded to the Inverse Initial Permutation. The criss-crossing of the two parts and the F-function are essential elements that it has borrowed from the Feistel Scheme. The general DES structure is illustrated in Fig. 1, while Fig. 2 presents a more detailed schematic view of the operations that are carried out in one round of processing, which are explained in the following subsections.

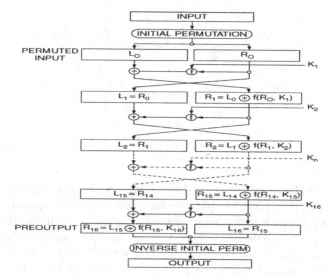

Fig. 1. DES Encryption Process [3]

2.3 Key Scheduling

As it was established, for each round we need to generate a unique 48 bit key from the main key. For this purpose, we use the Key Scheduling algorithm. A diagram of this algorithm is provided in Fig. 3.

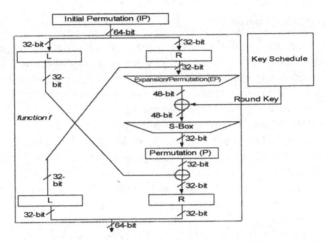

Fig. 2. Diagram of the first round of processing of DES algorithm [4]

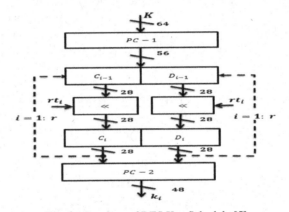

Fig. 3. Structure of DES Key Schedule [5]

The original 64 bit secret key is passed as an input to the Permuted Choice 1 function, which discards the eight parity bits and splits the remaining 56 bits into two 28 bit parts, called C_0 and D_0. On each of these parts we apply a circular left-shift operation (shifting all the bits one position to the left, with the very first bit getting shifted to the end). The results of this shift are C_1 and D_1, which we input into a Permuted Choice 2 function that rearranges the bits and selects 48 of them (24 bits are selected from C and the other 24 from D). These bits compose the first subkey. The same process is repeated for all the 16 rounds; however, for all iterations besides the first, second, ninth and the last one, we shift the bits by two positions instead of one. Each bit is used in approximately 14 out of the 16 subkeys.

2.4 Inside the F-function

The F-function gets as input the 48 bit Round Key generated by the Key Schedule, and the Right part of the data. It consists of four stages of processing. The first stage is the Expansion, where we apply an Expansion Function on the 32 bit block of data, transforming it into a 48 bit block by duplicating some of the bits in certain predetermined positions. In the next stage we have what is known as Key Addition or Key Mixing, where the output of the Expansion function is combined with the Round Key through an XOR operation, and a new 48 bit word is generated as a result. The third stage is Substitution, which splits the 48 bit word (block) into eight 6 bit words, and each of these words is passed through a substitution box (which we refer to as an S-box). An individual S-box takes 6 bits as an input and outputs 4 bits, so in the end we have 32 bits of output produced by all eight S-boxes. These 32 bits go through the final stage, a standard bit-wise Permutation. This permutation is designed in such a way that the outputs of each S-box of the current round are divided among four different S-boxes in the following round.

All four of the stages we just described can be seen in Fig. 2. For an alternative depiction of the F-function, which expands more on the S-boxes, you may refer to Fig. 4.

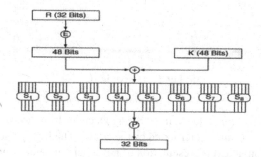

Fig. 4. The F-function [3]

2.5 Substitution Boxes

S-boxes are the non-linear part of DES because they map the 6 bits of input to 4 bits of output by performing a non-linear transformation, provided in the form of a lookup table. This non-linear transformation makes the algorithm highly resistant to analytical attacks. The S-box works by computing the x and y coordinates based on the input, and returning as an output the value found at that position in its lookup table. The x value is comprised of the four middle bits, while the y value is made up of the first and last bit. So for example, if our input was 100110, coordinate x would be 0011 = 3 and y would be 10 = 2, so the S-box would return the value at position (3, 2) in its lookup table. The lookup tables are different for each S-box.

3   Cryptool Implementation

CrypTool 2 provides an implementation of the DES algorithm, fully functional for both encryption and decryption, as well as an interactive step-by-step visualization of all the stages of processing the plaintext goes through to produce the ciphertext. In this section we will be explaining the CrypTool implementation and providing examples of encryption and decryption.

3.1   Encryption

Figure 5 depicts encryption using CrypTool 2. A few verses by Percy Bysshe Shelley serve as our plaintext in this illustration.

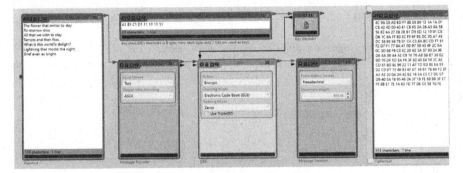

Fig. 5. Encryption

The Plaintext is first converted using a String Decoder from text to ASCII character representation, so that it can be interpreted by the cipher. The Key is also converted using a String Decoder, from a text representation of hexadecimal values into binary. Both of these are passed as input to the DES cipher, where we have selected "Encrypt" as the action to be performed. The poetry, which we want to encode here, is substantially longer than the block size, therefore we need to specify a Chaining Mode, which defines how DES will be used for each block and the dependency of the current block on the ciphertext generated for the previous block(s). The Electronic Code Book (ECB) mode which we have selected here, is the simplest and treats each block of plaintext individually and independently of the other blocks. Because of this, it is also the least secure. CrypTool provides other modes of operation besides ECB, such as Cipher Feedback (CFB), Output Feedback (OFB) and Cipher Block Chaining (CBC). The encrypted result of the cipher is then forwarded to a String Encoder, which converts it into a string (in hexadecimal representation).

3.2   Decryption

To decrypt the message we simply input the generated Ciphertext as Text Input, and change the input format of the Text Decoder to hexadecimal and the output format to text. We also change the action of the cipher to "Decrypt", which indicates to the algorithm that it will have to use the subkeys in reverse order. As shown in Fig. 6, we get the correct plaintext.

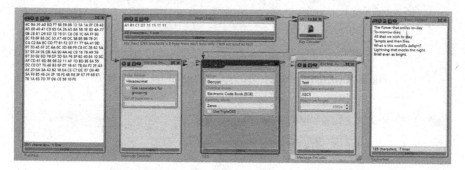

Fig. 6. Decryption

Next, we experiment by making small changes to the key. In Fig. 7 we have changed the last bit from 1 to 0, however the output is not affected at all. In Fig. 8 we make further changes, setting the 16th bit to 0 (from the hexadecimal value B1 of the second byte to B0) as well, and the output once again remains unaltered. This may seem surprising and counterintuitive at first, but the explanation is very simple. The key, as illustrated in Figs. 5, 6, 7, 8 and 9, is normally stored and transmitted in eight bytes, each byte having an odd parity bit at the end. In Figs. 7 and 8 we have only changed the least significant bit of the bytes, in other words, the bit that is used for parity checking and is not part of the effective key.

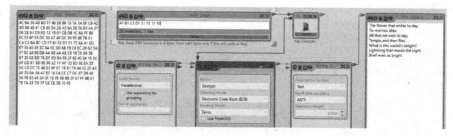

Fig. 7. Decryption with altered key (A1 B1 C1 D1 11 11 11 10)

If we were to change a more significant part of the key, for example as illustrated in Fig. 9 where we have changed the last byte from 11 to 21, the result of decryption is completely meaningless gibberish.

3.3 Visualization

In this subsection we will be illustrating each step of the DES Encryption Process, as presented in the CrypTool implementation. Through this visualization tool we can input

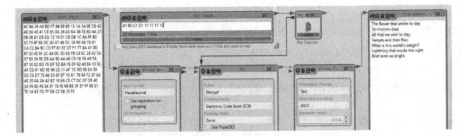

Fig. 8. Decryption with altered key (A1 B0 C1 D1 11 11 11 10)

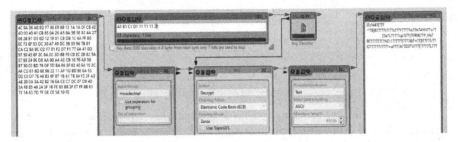

Fig. 9. Decryption with altered key (A1 B0 C1 D1 11 11 11 21)

only one block of plaintext. The inputted plaintext, the secret key and the generated ciphertext, in both hexadecimal and binary representations, are shown in Fig. 10.

Fig. 10. Encryption result

The process starts with the key schedule, where we input our key through the Permuted Choice 1 function and split it into the left and right half (C_0 and D_0), as depicted in Fig. 11.

The next step is the circular shift. Figures 12 and 13 illustrate the left-shift by only one bit position, because it is generating the subkey for round 1.

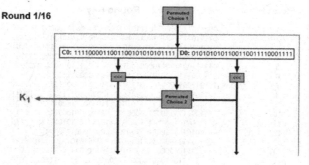

Fig. 11. Key Schedule

Cyclic Shift

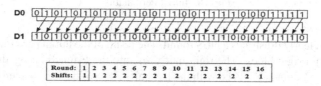

Fig. 12. Cyclic Shift of C0 producing C1

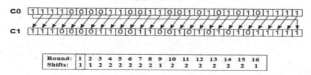

Fig. 13. Cyclic Shift of D0 producing D1

Then we move on to the Permuted Choice 2, which removes 4 bits from each half of the key and rearranges the rest, mixing them together, and producing subkey 1, as depicted in Fig. 14.

Permuted Choice 2

Fig. 14. Permuted Choice 2

This process is repeated until we obtain all 16 round keys as displayed in Fig. 15. The next step is the initial permutation of the plaintext, depicted in Fig. 16.

Round	Round Key
1	0001101100000010111011111111111000111000001110010
2	0111100110101110110110011101101111001001111100101
3	0101010111111100100010100100000101100111110011001
4	0111001010101101110101101101101100101010100011101
5	0111110011101100000001111110101101010011101010100
6	0110001110100101001111001010000011111011001011
7	1110110010000100101101111111011100001100010111100
8	1111011110001010001110101100000100111011111111011
9	1110000011011011111010111111011011111001110000001
10	1011000111110011010001111011101001000110010011
11	0010000101011111101001111011110110100011100000110
12	0111010101110001111101011001010001100111111101001
13	1001011111000101110100011111101010111010010001
14	0101111101000011011011111110010111001110011101
15	1011111110010001100011010011110100111111100001010
→ 16	1100101100111101100010110000111000010111111101010

Fig.15. All 16 subkeys

Initial Permutation

Fig. 16. Initial Permutation

Figure 17 clearly illustrates a DES round. The result of the initial permutation is split into a left and a right block. The right half goes into the F-function together with the subkey and the output is XOR-ed with the left half. The two halves are then exchanged, with the right part being forwarded unchanged.

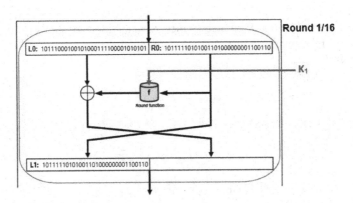

Fig. 17. DES Round 1

Figure 18 describes the f-function. The first stage here is the extension of the input from 32 to 48 bits (to bring it to the same length as the round key) as depicted in Fig. 19.

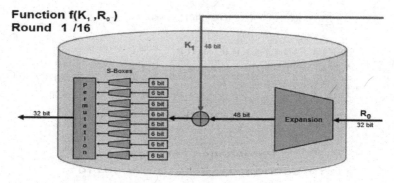

Fig. 18. F-function visualization

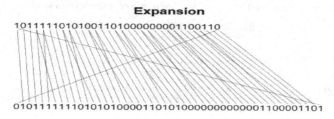

Fig. 19. Expansion

Then we move on to the Exclusive-OR logical operation, combining our current intermediate value with the subkey, whose result is inputed into the S-boxes (Fig. 20).

Fig. 20. XOR between subkey 1 and the result of the Expansion function

Figure 21 demonstrates how an S-box transformation works. Taking a block of 6 bits, it calculates the coordinates for the row (using the leftmost and rightmost bits) and column (using the middle bits) and outputs the binary representation of the number stored in that position in its lookup table. All the S-boxes function in the same way, but their lookup tables are different.

The 32 bit output of the S-boxes is then passed through a standard permutation function as depicted in Fig. 22.

The output of the F-function, which is the result of the aforementioned permutation, is combined with the Left block of data through an XOR operation (this calculation is illustrated in Fig. 23), producing an encrypted binary string which is going to serve as the new right part for the next round, as shown in Fig. 24.

[010001]001101 011111 100010 101111 000111 001101 111111

S1	0	1	2	3	4	5	6	7	8	9	10	11	12	13	14	15
0	14	4	13	1	2	15	11	8	3	10	6	12	5	9	0	7
1	0	15	7	4	14	2	13	1	10	6	12	11	9	5	3	8
2	4	1	14	8	13	6	2	11	15	12	9	7	3	10	5	0
3	15	12	8	2	4	9	1	7	5	11	3	14	10	0	6	13

Input: 010001
Row: 0___1   ≙ 1
Column: _1000_   ≙ 8
Output: 1010   ≙ 10

Fig. 21. S-box 1

Permutation Function

10101000000101101101001000011011

00101111111011100001101000000000

Fig. 22. Stage 4 of F-function: Permutation

L0:   10111000100101000111100001010101

⊕

f(R0):   00101111111011100001101000000000

R1:   10010111011110100110001001010101

Fig. 23. XOR between the Left part of data and the output of the F-function

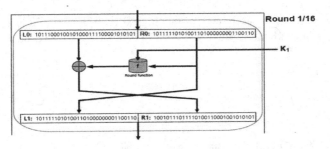

Fig. 24. DES Round 1 completed

After repeating this procedure for 16 rounds, we get the results that are listed in Fig. 25.

The final step is the Inverse Permutation, which is the mirror image of our initial permutation, as can be seen in Fig. 26, at the end of which we obtain our ciphertext.

Round	L	R
0	1011100010010100011110000101010101	1011111010100110100000001100110
1	1011111010100110100000001100110	1001011101111010011000100101010101
2	1001011101111010011000100101010101	0001111010101111101111111010110111
3	0001111010101111101111111010110111	1111010100100110110000100011000110
4	1111010100100110110000100110001110	0100011111100101010111101111011110
5	0100011111100101010111101111011110	1000101111010000110100011111000000
6	1000101110100001101000111110000000	0101000100100010110111011110111011
7	0101000100100010110111011101111110111	0010001000010000100011000101011000
8	0010001000010000100011000101011000	0010011011100001110100100001111010
9	0010011011100001110100100001111010	0111111100011110101110001100000110
10	0111111100011110101110001100001110	0010110000001011000110101000101010
11	0010110000001011000110101000101010	1100001111100100111111010101001010
12	1100001111100100111111010100101000	0001000001000001111000001101001
13	0001000001000001111000001101001	0101000111100000001100000111000001
14	0101000111100000001100000111000001	1110010001110000111101010101000000
15	1110010001111000011110101010001000	0001110010010100010101101011011110
➤ 16	0001110100010101001010110110111110	0010110001010110101111111010010

Fig. 25. Left and Right parts for each of the 16 rounds of processing

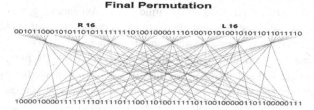

Final Permutation

R 16   L 16

0010110001010110101111111010010001010100101011011011110

100001000011111111011110111001101001111101100100000110110000111

Fig. 26. Inverse Permutation

4 CrypTool as a Learning Platform

CrypTool is a versatile and user-friendly software developed for educational and research purposes in the field of cryptography. It offers a comprehensive collection of cryptographic algorithms, visualization tools, and interactive tutorials that facilitate hands-on learning and experimentation.

4.1 Benefits of Using CrypTool for Teaching DES and Cryptography in General

The DES implementation, as demonstrated in this paper, is well-structured and easy to follow, making it ideal for educational purposes. It provides a clear representation of the basic operations involved in the algorithm. The visualization is done in binary encoding so the effect of each operation on every bit of the data is noticeable.

One of the biggest advantages of CrypTool is that it is open-source, thus enabling users to study and even alter, enhance and expand upon the current package. CrypTool follows a modular design pattern. The code is divided into separate modules, each responsible for a specific task (such as key scheduling). This not only makes it easier to maintain, but also easier to study the code of a specific component. The modular structure also allows to users to easily modify and extend the implementation to suit their needs or use the available modules in a new projects altogether.

CrypTool comprises over 160 different components for encryption, decryption and cryptanalysis, many of which are accompanied by a visualization and a concise description. It also includes over 200 predefined templates, where by template we mean a workspace where all the components of a certain cipher of cryptanalysis scenario are already in place and properly connected. This provides the students with plenty of examples of both classical ciphers (like Caesar, Vinegar, Enigma ect.) and modern cryptography standards like AES (symmetric) and RSA (asymmetric).

The primary strength of CrypTool lies in its visual programming approach, which makes it an ideal educational tool for teaching cryptography. With its intuitive graphical interface, students can easily create workflows by dragging and dropping cryptographic components onto the workspace. Every component within the workspace possesses input and output connectors, facilitating the communication between those components that are compatible. Specifically, in the context of the DES encryption, the input connectors are the parts where the arguments (key and plaintext) are imputed. The output connector is responsible for displaying the algorithm's final result, which is the DES ciphertext. By clicking on any of the objects, users can conveniently access options, allowing them to configure and experiment with additional parameters, such as the padding scheme or the mode of operation in this example. This dynamic interaction encourages active learning, allowing students to see how different elements of encryption algorithms fit together.

CrypTool's interactive nature fosters an atmosphere of experimental learning, encouraging students to actively engage with cryptographic methods, practically implementing the concepts learned during theoretical classes. Through hands-on practice and exploration, students gain valuable insights into the intricacies of encryption and decryption processes. This experiential approach allows them to grasp theoretical concepts in a more meaningful and tangible manner. In many traditional cryptography courses students get little exposure to security tools and algorithms and they acquire the concepts in an abstract manner. This lack of practical application also often leads to disinterest in the subject. Providing a platform for students to directly interact with cryptographic algorithms kindles their curiosity and makes the subject more appealing.

Moreover, the study of cryptographic systems generally calls for a strong foundation in mathematics, especially on disciplines like abstract algebra, number theory, probability, and statistics. While that is absolutely necessary to achieve a real and deep understanding of the process, CrypTool offers an accessible and user-friendly approach. Even without extensive mathematical expertise, students can engage with the various cryptography algorithms and experiment with them by using off the shelf components and modules from CrypTool's library. This makes cryptography more accessible.

Incorporating CrypTool in the curriculum could also be used to produces a shift towards a more student-centric, outcome-based assessment, focusing on enhancing and measuring the demonstrated and applicable skills of the students and their critical-thinking and problem-solving abilities, rather than memorization of the syllabus material. Asking the students to demonstrate the process of encryption and decryption of some cipher and analyze its vulnerabilities by implementing several types of attacks against it is a better assessment of their competences.

4.2 Limitations of the DES implementation in CrypTool

While the implementation of the DES algorithm is a great learning resource, it has a few limitations.

Firstly, the visualization feature is limited to only the encryption process. It does not support decryption. Additionally, it does not allow for customization of the input data or allow the user to change the mode the operation.

Secondly, the implementation does not support more modern and advanced modes of operation like such as Counter (CTR) and Galois Counter Mode (GCM). These modes are more secure, thus are commonly used in modern cryptographic applications. While the implementation does at least support four different modes (ECB, CBC, CFB and OFB) the visualization feature is even more limited as it only supports ECB, the simplest of the modes, which is generally considered insecure because it doesn't provide adequate protection against attacks that take advantage of repeating patterns in the plaintext.

Thirdly, CrypTool does not support hardware acceleration, such as the utilization of GPUs or FPGAs. This slows down the processes involved in the implementation, which could otherwise be significantly expedited.

Finally, the implementation is primarily intended for educational purposes and therefore is not optimized for large-scale use. CrypTool prioritizes user-friendliness and visualization over performance. Consequently, its DES implementation is unsuitable for real-time encryption or decryption, especially when dealing with extensive amounts of data.

4.3 Limitations of CrypTool as a Learning Platform

Cryptool employs simplified visual representations to explain intricate cryptographic processes. However, this approach may oversimplify certain concepts, failing to capture the complexities and challenges encountered in real-world cryptographic implementations. Although CrypTool provides simulations, they do not encompass the full scope of the real-world obstacles and constraints present in practical cryptographic systems. As a result, students may fail to comprehend the full implications of applying cryptographic techniques in real-life scenarios.

Moreover, CrypTool is a software-based tool, and it's important to note that students do not gain practical experience with hardware-based cryptographic implementations which can be crucial in certain real-world scenarios.

Relying solely on CrypTool for teaching may also create a dependence on the software and impede students' comprehension of the fundamental mathematical principles behind cryptography. An excessive emphasis on using CrypTool could result in students attaining proficiency with the tool itself, while sacrificing a deeper understanding of cryptographic concepts and theories.

As a learning platform, CrypTool lacks built-in assessment or evaluation tools for measuring the students' progress and understanding. Additionally, it does not integrate gamification elements or rewards to enhance motivation and engagement.

Lastly, while it does include a versatile range of algorithms, protocols and cryptanalysis techniques, CrypTool primarily focuses on classic ciphers and symmetric algorithms. The only asymmetric algorithm currently implemented as a template in the platform is the RSA cipher. Moreover, because of complexities that exceed the capabilities of the environment, CrypTool does not enable implementation of contemporary cryptographic protocols such as SSL and IpSec.

5   The Quest to Break DES and Conclusion

The selection of DES as a federal standard was followed by numerous objections and critiques. According to Whitfield Diffie and Martin Hellman, the pioneers of public-key cryptography, DES could theoretically be broken in just about twelve hours of computation, using a machine made up of a million VLSI chips, specifically designed to perform exhaustive search cryptanalytic attacks, all working in parallel and searching one key per microsecond. The authors estimated the cost of such a machine to be $20 million in the 70s, but they predicted that this cost would drop down to the $200,000 range in the following 10 years. Based on these assumptions, they concluded that DES would be replaced as a standard in approximately 5 to 10 years. As we know, this conclusion did not stand the test of time. In the discussion section however, they call for the use of a 128 bit or larger key [6], which was implemented by the successors of DES: Triple DES and AES.

In 1993, Eli Biham and Adi Shamir came up with a Differential Cryptanalysis attack, which analyses and exploits the effect that differences between pairs of plaintext have on the differences between their corresponding ciphertext pairs. It was the first known attack able to break the complete 16-round DES in less time than required to perform an exhaustive search of the keyspace with an average 2^{55} time complexity. Instead, the proposed attack needs to analyze only 2^{36} ciphertexts (selected from a pool of 2^{47} chosen plaintexts) in order to compute the key [7]. However, the requirement for such a massive number of known plaintexts makes this type of attack infeasible in practice. One year later, Mitsuru Matsui developed a known-plaintext attack that identified relationships between the sums of bits of the plaintext and ciphertext, which when combined provided information regarding the sum of the key bits. His algorithm could break an 8-round version of DES in 40 s, by analyzing 2^{21} known-plaintext. For a 12-round cipher 2^{33} plaintexts were required and the computation time increased to 50 h. In order to break the full 16-round DES, 2^{47} known-plaintexts were required. Since these are "known" and not "chosen" plaintexts they are easier to obtain. Still, it is a substantial amount of data and processing, even though the computation time was determined to be less than it would take to perform an exhaustive search [8].

In 1997, the DESCHAL Project (short for DES Challenge), was the first successful attempt at publicly breaking a Des-encrypted message through Brute Force attack. They were able to break the cipher at a very low cost, as instead of using dedicated hardware or supercomputers, the DESCHAL Project employed internet-based distributed computing, performing large computations by utilizing the power of otherwise unused CPU cycles. Searching at a rate of around 7 billion keys per second, they managed to solve the challenge in 96 days [9]. The following year, the Electronic Frontier Foundation solved the second DES challenge in just 56 h, with a machine of 1536 custom designed ASIC chips, built for a total cost of less than $250,000 [10].

In a 2006 paper, the authors describe the design and implementation of a FPGA-based parallel processing machine called COPACOBANA, which was able to break the DES cipher in an average search time of less than 9 days, outperforming conventional computers by several orders of magnitude. It was made up of 120 FPGAs, each designed to perform an extensive search attack of the 2^{56} keyspace. Moreover, COPACOBANA had a very cost-efficient hardware architecture, with all costs adding up to a total of

€8,980 [11]. Two years later, the same researchers published another paper where they demonstrated that after some software improvements the average time in which a DEC-encrypted message could be broken had been reduced to approximately 6.4 days [12]. Nowadays there exist websites such as crack.sh, which offer to crack DES keys for a very small fee, ranging from 20–100$ [13]. They have designed a system of 48 low-cost FPGAs which can exhaustively search the entire 56-bit DES keyspace in about 26 h.

With continuous developments in technological competence and enhanced computer processing capacity, all security algorithms inevitably become obsolete within a few years. DES has been a fundamental encryption standard for a long time and it has played an essential historical role in data security. However, as processing power and technical know-how have improved, it has become abundantly clear that it can no longer be a part of our future, and it has to be completely supplanted in all applications by more powerful algorithms such as triple-DES and particularly AES. All of this considered, the author believes that while the real-world use of the algorithm is bound to die out before long, the study of DES shall remain relevant and important, as by examining its strengths and vulnerabilities researchers can obtain vital insights which then serve as an inspiration for the development of more advanced and robust encryption algorithms like those in use today. Only after having acquired a deep understanding of the significant milestones of encryption history can we be able to adapt to evolving security threats.

References

1. Data Encryption Standard: Federal information processing standards publication 46. National Bureau of Standards, US Department of Commerce, vol. 23, pp. 1–18 (1977)
2. Luby, M., Rackoff, C.: Pseudo-random permutation generators and cryptographic composition. In: Proceedings of the Eighteenth Annual ACM Symposium on Theory of Computing, pp. 356–363 (1986)
3. Biryukov, A., De Cannière, C.: Data Encryption Standard (DES). In: van Tilborg H.C.A., Jajodia S. (eds.) Encyclopedia of Cryptography and Security, p. 296. Springer, Boston, MA (2011)
4. Moratelli, C., Cota, E., Lubaszewski, M.: A cryptography core tolerant to DFA fault attacks. In: SBCCI 2006 – 19th Symposium on Integrated Circuits and Systems Design, pp. 190–195 (2006)
5. Noura, M., Noura, H., Chehab, A., Mansour, M., Couturier, R.: S-DES: An efficient & secure DES variant. In: IEEE Middle East and North Africa Communications Conference (MENACOMM) (2018)
6. Diffie, W., Hellman, M.E.: Special feature exhaustive cryptanalysis of the NBS data encryption standard. Computer **10**(6), 74–84 (1977)
7. Biham, E., Shamir, A.: Differential Cryptanalysis of the Full 16-Round DES. In: Brickell, E.F. (ed.) CRYPTO 1992. LNCS, vol. 740, pp. 487–496. Springer, Heidelberg (1993). https://doi.org/10.1007/3-540-48071-4_34
8. Matsui, M.: Linear cryptanalysis method for DES cipher. In: Helleseth, T. (ed.) EUROCRYPT 1993. LNCS, vol. 765, pp. 386–397. Springer, Heidelberg (1993). https://doi.org/10.1007/3-540-48285-7_33
9. Curtin, M., Dolske, J.: A brute force search of DES keyspace. In: 8th Usenix Symposium, January, pp. 26–29 (1998)
10. Foundation, Electronic Frontier. Cracking DES: Secrets of encryption research, wiretap politics and chip design (1998)

11. Kumar, S., Paar, C., Pelzl, J., Pfeiffer, G., Rupp, A., Schimmler, M.: How to Break DES for BC 8,980. In: SHARCS '06–Special-purpose Hardware for Attacking Cryptographic Systems, pp. 17–35 (2006)
12. Güneysu, T., Kasper, T., Novotný, M., Paar, C., Rupp, A.: Cryptanalysis with COPACOBANA. IEEE Trans. Comput. **57**(11), 1498–1513 (2008)
13. crack.sh The world's fastest DES cracker Homepage. https://crack.sh/. Last accessed on 19 June 2023

On the Design and Performance Evaluation of Android Based Alarming Applications

Sara Rexha[1] and Dimitrios A. Karras[1,2]([⊠])

[1] Canadian Institute of Technology, Tirana, Albania
dimitrios.karras@gmail.com, adimitrios.karras@cit.edu.al
[2] National and Kapodistrian University of Athens, Athens, Greece

Abstract. The aim of this paper is to investigate and discuss issues on the design and performance evaluation of Android applications concerning alarming systems that would serve users in emergency or dangerous situations to be able to send text messages in real time giving information about their location and about their needs in searching for help. The user, for instance, could send a message to their chosen contacts just by shaking the phone a predefined number of times or following any other pattern of action involving the smartphone. The application designed has, also, some other features like sounding an alarm for 10 s, automatically opening the hospital map searching for hospitals in the area and automatically opening the police map searching for police stations nearby. While opening each of the maps mentioned, the user could check their location as well. Many other similar features could be added in the designed application. But the main goal of the paper is to investigate design issues in Android applications regarding real time performance as well as to evaluate performance in such time critical applications. Therefore, the contribution of this paper lies on comparing real time performance of different implementations of such an alarming application as well as on presenting step by step design, architectural and implementation issues of it.

Keywords: Android applications design · time critical applications · performance evaluation · alarming systems · emergency applications

1 Introduction

Alarming application development in the operation of critical environments like for instance Hazardous Gases and Volatile Chemicals in Laboratories and Industrial Locations has attracted many researchers in recent years [1]. Such specific applications need the integration of special platforms, including robotics and special sensing systems. However, alarming applications present a great potential for widespread usage in much simpler, everyday life cases. For instance, it is well known that an SOS alarm is a signal supposed to tell other people that a specific user is in dangerous situation and he/she needs help quickly. It stands for Save Our Ships or Save Our Souls and was firstly used as an International Morse distress signal (a signal from a ship or aircraft that is in danger). Nowadays the signal is not limited to navigation only but also to notify about a

© ICST Institute for Computer Sciences, Social Informatics and Telecommunications Engineering 2024
Published by Springer Nature Switzerland AG 2024. All Rights Reserved
M. H. Miraz et al. (Eds.): iCETiC 2023, LNICST 538, pp. 161–179, 2024.
https://doi.org/10.1007/978-3-031-50215-6_11

dangerous situation that demands quick attention. Given that nowadays communication platforms and infrastructures are available to assist people in issuing alarms about their situation, the necessity for designing alarming mechanisms and systems for everyday life becomes much greater. A Smartphone is one such very popular infrastructure for alarming systems development and is met in several different platforms, as for instance in [2]. The Android platform is the most popular operating system serving more than 2.5 billion users in more than 190 countries. Therefore, developing and evaluating an Android alarming application is a reasonable decision. Moreover, Android Operating System is open source, easy and quick to learn. Its flexible methods for development factors along with Android's open working model and easy availability of resources make it extremely easy and quick to develop customizable apps. Additionally, it offers better flexibility since through its open platform developers have more freedom to modify it and provide the features and functionality that users want [3, 4]. Moreover, it can target other platforms being simpler to convert an Android software to other platforms like Ubuntu (Fig. 1).

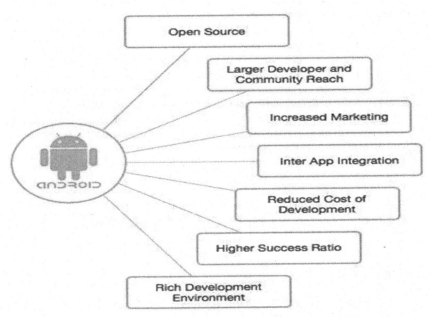

Fig. 1. Android features overview (https://www.tutorialspoint.com/android/android_overview. htm, reached 31/8/2023)

1.1 Android Application Development Architecture

There are five different software layers that make up the Android operating system architecture and are important for applications development as follows [3–8].

The following are the primary elements of the Android architecture relevant to mobile applications development [3–8]:

Applications – Applications make up the top layer of the android architecture. Numerous pre-installed programs, such as contacts, galleries and cameras, as well as apps downloaded from the Play Store are offered via this layer. It functions within the Android run time with the aid of the classes and services made available by the application framework.

Application Framework – This layer was created using Java, and the developer can make use of various common class files. These classes can be used and interact directly with an application. The ap-plication framework offers the phone's most essential features, including the location manager, content providers, resource manager, and others (Fig. 2).

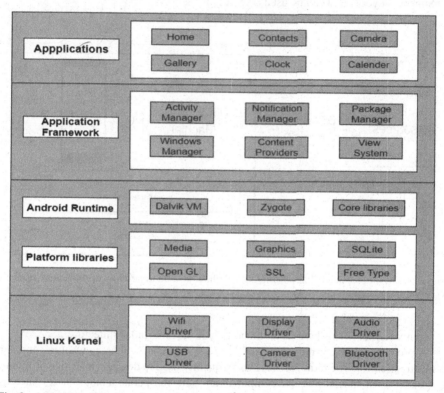

Fig. 2. Android Architecture for application development (https://www.geeksforgeeks.org/android-architecture, reached 31/8/2023)

Android Runtime – It primarily serves as the foundation for the framework and, with the aid of the core libraries, runs the application. The Dalvik virtual machine (DVM) and core libraries are also included. The Java Virtual Machine (JVM) and Dalvik Virtual Machine (DVM) are quite similar, but Dalvik Virtual Machine (DVM) is built for mobile devices with limited processing and memory. With the help of the core libraries, applications developers could create mobile applications for Android using either the Java or Kotlin programming languages.

Platform Libraries – It includes some Java based libraries and some core C and C++ libraries like Graphics, OpenGL, etc. to support the development.

1. To record and play audio and videos the user can involve Media library.
2. To provide a display management the user can involve Surface manager library.
3. For 3D or 2D graphics the user can involve SGL and OpenGL.
4. For database support the user can involve SQLite.
5. For font support the user can involve FreeType.
6. Web-Kit – A web browser engine that can show web content and simplifies page loading.
7. To provide security to the transferred data between web browser and server Secure Sockets Layer (SSL) can be used (Fig. 3).

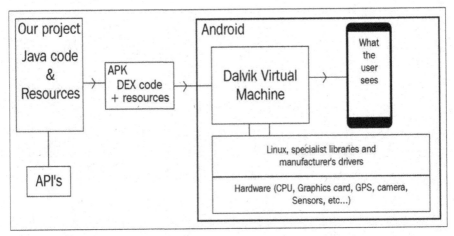

Fig. 3. DVM (https://wajahatkarim.com/2019/01/how-java-and-android-work-together/, reached 31/8/2023)

Linux Kernel – This layer is at the bottom of the Android architecture.

A program, also referred to as a set of predefined instructions, is what a computer is mostly used for. The term "process" is frequently used to describe an active program. Currently, most special purpose computers are built to operate a single task, whereas general purpose computers are built to run numerous processes simultaneously in a complex system. Hardware resources like memory, processor time, storage space, etc. are needed for every type of process. A middle layer in a general-purpose computer that has multiple processes running at once to manage the efficient and equitable distribution of the hardware resources among all the processes is required. This middle layer is referred to as the kernel. In essence, the kernel virtualizes the computer's shared hardware resources to provide each process access to its own virtual resources. This gives the impression that the process is the only one active on the computer. Additionally, the kernel is in charge of avoiding and resolving conflicts between various programs.

The Linux kernel's characteristics are:

1. Security: It manages the system's and application's security.
2. Memory Management: It successfully maintains memory, enabling developers to freely develop their applications.
3. Process Management: Processes are properly managed, and re-sources are assigned to them as needed.
4. Network Stack: Handles network communication effectively.
5. Driver Model: It guarantees that the application on the device will run properly (Fig. 4).

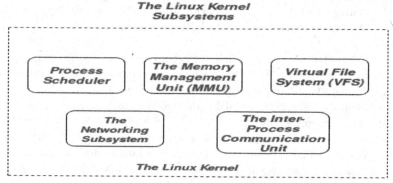

Fig. 4. Linux Kernel Subsystem. (https://www.geeksforgeeks.org/the-linux-kernel/, reached 31/8/2023)

Regarding the herein mobile application development Java has been used instead of Kotlin.

A more contemporary version of Java called Kotlin was released in 2011. It is a general-purpose, open source, statically typed, pragmatic programming language made for the JVM and Android. To create programs quickly, it blends object-oriented and functional programming techniques.

As previously noted, one of the elements that programmers look for when designing trustworthy systems with the possibility for error recovery is Java's verified exception functionality. Even though it was eliminated by Kotlin to encourage conciseness, this functionality is still a favorite among developers.

While Java allows for static members and shares all instances of the variable with the class, Kotlin does not. The static keyword indicates that the declared variable does not belong to a class as a result.

The wildcard type feature, a unique form of argument that regulates the type of safety of the use of parameterized types, is available in Java. When compared to Kotlin, Java stands out because of this feature. Field, parameter, and local variable types can all be used as wildcard types.

1.2   The SQLite Component in the Applications Framework Development

A compact, 275 kB or so, C programming library called SQLite contains an embedded relational database management system that com-plies with ACID standards. The majority of the SQL standard is implemented by SQLite, although it does not ensure the integrity of the domain because it uses a dynamic and loosely typed SQL syntax. Unlike other database management systems, SQLite is a core component of the client program and is not accessed as a separate process from it. While writes in SQLite can only be carried out sequentially, read operations can be multi-threaded. SQLite's source code is available for public use.

SQLite is a well-liked choice for local/client storage in web browsers. Numerous programming languages are tied to it. Given that it is currently utilized by a number of popular operating systems, embedded systems, and browsers, among others, it is likely the most commonly used database engine. It has no external dependencies and is totally independent.

It debuted in PHP V4.3 as an option and is built into PHP V5. The majority of the SQL92 standard is supported by SQLite, which also operates on all popular operating systems and supports all the top programming languages. Since the beginning of the commercial application market several decades ago, databases have been a crucial component of software applications.

As important as database management systems are, they also have a huge environmental impact and a high administrative cost. A new kind of database might be more appropriate than the bigger and more sophisticated conventional database management systems as software programs become less monolithic and more modular. Embeddable databases allow zero-configuration run modes, direct application process execution, and extremely compact footprints. In this article, the well-known SQLite database engine is introduced, and usage guidelines are provided.

The SQL92 standard is supported by SQLite and contains indices, constraints, triggers, and views. However, SQLite does handle Atomic, Consistent, Isolated, and Durable (ACID) transactions. Foreign key constraints are not supported by SQLite.

The major advantages of SQLite over other database management systems are:

1. A separate processor server system is not necessary for man-aging the storage with SQL database administration.
2. There is no setup for administration, SQLite has no configurations.
3. On SQLite, data can be stored in a single platform disk file.
4. The self-contained nature of the SQLite database eliminates the need for any external dependencies.
5. Almost all operating systems are supported by SQLite.
6. It provides an easy to use API.

The majority of SQL92's query language capabilities are supported by SQLite. It offers a straightforward and user-friendly API and is compatible with Linux, Mac, OS X, Android, iOS, and Windows. Some SQL92 features are not supported by SQLite.

They are shown in the following Table 1:

Table 1. Features that are not supported in SQLite

Nr.	Not supported feature
1	RIGHT OUTER JOIN
2	FULL OUTER JOIN
3	ALTER TABLE
4	Trigger support – only FOR EACH ROW triggers are supported
5	VIEWs –It is not possible to execute INSERT, DELETE or UPDATE
6	GRANT and REVOKE – The default file access permissions of the underlying operating system are the only access permissions that can be applied

1.3 The Alarming Mobile Application Characteristics and Requirements

The purpose of this application is to protect personal safety and to get emergency helpline with instant help by using the application through shaking the phone and when possible, opening the app for more features. Such an application might luckily prevent dangerous situations from happening [1, 2].

Requirement gathering is usually regarded as a part of developing software applications. It is the process of understanding what the herein paper is trying to build and why it should be built. The phase explains what the application is intended to do.

For the Alarming application, the authors thought about the most important features needed in a danger situation, comparing, also, with some SOS applications that already exist investigating an optimal way to develop the app. [2].

Below is a list with the functional requirements for the studied application:

a. The user should be able to send a notification if they are in danger in the easiest way possible.
b. The user should be able to add the contacts to whom the message will be sent.
c. The user should be able to delete contacts from the list.
d. The user should be able to check the map for the nearest hospitals.
e. The user should be able to check the map for the nearest police stations.
f. The user should be able to see their current location while checking for the hospitals or police stations.
g. The user should be able to sound an alarm, only when if they think it is safe (not automatically when they shake the phone).

The non-functional requirements for the application are:

a. Providing the simplest UI. In this way the user will find it much easier to search for whatever feature in a panic situation.
b. Providing a list for all the contacts.

1. The Alarming mobile application Design characteristics

Alarming app is a mobile app designed to work with the Android operating system. The main design features of the application according to the previous analysis are:

a. Shaking phone when in danger – it will automatically send a message with user's location to the chosen contacts from the contact list.

b. After opening the app, users can click the "ADD CONTACT" button to add contacts from their contact list. They can choose up to 5 contacts.

c. The user can also delete emergency contacts from the application.

d. The user can click a button which will sound a panic alarm for a few seconds and then it will stop. The user can click it many times.

e. The user can click a button which will show a map with the users' exact location and all the closest hospital buildings to them.

f. The user can click a button which will show a map with the users' exact location and all the closest police stations to them (Figs. 5 and 6).

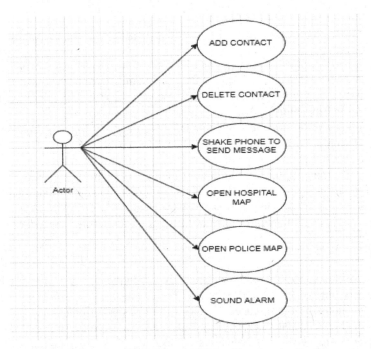

Fig. 5. Use Case UML Diagram of the Alarming Application

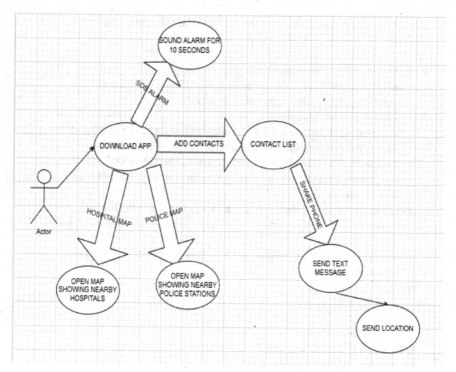

Fig. 6. Use Case UML Diagram of the SOS Application

2 Android Framework for the Development, Implementation and Deployment of the Alarming Mobile Application

Applications must be given permissions during the installation process in order to share data with other applications and system services. The necessary permissions are added in the Manifest file to accomplish this.

2.1 AndroidManifest.xml

Important information about the app is described in the AndroidManifest file for the Android operating system, the Android build tools, and Google Play.

Declaring the app's components in the file is necessary. All actions, services, broadcast viewers, and content suppliers are included. Intent filters and capabilities that specify how the component can be launched can also be declared.

To access restricted areas of the system or other apps, such as contacts, images, and so forth, the app needs authorization. The manifest file also contains a declaration of these permissions.

Following is the AndroidManifest file for the Alarming application:

```xml
<?xml version="1.0" encoding="utf-8"?>
<manifest xmlns:android="http://schemas.android.com/apk/res/android"
    xmlns:tools="http://schemas.android.com/tools"
    package="com.example.sos">
    <uses-permission android:name="android.permission.READ_CONTACTS"/>
    <uses-permission android:name="android.permission.VIBRATE"/>
    <uses-permission android:name="android.permission.SEND_SMS"/>
    <uses-permission android:name="android.permission.ACCESS_FINE_LOCATION"/>
    <uses-permission
android:name="android.permission.ACCESS_COARSE_LOCATION"/>
    <uses-permission android:name="android.permission.FOREGROUND_SERVICE"/>
    <uses-permission
android:name="android.permission.ACCESS_BACKGROUND_LOCATION"/>
    <uses-permission
an-
droid:name="android.permission.REQUEST_IGNORE_BATTERY_OPTIMIZATIONS"/>
    <application
        android:allowBackup="true"
    android:label="@string/app_name"
    android:icon="@mipmap/ic_launcher"
        android:theme="@style/Theme.SOS"
        android:roundIcon="@mipmap/ic_launcher_round"
        android:supportsRtl="true">
        <receiver
    android:name=".ShakeServices.ReactivateService"
    android:enabled="true"
    android:exported="true"/>
<service
    android:name=".ShakeServices.SensorService"
    android:enabled="true"
    android:exported="true" />
<activity android:name=".MainActivity">
    <intent-filter>
        <action android:name="android.intent.action.MAIN" />
        <category android:name="android.intent.category.LAUNCHER" />
    </intent-filter>
</activity>
</application>
</manifest>
```

2.2 Activities

Engaging a user in a task is the first step in connecting with them. It stands for a user interface with just one screen. For instance, an email app might offer three distinct features: the ability to write, read, and view a list of new emails. All of the activities stand alone even though they work together to produce a smooth user experience in the email app. Therefore, another app may initiate any of these operations if the email app authorizes it. To send an image, for instance, a camera app may trigger an email app's action to start a new message. An activity enables the following significant interactions between a system and an app:

1. Monitoring the user's current focus (what is visible on the screen) to make sure the system doesn't stop the process that is hosting the activity.
2. Putting more importance on maintaining previously utilized processes since they contain items the user may come back to (stopped activities).
3. Providing assistance to the app in handling the termination of its process so that the user can resume activities with their former state restored.
4. Enables the system to manage user flows by providing apps with a way to implement user flows between one another.

2.3 Services

An entry point with several functions called a service can be used to keep a program running in the background while serving a number of different functions. It is a part that performs background operations on time-consuming tasks or on behalf of distant processes. A service does not provide a user interface. For instance, a service might play music in the background while the user is using another app or gather data over the network while the user is interacting with another app. The service may be bound to for interaction or may be started and allowed to operate by another component, such as an activity. There are two types of services that tell the system how to operate an app: initiated services and bound services (Fig. 7).

When an application component, such as an activity, calls startService on a service, the service is said to be started (). Even if the component that launched the service is deleted, it can continue to function in the background indefinitely once it has been started.

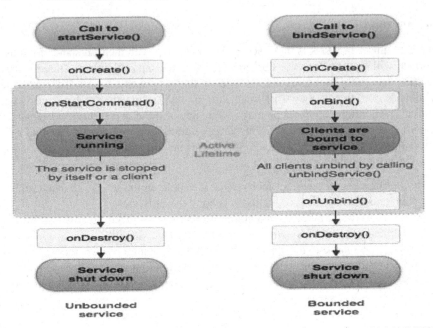

Fig. 7. Services (https://developer.android.com/guide/components/services, reached 31/8/2023)

A service is considered to be bound() when an application component invokes bind-Service to attach to it. A bound service offers a client-server interface so that other components can talk to it, send requests, and get responses. Through interprocess communication, they are even able to do this across processes.

2.4   Intent

The three of the four component types that are activated by an asynchronous message known as an intent are activities, services, and broadcast receivers. Intentions connect several components at runtime. They frequently serve the following functions:

1. The startActivityForResult() method should be used to start the Activity rather than the startActivity() method if the caller Activity anticipates a result from the Activity being called.
2. calling the startService() function to start a service Services are frequently employed to carry out time-consuming background tasks that don't call for a front end.
3. to send a broadcast message to various app components that have the corresponding Intent filter declared, whether they are inside the same app or not.

With the help of the Intent object, an intent is built that describes a message to activate either a particular component or a particular kind of component.

i. Explicit – The user can involve these Intents to start a specific app component. The user must define the component name Intent object while establishing this intent. The Android system then locates the component with the given name and launches it right away, providing it any further information that may have been provided.

ii. Implicit – These Intents define an activity that may be carried out by any app. The Android system then matches the action against the component's Intent Filter to discover a component that can carry out the desired action from other apps (Fig. 8).

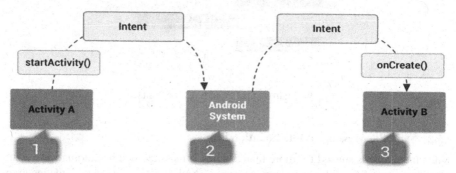

Fig. 8. Intent states (https://developer.android.com/guide/components/intents-filters, reached 31/8/2023)

2.5 Sample Functionalities

2.5.1 Add/Delete Contact Feature

When clicked the "ADD CONTACT" button the user could choose up to 5 contacts from his/her contact list to send an emergency message in case of danger (Fig. 9).

```
contact.setOnClickListener(new View.OnClickListener() {
@Override
        public void onClick(View v) {
            if(database.count()!=5) {
                Intent    intent    =    new    Intent(Intent.ACTION_PICK,    ContactsCon-
tract.Contacts.CONTENT_URI);
                startActivityForResult(intent, PICK_CONTACT);
            }else{
                Toast.makeText(MainActivity.this,  "Can't  Add  more  than  5  Contacts",
Toast.LENGTH_SHORT).show();
            } } }
```

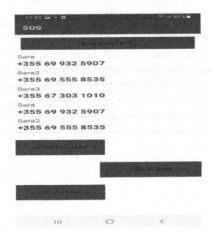

Fig. 9. Main page after adding all 5 contacts

2.5.2 Send the Message While Location is on

When the phone is shaked for more than 5 times, a message will be automatically sent [9] with the text "Please help me I am in danger." And a link is sent too with the location in the moment of shaking (Fig. 10).

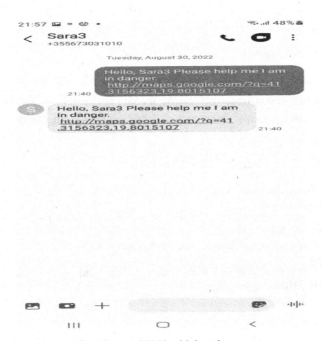

Fig. 10. Send SMS with location on

2.5.3   Open Hospital Map

When the "HOSPITAL MAP" button is clicked, it will redirect the user to Google Maps. It will show user's location with a blue circle and all nearest hospitals in the area with a red pin (Fig. 11).

```
hospital.setOnClickListener(new View.OnClickListener() {
        @Override
        public void onClick(View v) {
            String                          theurl                    =
"http://maps.google.com/maps?q=hospital&mrt=yp&sll=lat,lon&output=kml";
            Uri urlstr = Uri.parse(theurl);          Intent urlintent = new Intent();
            urlintent.setData(urlstr);           urlintent.setAction(Intent.ACTION_VIEW);
            startActivity(urlintent);          }        });
```

2.5.4   Sound Alarm Button

```
alarm.setOnClickListener(new View.OnClickListener() {
        @Override
        public void onClick(View view) {
          alarmSound.start();
        } });
```

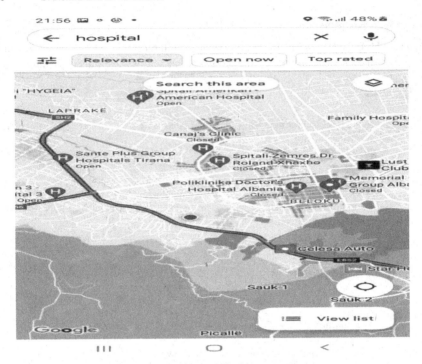

Fig. 11. Hospital map

3 Application Performance Testing

When an Android app is developed, different features are applied using different methods. If during the execution of these methods there are delays, then the application will be less useful especially in the situations of emergency.

It is possible to determine how long each method takes to execute in order to improve the application's performance. The app will operate more quickly as a result. There are two methods for calculating a method's execution time [10–13]:

a. One of the easiest methods is by using HUGO. It is possible to use the Hugo library and apply the @DebugLog annotation to the method.

The library could be used after adding it to the project under consideration in the build.gradle file.

```
buildscript {
    repositories {
        google()
        jcenter()   }
    dependencies {
        classpath 'com.android.tools.build:gradle:3.5.0'
        classpath 'com.jakewharton.hugo:hugo-plugin:1.2.1'
    } }
    dependencies {
        ...          }
    apply plugin: 'com.android.application'
    apply plugin: 'com.jakewharton.hugo'
```

b. Using System.currentTimeinMillis() or using System.nanoTime().

System.nanoTime() has been herein used because it returns the most precise value in nanoseconds while System.currentTimeMillis() is less precise.

The code used in the methods is:

```
//the first line is used in the beginning of the method and the other three lines
are in the //end
long startTime = System.nanoTime();
...
long endTime = System.nanoTime();
long result = endTime - startTime;
Log.d("Time", "Value = " + result);
```

The first method tested was the onSuccess method (when we shake the phone it automatically sends a message depending if the location is on) on the SensorService class. Then the test for the alarm button followed with, hospital map button and police map button. While doing the first tests only 2 contacts have been considered in the contact list. The results are shown in the table below in nanoseconds, comparing performance in Java and Kotlin platforms:

Table 2. Performance testing, 2 contacts

Tested	Value in nanoseconds when Jave coding	Value in nanoseconds when Kotlin coding
onSucces (location on)	92594539 ns	91894788 ns
onSuccess (location off)	128400692 ns	125212683 ns
Sos alarm	2505461 ns	2307942 ns
Hospital map	25701308 ns	22913506 ns
Police map	26860308 ns	24379319 ns

The same tests for each method were running but at this second time the maximum number of contacts (supposed to be 5) in the contact list have been used. Tables 2 and 3 show that performances of the application under Kotlin platform slightly improve Java platform ones. Of course these are preliminary results and need to be verified in larger scale studies.

Table 3. Performance testing, 5 contacts

Tested	Value in nanoseconds when Jave coding	Value in nanoseconds when Kotlin coding
onSucces (location on)	210741307 ns	204925879 ns
onSuccess (location off)	258219308 ns	244396827 ns
Sos alarm	3286461 ns	2968843 ns
Hospital map	22829615 ns	1896789 ns
Police map	30086846 ns	28848932 ns

4   Conclusions and Future Work

Alarming mobile applications are very important ones that it would be beneficial and for great value for everybody to have them on their phone. They are personal security apps that are designed to send text messages to selected people from users contact list without even opening the phone, involving minimum only actions from user side. Such applications make it easier for the user to check his/her location and all nearby hospital buildings and police stations as well. The user could also sound an alarm so that other people can hear it and find him/her. The text message is equipped with user location information, which is absolutely essential in dangerous situations, for the possible help to come.

The herein presented and evaluated mobile app software contains many extremely useful functions that would be used in case of danger and emergency situations, such as sending text messages without having to open the phone or other apps, opening both hospital and police maps, and ringing an alert. But it is of course preliminary, and many more functions could be integrated. Some only improvements, out of the many possible ones, could be for example:

a. While sounding the alarm, the flashlight could turn on and off continuously. In this way not only can the user be heard, but people can also see the light.
b. When shaking phone, the police or emergency cases dept. of hospital care or even both could be called directly and automatically, depending on a simple click or different shaking of the phone. This feature can be useful because the user will not have to wait for his/her emergency contact to get the message and then call the police.
c. When shaking phone, the user could automatically start recording a video so that he/she could have proof to show to the police.

d. Setting up a password would be beneficial too, so that the user could stop the application in situations he/she think will not need it.

The performance evaluation, also, strategy, herein presented for alarming applications should be improved and be much more extensive.

References

1. Al-Okby, M.F.R., Neubert, S., Roddelkopf, T., Thurow, K.: Mobile detection and alarming systems for hazardous gases and volatile chemicals in laboratories and industrial locations. Sensors **21**(23), 8128 (2021). https://doi.org/10.3390/s21238128
2. Faiz, A.B., Imteaj, A., Chowdhury, M.: Smart vehicle accident detection and alarming system using a smartphone. In 2015 international conference on computer and information engineering (ICCIE), pp. 66–69. IEEE (2015)
3. Sarkar, A., Goyal, A., Hicks, D., Sarkar, D., Hazra, S.: Android application development: a brief overview of android platforms and evolution of security systems. In: 2019 Third International conference on I-SMAC (IoT in Social, Mobile, Analytics and Cloud) (I-SMAC), pp. 73–79. IEEE (2019)
4. Brahler, S.: Analysis of the android architecture, vol. 7, no. 8. Karlsruhe Institute for Technology (2010)
5. Sihag, V., Swami, A., Vardhan, M., Singh, P.: Signature based malicious behavior detection in android. In: Chaubey, N., Parikh, S., Amin, K. (eds.) COMS2 2020. CCIS, vol. 1235, pp. 251–262. Springer, Singapore (2020). https://doi.org/10.1007/978-981-15-6648-6_20
6. Hoog, A.: Chapter 3 – Android software development kit and android debug bridge, Android Forensics, Investigation, Analysis and Mobile Security for Google Android, pp. 65–103 (201)
7. Cheon, Y.: Multiplatform application development for Android and Java. In: Departmental Technical Reports (CS). 1328, appeared in the 17th IEEE/ACIS International Conference on Software Engineering Research, Management and Applications, Honolulu, Hawaii, 29–31 May 2019
8. Makaji, A.: Android architecture components. Zbornik radova Fakulteta tehničkih nauka u Novom Sadu **35**(11), 2002–2005 (2020). https://doi.org/10.24867/10BE36Makaji
9. Primorac, S., Russo, M.:Android application for sending SMS messages with speech recognition interface. In: 2012 Proceedings of the 35th International Convention MIPRO, Opatija, Croatia, pp. 1763-1767 (2012)
10. Geyer, K., Ellis, D.A., Shaw, H., et al.: Open-source smartphone app and tools for measuring, quantifying, and visualizing technology use. Behav. Res. **54**, 1–12 (2022). https://doi.org/10.3758/s13428-021-01585-7
11. Fernandes, T.S., Cota, E., Moreira, Á.F.: Performance evaluation of android applications: a case study. In: 2014 Brazilian Symposium on Com puting Systems Engineering, pp. 79–84. IEEE (2014)
12. Andrews, S., Ellis, D.A., Shaw, H., Piwek, L.: Beyond selfreport: tools to compare estimated and real-world smartphone use. PLoS ONE **10**(10), e0139004 (2015)
13. Keil, T.F., Koschate, M., Levine, M.: Contact Logger: measuring everyday intergroup contact experiences in near-time. Behav. Res. Methods **52**(4), 1568–1586 (2020). https://doi.org/10.3758/s13428-019-01335-w

Cloud, IoT and Distributed Computing

Investigation of Air Effluence Using IoT and Machine Learning

Shalah Uddin Perbhez Shakil[1], Mohammod Abul Kashem[1],
Md. Monirul Islam[2], Nasim Mahmud Nayan[3], and Jia Uddin[4]

[1] Department of Computer Science and Engineering, Dhaka University of Engineering and Technology, Gazipur 1707, Bangladesh
[2] Department of Software Engineering, Daffodil International University, Daffodil Smart City (DSC), Birulia, Savar, Dhaka 1216, Bangladesh
monirul.swe@diu.edu.bd
[3] Department of Computer Science and Engineering, University of Information Technology and Sciences (UITS), Dhaka 1212, Bangladesh
[4] AI and Big Data Department, Endicott College, Woosong University, Daejeon, South Korea
jia.uddin@wsu.ac.kr

Abstract. Air pollution poses a significant issue in numerous cities worldwide, impacting public health and the environment. We study three significant cities under the Dhaka division, including Kuril Bishow Road, Uttara, and Tongi. Traditional air quality monitoring methods often need more coverage and accuracy. Leveraging Internet of Things (IoT) technology as well as machine learning (ML) algorithms, this study deploys an IoT-based sensor network using Arduino boards and various devices, including MQ135, DHT22, PM2.5, MQ9, and dust sensors to gather real-time values on air pollutants. The gathered data, including sulfur dioxide, ozone, particulate matter 2.5, nitrogen dioxide, particulate matter 10, as well as carbon monoxide, provides a comprehensive view of city pollution levels. ML models such as linear regression, decision trees, K-Nearest Neighbors (KNN), Naive Bayes (NB), Gradient Boosting (GB), and Random Forest classifiers are applied to predict pollution levels using environmental parameters. The Random Forest classifier achieves an impressive prediction accuracy of 97.2%. Evaluation metrics, including precision, recall, F1 score, Kappa score, mean square error (MSE), root mean square error(RMSE), along mean absolute error (MAE), are used to assess the performance of the models. This study demonstrates the potential of IoT technology along with ML algorithms in accurately predicting air pollution levels, aiding in environmental management and public health efforts in urban areas.

Keywords: Air pollutant components · IoT · Machine Learning · Sensors · Prediction · Real-time data

© ICST Institute for Computer Sciences, Social Informatics and Telecommunications Engineering 2024
Published by Springer Nature Switzerland AG 2024. All Rights Reserved
M. H. Miraz et al. (Eds.): iCETiC 2023, LNICST 538, pp. 183–202, 2024.
https://doi.org/10.1007/978-3-031-50215-6_12

1   Introduction

People in many cities worldwide are impacted by air pollution, a severe environmental and public health concern. Respiratory sickness, heart disease, and cancer are among the various health problems that can be caused by air pollutants like SO2 (sulfur dioxide), NO2 (nitrogen dioxide), PM (particulate matter), O3 (ozone), and CO (carbon monoxide) [1]. Traditional air quality monitoring methods rely on stationary sensors that may not provide a comprehensive or accurate view of pollution levels in a given area [2]. IoT can be applied in research fields including smart storage systems, aqua fisheries, and drinking water [3–6]. Advancements in IoT technology and ML algorithms have made it possible to collect and analyze significant volumes of air quality data in recent years, leading to a more intricate and precise understanding of the levels of air pollution [7]. This investigation aims to analyze air pollution levels in a significant urban area using an IoT-based sensor network and machine learning algorithms [8].

We use a network of sensors throughout the Dhaka division from three different cities(Kuril Bishow Road, Uttara, and Tongi) to gather information on several air pollution parameters, including CO, SO2, PM2.5, NO2, and PM10. Using machine learning algorithms, we analyze the collected data to predict pollution levels based on these environmental factors [9,10]. Our study has several potential applications, including public health, urban planning, and environmental policy. Precise and up-to-the-minute tracking of air pollution levels can assist policymakers in making well-informed choices to minimize air pollution and safeguard public health [11]. Additionally, the detailed and comprehensive data provided by our IoT-based sensor network can help urban planners identify areas of the city that are particularly susceptible to air pollution and develop targeted interventions to mitigate the problem.

Overall, our study highlights the potential of IoT and machine learning for addressing complex environmental challenges and improving public health outcomes. Combining cutting-edge technologies and comprehensive data collection methods can help us better understand and address the pressing issue of air pollution in cities worldwide. Primary pollutants include:

- Particulate Matter (PM): The inhalation of PM can result in respiratory and cardiovascular issues, such as asthma, bronchitis, lung cancer, and heart disease, as it can infiltrate profoundly into the lungs and even enter the blood circulating. It is crucial to note that the outcome of PM on health can be severe. PM can also irritate the eyes, nose, and throat and exacerbate health conditions [12].
- Sulfur oxide (SOX): In the presence of other compounds in the atmosphere, SOx can react to create acid rain, which can damage buildings, crops as well as bodies of water. SOx can also contribute to the formation of particulate matter, which can harm the respiratory system and cause lung disease [13].
- Nitrogen oxide (NOX): NOx plays a part in generating ground-level ozone, which has been known to cause respiratory problems, particularly in susceptible groups like children, the elderly, and those with pre-existing medical

conditions. Exposure to high levels of NOx can also aggravate asthma and other respiratory diseases [14].

- Carbon monoxide (CO): CO is especially harmful. It can only be detected with sophisticated equipment because it has no smell or color. Exposure to elevated concentrations of CO may result in symptoms like headaches, dizziness, and nausea. In severe cases, it can even lead to fatalities [15].

The study makes several notable contributions, which are outlined as follows:

- Data Collection: IoT devices, including sensors and Arduino boards, collect real-time data. This approach enables the continuous monitoring of various air pollutants.
- Machine Learning Model Application: Different ML algorithms are examined to analyze the collected data. The models leverage advanced algorithms to predict and gain insights into air pollution levels.
- Evaluation Metrics: Various evaluation metrics are utilized to assess the performance of the machine learning models. These metrics include precision, recall, F1 score, Kappa score, and regression metrics to evaluate the accuracy as well as the effectiveness of the predictions made by the models.

Overall, the paper highlights the potential of IoT and machine learning for addressing complex environmental challenges and improving public health outcomes. Combining cutting-edge technologies and comprehensive data collection methods can help us better understand and address the pressing issue of air pollution in cities worldwide.

The remainder of this paper is structured as follows: Sect. 2 explores related works, Sect. 3 outlines the proposed methodology, Sect. 4 delves into the results and discussion, and Sect. 5 provides the paper's concluding remarks.

2   Related Tasks

Industrialized and developing countries struggle with air pollution, especially in the metropolitan areas of the latter, where industrialization is still taking place [16]. The frequency of air pollution-related health issues has risen more quickly [17]. As a result, monitoring air contaminants has drawn much interest in increasing public awareness of air quality. In addition to threatening human health, air pollution can adversely affect the environment and ecosystem [18]. Saini et al. [19] seeks to create a dataset by employing IOT devices to monitor the levels of carbon monoxide (CO) as well as nitrogen dioxide (NO2) in the city of Dhaka. It displays the CO and NO2 emissions variation based on the effects of various sessions and the measured value. However, this method has the disadvantage of ignoring essential factors like PM2.5 or PM10 and not applying machine learning algorithms to predict air pollution. Rajkumar et al. [20] proposed a method that, based on a data set (obtained from the UCI repository) makes of the daily atmospheric situation in a particular town, attempts are made to estimate just the PM2.5 level and identify air quality. On a monthly, weekly, or daily basis, the data is shown. Also, once the numbers are predicted, they are unaffected by a sudden change in the weather or an unexpected boost in traffic. In their research, Payne et al. [21] suggested that they contrasted supervised algorithms including decision trees (DT), K-Nearest Neighbor (K-NN), and Support Vector Machines (SVM), with unsupervised neural network algorithms whose output is unknown. While neural networks outperform these algorithms regarding overall performance, their use of pre-existing datasets prevents them from making hourly predictions of air pollution levels. Parmar et al. [22], compared to other methods like artificial intelligence networks (ANN), Random Forest (RF), DT, Least Squares SVM Model, and Deep Belief Network (DBN), require hourly data prediction. However, a disadvantage is that there are several problems with sensor quality because of manufacturing flaws in the device. Ali et al. [23] suggested that machine-learning algorithms play a significant role in adequately calculating the air quality index. The levels of PM2.5 may be determined using auto-regression, ANN, and logistic regression. The best findings in the article go to ANN.

According to Saini et al., a unique mix of an AI-based prediction model and an IoT-based monitoring system can assist building occupants in taking preventative action to lessen the effects of air pollution [24]. Bu Zhao et al. collect the most extensive mobile sensor data for monitoring urban air quality, supplemented by cutting-edge machine-learning approaches to produce high-quality urban air pollution maps [25], according to R. Jha et al. Advanced real-time air quality reporting systems that reliably detect gases like NO2, CO, and PM2.5 can be implemented in real systems. It can incorporate real-time data into a mobile phone app. These systems use IoT architecture [26]. Rakib et al. suggested a solution combining IoT and machine learning. It properly forecasts air pollution levels with an accuracy of 90% or higher for all criteria, making it a viable tool for extensive installation [27]. Zhang et al. proposed a method that effectively models air quality patterns in a specific area using stationary and mobile IoT sensors. This gives users a thorough understanding of air pollution in their immediate surroundings. It also shows promising real-time air quality monitoring and prediction results in innovative city applications [28]. Moses et al. recommend that A person can be automatically rerouted to a pollution-free environment using a cloud-based IoT system for air quality monitoring that uses sensors to calculate pollution levels and environmental conditions, a web-based application with a Google map API for frequent updates, and prediction analysis for PM using neural network Multi-Layer perceptron as well as SVM regression (SVMR) learning model [29].

In [30,31], authors provide predictions for the air quality index using several ML techniques, including decision trees and random forests. The Random Forest method provides better predictions of the air quality index, according to the results. Esquiagola et al. [32], compared to the existing model, the authors' suggested approach, which uses the deep learning model BILSTM, predicts PM2.5 with superior performance and produces excellent MAE and RMSE. Jo and Firdhous and their colleague [33,34] employed big data analytics and machine learning to establish their prediction model findings, making comparing and contrasting earlier air quality measurements easier. The DT algorithm produced the best results out of all the methods.

3   Methodology

Table 1 shows the chart lists the maximum allowable concentrations of various contaminants for rural and ecological regions throughout different periods. The concentration restrictions are represented in a variety of measures, including micrograms per cubic meter (g/m^3) for lead (Pb) and particulate matter (PM2.5, PM10) and parts per million (ppm) for gases, including SO2, NO2, CO, and O3. These concentration limits provide crucial data for policymakers, environmental authorities, and researchers in assessing and managing air pollution levels to protect public health and the environment. They also serve as regulatory standards to maintain acceptable air quality levels in rural and ecological areas.

Table 1. Who air quality standards [35]

Pollutant Component	Time avg.	Rural area	Ecological area
Sulphur Dioxide (SO2)	24-h	0.05 ppm	0.02 ppm
Nitrogen Dioxide (NO2)	Annual	0.053 ppm	0.020 ppm
Particulate Matter (PM2.5)	Annual	$10\ \mu g/m^3$	$5\ \mu g/m^3$
Particulate Matter (PM10)	Annual	$20\ \mu g/m^3$	$10\ \mu g/m^3$
Carbon Monoxide (CO)	8-h	10 ppm	5 ppm
Ozone (O3)	8-h	0.100 ppm	0.080 ppm
Lead (Pb)	Annual	$0.5\ \mu g/m^3$	$0.5\ \mu g/m^3$

N.B. ppm = parts per million, $\mu g/m^3$ = micrograms per cubic meter

The workflow diagram 1 visually represents this paper's sequential steps and interactions. It provides a clear and structured overview of how tasks are completed, decisions are made, and information flows within the system.

3.1   IoT Tools for Monitoring Air Pollution

The MQ135 sensor, DHT22 sensor, PM2.5 sensor, MQ9 sensor, and dust sensor are a few of the often used sensors for air quality monitoring. MQ-135 sensor measures the air quality, detecting various air pollutants, including benzene, alcohol, smoke, CO2, and NH3 [36]. It is a less expensive sensor that easily interfaces with Arduino and other microcontrollers. To connect the MQ-135 sensor with the Arduino, We had to follow these steps:

- Connect the MQ-135 (Vcc) to the Arduino (5 V) pin.
- Connect the MQ-135 (GND) to the Arduino (GND).

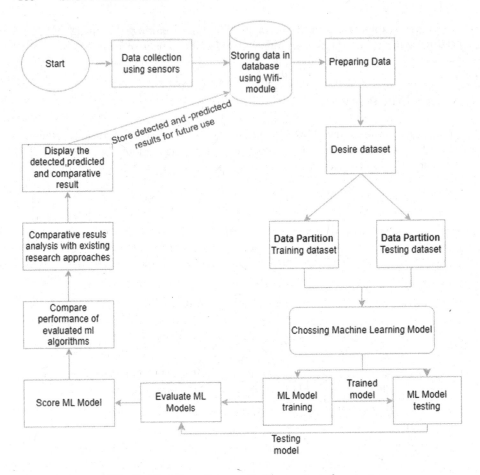

Fig. 1. Workflow diagram for the projected system

– Connect the MQ-135 (A-out) to the Arduino (A0).
– Connect the MQ-135 (D-out) to the Arduino (2).

The MQ-9: Methane (CH4), carbon monoxide (CO), and LPG gases are among the gases that the MQ-9 sensor can detect [37]. Real-time air quality monitoring can be performed by connecting the MQ-9 sensor to an Arduino board. The connection of MQ-9 is similar to MQ-135. A dust sensor is an air quality sensor that measures the dust or particulate matter (PM) concentration in the air [38,39]. These sensors are commonly used in air quality monitoring systems to identify PM 2.5 as well as PM 10 particles. To connect a dust sensor to an Arduino board, follow these steps:

– Connect the sensor's VCC to the Arduino's 5 V.
– Connect the sensor's GND to the Arduino's GND.

Connect the sensor's digital output pin to any digital pin on the microcontroller. This research connected sensors to an Arduino UNO microcontroller, facilitating data transfer via WIFI using the Arduino WiFi shield. The full hardware setup can be observed in Fig. 2.

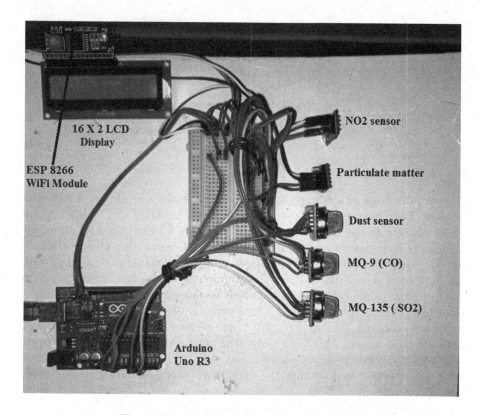

Fig. 2. Combined circuits with all the sensors

3.2   Data Collection

IoT devices were used in the data-gathering procedure to get real-time information on air pollution in Dhaka. The hardware design was made to ensure that suitable sensors were fitted to detect the levels of carbon monoxide, nitrogen dioxide, ozone, particulate matter 2.5, and particulate matter 10. To facilitate connectivity with the IoT devices, the Arduino IDE code was uploaded. The appropriate Excel file was opened after starting the Excel data streamer. The Arduino IDE chose the proper COM port to connect the IoT devices to the PC.

The gathered data were stored in a designated file location to facilitate analysis and interpretation. This approach enabled future research and decision-making procedures about air pollution in Dhaka. It also ensured continuous monitoring and complete assessment of air quality metrics.

Figure 3 shows a sample of our dataset, including the target variable and all dataset parameters.

	Address	SO2	NO2	CO	PM2.5	PM10	O3	soi	noi	coi	pmi	AQI	AQI_Range	
0	Kuril Bishow Road, Dhaka, Bangladesh	0.04	0.059	1.2	57	73	0.002	0.0500	0.07375	2.0	58.75	58.75	Moderate	
1	Kuril Bishow Road, Dhaka, Bangladesh	0.04	0.058	1.2	59	71	0.002	0.0500	0.07250	2.0	61.25	61.25	Moderate	
2	Kuril Bishow Road, Dhaka, Bangladesh	0.04	0.056	1.2	59	70	0.002	0.0500	0.07000	2.0	61.25	61.25	Moderate	

Fig. 3. Sample of dataset

3.3 Read Dataset and Pre-processing

The required libraries are imported before the dataset is read into our Python function. This dataset contains sensor values of SO2, NO2, CO, O3, PM2.5, and PM10, along with the respective air quality ratings for the values registered by the sensors at the current location. Therefore, this dataset has eleven columns, and the number of rows depends on how long it records data. Finally, we save this dataset as a .csv file in Excel. Data from the source has more noise than usual, as some of the data from the stations was marked as NAN or unavailable. To combat this, we pre-processed it to remove outliers. These anomalous data points are primarily a result of malfunctioning sensors or errors in transmission, and they exhibit more significant variability in contrast to regular and accurate results. We applied boundary value analysis (BVA) to the data set to identify these outlier points to determine the upper and lower quartile ranges.

3.4 The Dataset into Training and Testing Sets

The model is taught using the training set, while the testing set helps establish whether the model can generalize newly seen data well. Optimal results are attained when 20–30% of the data is devoted to testing and 70–80% to training. One must import the train_test_split library from Sci-kit, where an 80/20 split of training and testing is used, respectively. Linear regression, DT regression, and random forest regression are some examples of ML methods for air pollution regression issues. The models chosen for classification for predicting air pollution include logistic regression, decision trees, random forests, and KNN.

3.5   Machine Learning Model

Implementing a machine learning algorithm can help predict air pollution. ML is part of AI and allows applications to be reliable in forecasting outcomes without needing to be specially coded. To forecast new outcomes, ML algorithms use existing data as input. With ML, a computer program can receive much data and conclude it without any additional instructions. Linear regression: In simple terms, linear regression (LR) involves fitting a straight line through a scatter plot of data points such that the line best represents the trend or pattern in the data. The equation of the line is typically represented as:

$$y = mx + b \tag{1}$$

where: y is the target variable, x is the predictor variable, m is the slope of the line, and b is the $y$intercept of the line.

Decision tree: A decision tree is a non-linear, non-continuous construction. It operates as a model that generates a choice as an output from a vector of attribute values as an input. The supervised learning family of machine learning algorithms includes decision trees, which may be used to address both classification and regression issues. A decision tree uses a sequence of operations to reach judgments depending on the input data [40].

Random forest: Random forest (RF) is a machine learning ensemble learning approach that blends many decision trees for more precise predictions. It builds many decision trees during training and then merges their predictions for a more reliable and accurate outcome. A random sample of the data with replacement (bootstrap sampling) and a random subset of the characteristics are used to train each tree in the random forest. Depending on whether the problem is one of regression or classification, the final prediction is produced by averaging or by taking a majority vote of the predictions from all the trees in the forest. Random Forest is known for handling high-dimensional data, handling missing values, and reducing the risk of overfitting. It is a powerful and popular algorithm for various machine-learning tasks [41].

K-Nearest Neighbors (KNN): KNN is a lazy learning algorithm. It does not build an explicit model during training and instead stores the entire training dataset for making predictions during testing. KNN is simple to implement, does not require assumptions about the underlying data distribution, and can be used for binary and multiclass classification and regression tasks [42,43]. However, it can be computationally expensive, sensitive to the choice of K and the distance metric, and may need to perform better with large datasets or noisy data.

4   Result and Discussion

This section presents the findings and outcomes of the study. This section typically includes statistical analyses, Simulation, visual representations (tables, graphs, charts), and textual descriptions to present the results clearly and organized.

4.1 Simulation and Calculation of Air Quality Index (AQI)

The following two phases are involved in AQI formation: Subindex Calculation: According to the linear segmentation principle, the general equation for the subindex (Ii) for a certain pollutant concentration (Cp) is determined as follows [7],

$$Ii = [(Imax - Imin/Bmax - Bmin) * (Cp - Bmin)] + Imin \qquad (2)$$

where Bmax = Breakpoint >= given Concentration. Bmin = Breakpoint <= given Concentration. ImaxI = AQI value corresponding to Bmax. Imin = AQI value corresponding to Bmin. Cp = Pollutant Concentration.

Table 2. Breakpoint concentration of a certain contaminant [44]

AQI Category (Range)	PM2.5 24-h	NO2 24-h	O3 8-h	CO 8-h	SO2 24-h
Good (0–50)	0–30	0–40	0–50	0–1.0	0–40
Satisfactory (51–100)	31–60	41–80	51–100	1.1–2	41–80
Moderate (101–200)	60–90	81–180	101–168	2.1–10	81–380
Poor (201–300)	91–120	181–280	169–208	10.1–17	381–800
Very Poor (301–400)	121–250	281–400	209–748	17.1–34	801–1600
Severe (401–500)	250+	400+	748+	34+	1600+

Note: While CO is in mg m-3 and others is in μg m-3

Table 2 lists the AQI categories as well as the ranges for pollutants such as PM2.5, NO2, O3, CO, and SO2 in each category. While PM2.5, NO2, O3, and SO2 are all measured in g/m3, CO is measured in mg/m³. The pollutant concentration ranges for each AQI category are shown in the table.

Calculation of the aggregate index [7]:

$$Agg.Index = AQI/I = Max(I1, I2 \ldots In) \qquad (3)$$

There are other methods or formulas for calculating AQI; however, this is a more popular or often-used form. Figure 4 can display the AQI range and associated health effects. The information we collected contains various columns of sensor data from Tongi, Uttara, and Kuril in Dhaka. Each pollutant index indicates the relationship between the Concentration and the corresponding index. An example of an individual AQI calculation for CO is illustrated in this code.

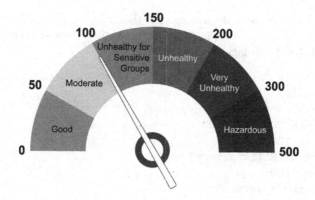

Fig. 4. WHO AQI standard level

```
## CO Sub Index calculation
def co_subindex(s):
    if s <= 1:
        return s * 50 / 40
    elif x <= 2:
        return s + (s - 1) * 50 / 40
    elif x <= 10:
        return 100 + (s - 2) * 100 / 8
    elif x <= 17:
        return 200 + (s - 10) * 100 / 7
    elif x <= 34:
        return 300 + (s - 17) * 100 / 17
    elif x > 34:
        return 400 + (s - 34) * 100 / 17
    else:
        return 0;
```

We applied similar calculations to determine the individual AQI values for SO2, NO2, O3, PM2, and PM10 pollutants based on the calculation method used for the AQI of CO. A location's AQI is established by the highest value of pollutants found in that area. The maximum sub-index of all pollutants forms the AQI for that location, which will be shown below.

```
df["AQI"] = round(df[["PM2.5_SI", "PM10_SI", "SO2_SI", "NO2_SI",
"CO_SI", "O3_SI"]].max(axis = 1))
```

Now use an if-else statement and specify the AQI range based on the WHO AQI standard. After defining the AQI range, the final dataset included the AQI range. AQI Range Calculation is shown below.

```
## AQI Range Calculation
def AQI_level(s):
    if s <= 50:
        return "Good"
    elif s <= 100:
        return "Satisfactory"
    elif s <= 200:
        return "Moderate"
    elif s <= 300:
        return "Poor"
    elif s <= 400:
        return "Very Poor"
    elif s > 400:
        return "Severe"
    else:
        return np.NaN
```

A pair plot of the collected sensor data is shown in Fig. 5 to highlight the correlation between pairs of values received from various sensors. The plot visually examines the data by displaying the measured variables' patterns, trends, and correlations. It is possible to learn more about how the data from the various sensors relate to one another by looking at the placement and distribution of the dots on the plot. A more detailed overview, however, can only be given with access to the precise figure or the specifics of the sensor data.

4.2   Evaluation

We divide the dataset into dependent and independent columns to apply machine learning models. In regression, AQI is the target column, while in classification, AQI is an independent column with AQI_Range as the target. The dataset is separated into training as well as test data before applying machine learning. Figure 6 shows the AQI values according to the AQI range.

We assessed the regression model using the evaluation matrices RMSE, MAE, r2 score, and R-squared. If RMSE is low and R-squared is high, the model operates accurately. Here precision score, recall score, F1 score, and Kappa score are also evaluation matrices for the classification model. If the Kappa score is high, it indicates the high accuracy of the model. Furthermore, we evaluated the accuracy of the classifier model by computing accuracy scores for all the classification models employed in the study. Using this model, we can manually input the independent values and get the predicted air quality range. Based on the observations from Fig. 7, it is evident that the decision tree model is prone to overfitting, while the Random Forest model performs better as a regression model for prediction.

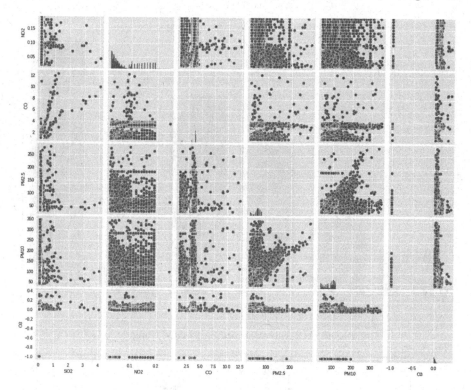

Fig. 5. Pair plot for all sensors

Additionally, as seen in Fig. 8, the accuracy of the classifier model is assessed, and the random forest classifier provides the most accuracy for predicting AQI ranges.

The accuracy ratings with Logistic Regression (LR) scoring is 93%, DT scoring is 95%, and K-NN scoring is 97.0%. Naive Bayes earned 94%, whereas Random Forest Classifier (RFC) attained a score of 97.2%. The most accurate algorithm is RFC, which beats all others. These results provide insightful information about how well various algorithms work, indicating that RFC may be particularly well-suited for the categorization issue. When choosing good algorithms

Table 3. Regression score for Ml model

ML Regressor Model			
Model	MAE	RMSE	R Squared
Linear Regression	9.43	20.04	0.505
Decision Tree Regressor	11.76	25.34	0.995
Random Forest Regressor	9.00	18.73	0.930
Gradient Boosting	8.34	17.86	0.60

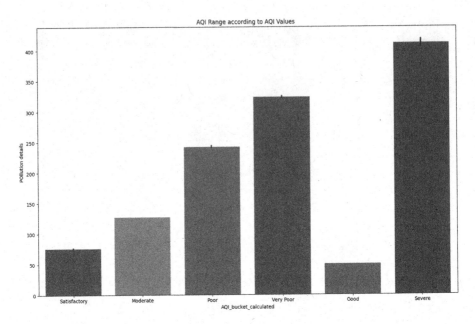

Fig. 6. AQI values according to AQI Range

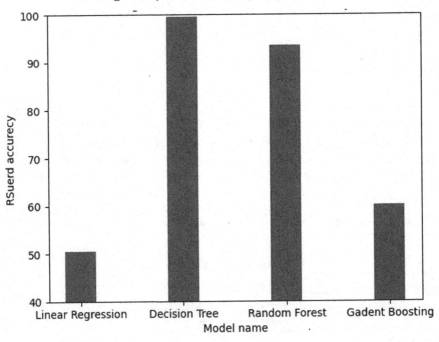

Fig. 7. R squared percentage to evaluate the model

for comparable jobs in the future, researchers and practitioners might consider these findings.

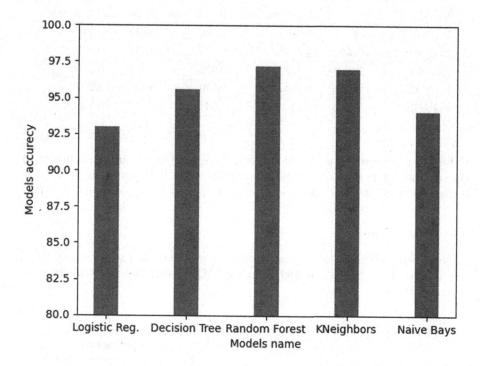

Fig. 8. Accuracy score to evaluate the model

LR, DT Regressor, RF Regressor, as well as Gradient Boosting, are the four models evaluated in the ML Regressor Model section shown in Table 3. A moderate performance was attained through linear regression, with an MAE of 9.43 and an RMSE of 20.04. The model's R-squared (R2) value was 0.505, accounting for around 50.5% of the variance. More significant mistakes were displayed by the Decision Tree Regressor, with an MAE of 11.76 and an RMSE of 25.34. It attained an astonishingly high R2 score of 0.995, indicating an excellent fit for the data. Better results were achieved by the Random Forest Regressor, with an MAE of 9.00 and an RMSE of 18.73. The model can account for almost 93% of the variation, according to the R2 value of 0.930. Gradient boosting was the technique that performed the best and had the fewest mistakes (MAE of 8.34 and RMSE of 17.86). The R2 score was 0.60, indicating that the model can account for almost 60% of the variation. The lowest errors and most excellent R2 value were attained by Gradient Boosting, which performed better than the other models overall. These results demonstrate the utility of gradient boosting in the regression problem.

Table 4 displays evaluation metric scores for various models, including Precision score, Recall score, F1 score, and Kappa score. The Random Forest Classifier

Table 4. Evalutaion Metrics score tabel

ML Classifier Model				
Model	Precision score	Recall score	F1_score	Kappa score
Logistic Regression	0.930	0.930	0.930	0.206
Decision Tree Classifier	0.954	0.954	0.954	0.671
Random Forest Classifier	0.972	0.972	0.972	0.787
KNN Classifier	0.970	0.970	0.970	0.760
Naive Bayes	0.94	0.94	0.94	0.65

showed the highest scores across all metrics, indicating strong performance in classification. The Random Forest model achieved a Precision score of 0.972%, a Recall score of 0.972%, an F1 score of 0.972%, and a Kappa score of 0.787%.

4.3 Prediction

Figure 9 depicts a graphical representation of the actual and predicted AQI using the decision tree regression model. Similarly, AQI predictions can be made using all the other regression models.

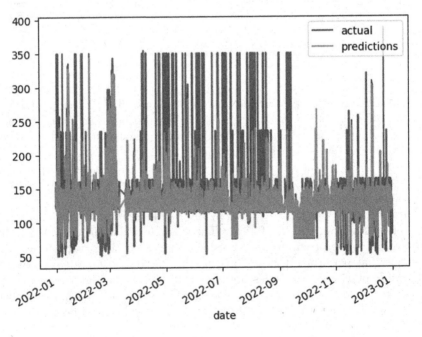

Fig. 9. Actual value vs. Predicted value of AQI

4.4   Comparison with Existing Works

This part compares our research with previous air pollution detection and forecasting studies. We must emphasize that our method uses different datasets than earlier research. In contrast to other studies that use secondary data, we only use real-time data in our research. Furthermore, our original dataset has never been used for such reasons. Our study stands out owing to its unique dataset and approach, despite several noteworthy studies in air pollution detection using IoT devices and prediction using machine learning or deep learning techniques. We offer a comparative analysis in Table 5 to give a thorough overview.

Table 5. A Comparison with Existing Works

Paper	Method	ML\DL Used?	Accuracy
[27]	IoT and Machine Learning	ML	90%
[45]	IoT and Deep Learning	DL	None
[46]	IoT Based Proposed System	None	None
[47]	IoT Based Proposed System	None	None
[29]	IoT and Machine Learning	ML	None
[28]	IoT and Machine Learning	ML	None
Our Work	IoT and Machine Learning	ML	97.2%

5   Conclusion and Future Works

In this work, we have collected real-time data on air pollutants named particulate matter 10, sulfur dioxide, ozone, nitrogen dioxide, particulate matter 2.5, as well as carbon monoxide using IoT devices from three different places in Dhaka city, the capital of Bangladesh. After that, we applied machine learning algorithms named regressor and classification models on the dataset. Among the classification models, Random Forest outperforms by achieving the 0.972% of accuracy. In a regression problem, we have shown MAE, RMSE, and R-squared metrics. In this case, Gradient Boosting performs well in MAE and RMSE metrics, and Linear regression performs well in R squared. Overall, the work demonstrates the potential for IoT and machine learning to provide a more comprehensive and accurate analysis of air pollution levels. The paper's results might be used to develop effective policies and initiatives to lessen the harmful effects of air pollution on the environment as well as public health.

References

1. Veljanovska, K., Dimoski, A.: Air quality index prediction using simple machine learning algorithms. Int. J. Emerg. Trends Technol. Comput. Sci. (IJETTCS) **7**(1), 025–030 (2018)

2. Saha, R., Hoque, S.N.M.A., Manu, M.M.R., Hoque, A.: Monitoring air quality of Dhaka using IoT: effects of COVID-19. In: 2021 2nd International Conference on Robotics, Electrical and Signal Processing Techniques (ICREST), pp. 715–721. IEEE (2021)
3. Islam, M.M., Rony, J.H., Akhtar, M.N., Shakil, S.U.P., Uddin, J.: Water monitoring using Internet of Things. In: Marques, G., González-Briones, A. (eds.) Internet of Things for Smart Environments. EAISICC, pp. 59–69. Springer, Cham (2023). https://doi.org/10.1007/978-3-031-09729-4_4
4. Islam, M.M., Uddin, J., Kashem, M.A., Rabbi, F., Hasnat, M.W.: Design and implementation of an IoT system for predicting aqua fisheries using Arduino and KNN. In: Singh, M., Kang, D.-K., Lee, J.-H., Tiwary, U.S., Singh, D., Chung, W.-Y. (eds.) IHCI 2020. LNCS, vol. 12616, pp. 108–118. Springer, Cham (2021). https://doi.org/10.1007/978-3-030-68452-5_11
5. Islam, M.M., Kashem, M.A., Uddin, J.: An Internet of Things framework for real-time aquatic environment monitoring using an Arduino and sensors. Int. J. Electr. Comput. Eng. **12**(1), 826 (2022)
6. Rony, J.H., Karim, N., Rouf, M.D.A., Islam, M.M., Uddin, J., Begum, M.: A cost-effective IoT model for a smart sewerage management system using sensors. J **4**(3), 356–366 (2021)
7. Mehta, Y., Pai, M.M.M., Mallissery, S., Singh, S.: Cloud enabled air quality detection, analysis and prediction-a smart city application for smart health. In: 2016 3rd MEC International Conference on Big Data and Smart City (ICBDSC), pp. 1–7. IEEE (2016)
8. Zhang, J., Ding, W.: Prediction of air pollutants concentration based on an extreme learning machine: the case of Hong Kong. Int. J. Environ. Res. Public Health **14**(2), 114 (2017)
9. Sharma, M., Jain, S., Mittal, S., Sheikh, T.H.: Forecasting and prediction of air pollutants concentrates using machine learning techniques: the case of India. In: IOP Conference Series: Materials Science and Engineering, vol. 1022, p. 012123. IOP Publishing (2021)
10. Kang, G.K., Gao, J.Z., Chiao, S., Lu, S., Xie, G.: Air quality prediction: big data and machine learning approaches. Int. J. Environ. Sci. Dev. **9**(1), 8–16 (2018)
11. Streatfield, P.K., Karar, Z.A.: Population challenges for Bangladesh in the coming decades. J. Health Popul. Nutr. **26**(3), 261 (2008)
12. Li, X., Peng, L., Yuan, H., Shao, J., Chi, T.: Deep learning architecture for air quality predictions. Environ. Sci. Pollut. Res. **23**, 22408–22417 (2016)
13. Seinfeld, J.H., Pandis, S.N.: From Air Pollution to Climate Change. Atmospheric Chemistry and Physics, p. 1326 (1998)
14. Greaver, T.L., et al.: Ecological effects of nitrogen and sulfur air pollution in the us: what do we know? Front. Ecol. Environ. **10**(7), 365–372 (2012)
15. Pasupuleti, V.R., Kalyan, P., Reddy, H.K., et al.: Air quality prediction of data log by machine learning. In: 2020 6th International Conference on Advanced Computing and Communication Systems (ICACCS), pp. 1395–1399. IEEE (2020)
16. Jeya, S., Sankari, L.: Air pollution prediction by deep learning model. In: 2020 4th International Conference on Intelligent Computing and Control Systems (ICICCS), pp. 736–741. IEEE (2020)
17. Eren, F., Ozturk, S.: Evaluation of the effect of air pollution on cognitive functions, cognitive decline, and dementia. Ann. Indian Acad. Neurol. **25**(Suppl 1), S9 (2022)
18. Dobrea, M., et al.: Machine learning algorithms for air pollutants forecasting. In: 2020 IEEE 26th International Symposium for Design and Technology in Electronic Packaging (SIITME), pp. 109–113. IEEE (2020)

19. Saini, R.K., Saini, H., Singh, S.: Air pollution quality monitoring system using Internet of Things for smart cities. Turk. J. Comput. Math. Educ. (TURCOMAT) **11**(2), 1077–1092 (2020)
20. Rajakumari, K., Priyanka, V.: Air pollution prediction in smart cities by using machine learning techniques. IJITEE **9**(5), 1272–1279 (2020)
21. Payne-Sturges, D.C., et al.: Healthy air, healthy brains: advancing air pollution policy to protect children's health. Am. J. Public Health **109**(4), 550–554 (2019)
22. Parmar, G., Lakhani, S., Chattopadhyay, M.K.: An IoT based low cost air pollution monitoring system. In: 2017 International Conference on Recent Innovations in Signal Processing and Embedded Systems (RISE), pp. 524–528. IEEE (2017)
23. Ali, H., Soe, J.K., Weller, S.R.: A real-time ambient air quality monitoring wireless sensor network for schools in smart cities. In: 2015 IEEE First International Smart Cities Conference (ISC2), pp. 1–6. IEEE (2015)
24. Saini, J., Dutta, M., Marques, G.: Predicting indoor air quality: integrating IoT with artificial intelligence. In: Internet of Things for Indoor Air Quality Monitoring. SAST, pp. 51–67. Springer, Cham (2021). https://doi.org/10.1007/978-3-030-82216-3_4
25. Zhao, B.: Urban air pollution mapping using fleet vehicles as mobile monitors and machine learning. Environ. Sci. Technol. **55**(8), 5579–5588 (2021)
26. Jha, R.: Air quality sensing and reporting system using IoT. In: 2020 Second International Conference on Inventive Research in Computing Applications (ICIRCA), pp. 790–793 (2020)
27. Rakib, M.: IoT based air pollution monitoring & prediction system. In: 2022 International Conference on Innovations in Science, Engineering and Technology (ICISET), pp. 184–189 (2022)
28. Zhang, D.: Real time localized air quality monitoring and prediction through mobile and fixed IoT sensing network. IEEE Access **8**, 89584–89594 (2020)
29. Moses, L.: IoT enabled environmental air pollution monitoring and rerouting system using machine learning algorithms. In: IOP Conference Series: Materials Science and Engineering, vol. 955 (2020)
30. Ali, S., Glass, T., Parr, B., Potgieter, J., Alam, F.: Low cost sensor with IoT LoRaWAN connectivity and machine learning-based calibration for air pollution monitoring. IEEE Trans. Instrum. Meas. **70**, 1–11 (2020)
31. Molinara, M., Ferdinandi, M., Cerro, G., Ferrigno, L., Massera, E.: An end to end indoor air monitoring system based on machine learning and SENSIPLUS platform. IEEE Access **8**, 72204–72215 (2020)
32. Esquiagola, J., Manini, M., Aikawa, A., Yoshioka, L., Zuffo, M.: Monitoring indoor air quality by using IoT technology. In: 2018 IEEE XXV International Conference on Electronics, Electrical Engineering and Computing (INTERCON), pp. 1–4. IEEE (2018)
33. Jo, J.H., Jo, B.W., Kim, J.H., Kim, S.J., Han, W.Y.: Development of an IoT-based indoor air quality monitoring platform. J. Sens. **2020**, 1–14 (2020)
34. Firdhous, M.F.M., Sudantha, B.H., Karunaratne, P.M.: IoT enabled proactive indoor air quality monitoring system for sustainable health management. In: 2017 2nd International Conference on Computing and Communications Technologies (ICCCT), pp. 216–221. IEEE (2017)
35. Soundari, A.G., Jeslin, J.G., Akshaya, A.C.: Indian air quality prediction and analysis using machine learning. Int. J. Appl. Eng. Res. **14**(11), 181–186 (2019)
36. Saranya, E., Maheswaran, T.: IoT based disease prediction and diagnosis system for healthcare. Int. J. Eng. Dev. Res. **7**(2), 232–237 (2019)

37. Dhanvijay, M.M., Patil, S.C.: Internet of Things: a survey of enabling technologies in healthcare and its applications. Comput. Netw. **153**, 113–131 (2019)

38. Babakerkhell, M.D., Pandey, N.: Analysis of different IoT based healthcare monitoring systems. Int. J. Innov. Technol. Explor. Eng. (IJITEE) **8**, 61–67 (2019)

39. Ahmadi, H., Arji, G., Shahmoradi, L., Safdari, R., Nilashi, M., Alizadeh, M.: The application of Internet of Things in healthcare: a systematic literature review and classification. Univ. Access Inf. Soc. **18**, 837–869 (2019)

40. Mustary, S., Kashem, M.A., Khan, M.N.I., Jewel, F.A., Islam, M.M., Islam, S.: LEACH based WSN classification using supervised machine learning algorithm. In: 2021 International Conference on Computer Communication and Informatics (ICCCI), pp. 1–5. IEEE (2021)

41. Islam, M.M., Kashem, M.A., Uddin, J.: Fish survival prediction in an aquatic environment using random forest model. Int. J. Artif. Intell. **10**(3), 614–622 (2021). ISSN: 2252-8938

42. Alam, M., Islam, M.M., Rokunojjaman, M., Akter, S., Hossain, M.B., Uddin, J.: Electrocardiogram signal analysis based on statistical approaches using K-nearest neighbor. In: Islam, A.K.M.M., Uddin, J., Mansoor, N., Rahman, S., Al Masud, S.M.R. (eds.) Bangabandhu and Digital Bangladesh. CCIS, vol. 1550, pp. 148–160. Springer, Cham (2021). https://doi.org/10.1007/978-3-031-17181-9_12

43. Sahidullah, M., Nayan, N.M., Morshed, M.S., Hossain, M.M., Islam, M.U.: Date fruit classification with machine learning and explainable artificial intelligence. Int. J. Comput. Appl. **975**, 8887 (2023)

44. Aditya, C.R., Deshmukh, C.R., Nayana, D.K., Vidyavastu, P.G.: Detection and prediction of air pollution using machine learning models. Int. J. Eng. Trends Technol. (IJETT) **59**(4), 204–207 (2018)

45. Wu, Z., Wang, Y., Zhang, L.: MSSTN: multi-scale spatial temporal network for air pollution prediction. In: 2019 IEEE International Conference on Big Data (Big Data), pp. 1547–1556. IEEE (2019)

46. Kiruthika, R., Umamakeswari, A.: Low cost pollution control and air quality monitoring system using Raspberry Pi for Internet of Things. In: 2017 International Conference on Energy, Communication, Data Analytics and Soft Computing (ICECDS), pp. 2319–2326 (2017)

47. Ghoneim, M., Hamed, S.M.: Towards a smart sustainable city: air pollution detection and control using Internet of Things. In: 2019 5th International Conference on Optimization and Applications (ICOA), pp. 1–6. IEEE (2019)

Exploring the Emerging Technologies Within the Blockchain Landscape

Mohammad Ali Tareq[1] , Piyush Tripathi[2] , Nurhayati Md. Issa[3],
and Mahdi H. Miraz[4,5,6(✉)]

[1] Universiti Malaya (UM), Kuala Lumpur, Malaysia
[2] Texas A&M University, College Station, College Station, TX, USA
[3] Yamaguchi University, Yamaguchi, Japan
[4] Xiamen University Malaysia, Selangor, Malaysia
m.miraz@ieee.org
[5] Wrexham University, Wrexham, UK
[6] University of South Wales, Pontypridd, UK

Abstract. Although blockchain technology was first introduced in 2008 and materialised in 2009, the early usage of blockchain were mainly limited to financial technologies, particularly cryptocurrencies. Later, blockchain became a widespread emerging technology, utilised in multifaceted sectors and applications. In fact, various new and innovative application of blockchain and distributed ledger technologies are still continuously being researched and explored. On the other hand, smart-contracts were first introduced in 1990s, however, it did not gain enough popularity until being integrated with blockchain technologies lately. The duo lately been seen as the key to many innovations in various industries and sectors. So, we took data from 1445 blockchain-related patent documents and tried to map out the historical and current trends in patenting activities in the blockchain field. This helps us get a better grasp of how blockchain technologies are evolving and being tracked. In addition to serving as an indicator of science and technology growth, patents are also used to judge the research potential and development of a particular technology.

Keywords: Blockchain · Smart-contract · Patent · IPC · Emerging Technology

1 Introduction

Szabo, an American lawyer as well as computer scientist, was the first to conceptualise smart-contracts as far back as the early 1990s [1]. Obviously, his version of smart-contracts was in the absence of today's blockchain or distributed ledger technologies. As a matter of fact, the idea of blockchain was first put forward by [2] in 2008 as an incidental result of the Bitcoin cryptocurrency, materialised in 2009. The earliest version of the blockchain, i.e. Blockchain 1.0 [3], was in fact orchestrated without the compatibility of smart contract. The fusion of both the blockchain and the smart-contracts was first transpired in Blockchain 2.0 [3]. Since then, the application of this duo has been

M. H. Miraz et al. (Eds.): iCETiC 2023, LNICST 538, pp. 203–215, 2024.
https://doi.org/10.1007/978-3-031-50215-6_13

exponentially increasing in various technological innovations beyond cryptocurrencies [4], as evident in various research publications and patent applications. Such implementation of smart contracts on blockchain' (distributed) ledgers not only assumes it immutability, transparency and extra layer of security, but also codify and automate the 'delivery' aspect of a contact, enabling secure and automated execution of any part of a project upon satisfaction of the predefined conditions, being verified by the peers of the distributed blockchain network utilising its consensus model. That being the case, such fusion of the blockchain and smart-contract technologies has been acting as a springboard for multitude of innovations in multifaceted disciplines. Therefore, to study the current trends and predict the future directions of technological innovations applying blockchain and smart-contracts, we have used the IPC Codes in this study to analyse subject trends of the blockchain related patents. This study tries to identify the technologies pertaining to the blockchain technology and further exploring the relationship among the technologies used in the development of blockchain. Our investigation utilizes this information to tackle our study query: which fields of knowledge play a role? The study is the initial step to map the overall technology space within the blockchain. This study will lay the groundwork by addressing the core technologies as well as the interrelationship among them, and also the assignees using these technologies.

The rest of this paper is as follows: literatures are discussed in Sect. 2. Section 3 explained the methodology of the paper. Findings are presented in Sect. 4 and conclusion follows in Sect. 5.

2 Literature Review

2.1 Blockchain Technologies

A distributed ledger of transactions, or blockchain, is an developing technology that can be traced back to 2008 when [2] introduced bitcoin [5–9]. Unlike traditional databases, blockchains are made up of blocks containing transactions validated by encryption mechanisms, and their information cannot be removed or altered by anyone. These blocks are consistently linked, resulting in an ever-expanding chain of blocks [10]. A blockchain technology is generally viewed as a cross between software engineering, cryptography, economic game theory, and decentralized computing.

Attention to cryptocurrencies has increased 2014 onward, and approximately 9,984 cryptocurrencies are listed in CoinMarketCap upto July 2023. A blockchain can be used for more than just cryptocurrencies. In today's world, blockchain technology is being used in a wide range of domains, including financial services [11–13], smart contracts [14], Internet of Things (IoT) [15, 16], identification services [9], security services [17], healthcare services [18–20], supply chain [21–25], etc. Diverse focus of blockchain technology warrants a proper technology mapping for a better understanding of the evolution in this field. Figure 1 shows a variety of blockchain applications in both financial and non-financial domains, as adopted from Casino, Dasaklis [26].

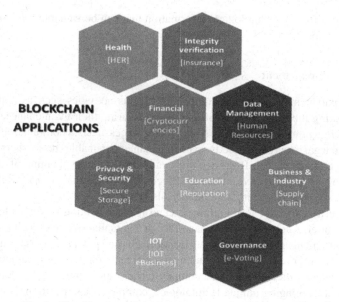

Fig. 1. Classification of blockchain applications by Casino [26]

2.2 Patent Analysis

The World Intellectual Property Organization (WIPO) defines a patent as a documentation showcasing a unique product, a pioneering procedure for product creation, or an inventive answer to a specific issue. This document grants inventors the exclusive rights and legal protection for a specified period, playing a crucial role in promoting equitable technology development and distribution [27, 28]. A patent document typically includes essential technological details such as the patent number, issuance date, inventor's name, assignee (the entity granted the patent rights), abstract, title, and an International Patent Classification (IPC) code that categorizes the technology's subject matter.

Patents serve as a crucial gauge of innovation, assessing the advancement of technology, inventive endeavours, and creative accomplishments related to novel technologies, products, and processes. Utilising patent intelligence offers a valuable means of comprehending a nation's knowledge-driven economy. Despite their limitations, patent indicators remain an unparalleled source for analysing the strides made in technology innovation.

By providing detailed technical information, patents offer new knowledge and insights. For nearly two decades, experts and researchers in technology management and technology forecasting have employed the analysis of patent documents as a method to identify and understand the technologies associated with various industries [28–33]. Analysing patents helps prevent researchers from duplicating efforts in specialized fields and empowers them to create novel technological advancements based on existing information. This approach has proven valuable in gaining insights into technological trends and advancements within specific sectors. In essence, a patent document serves as an extensive repository of technological information that can be valuable for research and innovation purposes.

2.3 Patent Management

Traditional patent management encompasses various activities such as applying for patents, securing their issuance, obtaining them, ensuring their maintenance, and safeguarding them against infringement. This process necessitates a combination of robust technical and legal expertise. Effective patent management enables researchers and firms to gauge the efficacy of their R&D activities, aiding in strategic planning. It also serves as a means to gain a competitive advantage concerning intellectual property rights within the industry, setting them apart from their rivals.

To devise a successful R&D strategy, careful consideration of future technology trends is essential. Analysing patents can serve as a valuable source of technology forecasting, providing insights into emerging technologies and potential areas for investment and development. For any firm, introducing a novel technology is of paramount importance, as it can significantly enhance competitiveness in the market. By continuously innovating and leveraging unique technologies, companies can position themselves as industry leaders and gain a distinctive edge over competitors.

Compared to scholarly articles, patents offer more comprehensive details on various technologies. Examining the data gleaned from patent documents has given rise to strategic organization, handling of technology, analysis of business rivals, and managing research and development divisions [28, 29, 34]. Analysing patent data has been instrumental in strategic planning, as it allows organizations to identify technological opportunities, potential areas of growth, and emerging trends. It aids in effective technology management, helping companies align their R&D efforts with market demands and innovation goals. Besides, through competitor analysis, organizations can better understand the technological landscape and the strengths and weaknesses of their rivals, enabling them to make informed decisions in the market [29]. An analysis of competitors' patents and a new exploration of technology opportunities can be achieved from patents' bibliographic information such as inventors, publication dates, applicants, and other specifications [29, 32, 35, 36]. Analyzing patents can be advantageous in predicting technology trends and forecasting, crafting technology roadmaps, and identifying countries that are pioneers in innovative technology [29].

2.4 R&D, Technology and IPC

Researchers, investors, and public agencies are taking a close look at blockchain technology, which has a variety of impressive applications. A good way to make an informed technology investment and selection decision is to recognize the future trend of technologies. It is the potential for technological advancement in general or within a particular field that affects the overall industry and individual companies. Different industries' R&D intensity is affected by different technological opportunities, which leads to heterogeneous R&D productivity. Different enterprises have different R&D productivity and operating results in response to technological opportunities at the firm level.

The International Patent Classification (IPC) is the world's main system for categorizing patents, as recommended by the World Intellectual Property Organization (WIPO). Each IPC comes with a matching technology category. By evaluating IPC classification distributions, it is possible to assess the overall technology trend by analysing the technology classification distributions of patents.

IPC codes can be used to pre-defined technologies and can be used to investigate their trends, i.e.; the sequence of technology definition. In investigating IT and BT areas, [37] used IPC codes to assign relevant patents to information technology (IT) and biotechnology (BT), and analysed the characteristics of patents in each of the IPC codes to identify emerging technologies by defining one IPC code as one technology.

The Strasbourg Agreement of 1971 initiated the establishment of an ordered patent classification known as the IPC [23]. The International Patent Conversation (IPC) codes have been overseen by the World Intellectual Property Organization (WIPO). These codes function as a technological categorization term that gives testament to the subject of the invention. In this paper, we use the 4th level of IPC code such as G10D 1/02 as in Table 1:

Table 1. Hierarchical structure of IPC codes

IPC Hierarchy	Description
G	: Section G - Physics
G10	: Musical Instruments; Acoustics
G10D	: Stringed musical instruments; Wind-Actuated musical instruments; Accordions or concertinas; Musical Instruments not otherwise provided for;
G10D 1/02	: of violins, violas, violoncellos, basses

2.4.1 Necessity of Technology Analysis

The trends in research and development (R&D) paradigms highlight the importance of dominant designs for shaping the development of next-generation products and the significance of discontinuous innovation for creating breakthrough products [38]. Innovative ideas can originate from various sources, and while internal sources have traditionally been considered the primary suppliers of new ideas, recent studies suggest that customers and users play a significant role in generating a majority of ideas in many industries. Moreover, suppliers and even competitors can also offer valuable insights that contribute to the innovation process. Discontinuous innovation involves radical shifts and ground-breaking developments that result in entirely new products or solutions.

These innovations disrupt the existing market and can revolutionize entire industries. The Blockchain is regarded as one of the emerging technologies that has the potential to disrupt the entire ecosystems in different areas where blockchain is involved in as shown by [26]. This has opened up the necessity to explore the technology development within the blockchain ecosystems. The escalating significance of blockchain technology and its promising future has prompted key research to examine patents within this sector [39].

What then becomes crucial is how to identify these newer innovations that transform raw data into information that can be used for innovation, regardless of source. From macrolevel analysis of strategy to microlevel modelling of specific emerging technologies, patents are useful sources of information about technical progress and innovative activity [30, 33, 40]. Analysing patents can reveal technological details, reveal business trends, inspire new industrial solutions, and guide investment decisions [27, 31, 34, 41].

3   Methodology

The prime objective of this paper is to explore the technology landscape of patents related to blockchain. The sample of this paper consists of 1,445 patents from 2020 and 2021. This sample will allow is to have an idea on the current development as well as the impact of these technologies. The patents were handpicked after careful review of the abstracts and the claims in order to avoid auto-generated samples containing near keywords 'chainsaw', 'building block' and alike. After curation and sorting of the sample, necessary information (Publication number, Dates, Assignee, Country, Abstracts and IPC codes) from 1,426 patents are collected for further analysis. Excel, Python and Gephi are used to analyse the curated and sorted data and to create graphical presentations. Figure 2 presents the flow of methodology for the paper.

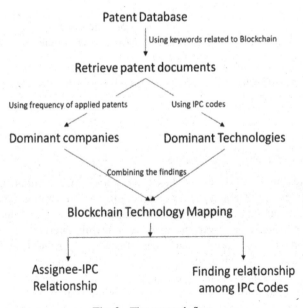

Fig. 2. The research flow

4   Findings

Figure 3 shows the trends in patenting activities for blockchain related patents documents over the years. The spike in the blockchain patents started from around 2016 with an increasing trend. Interesting to see the decline in the number of application post-2021.

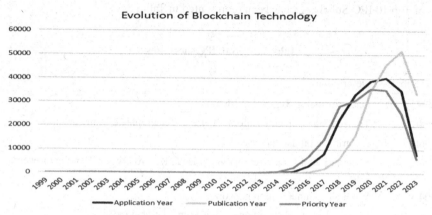

Fig. 3. Trend in patenting activities

The top owners of patents in the blockchain field are the E-commerce giant ALIBABA, Chinese Technology Company Tencent, IBM technology firm, Ping An tech, Nchain Holding, Advanced New Technologies, and Alipay finance services. Surprisingly, majority of the assignees of the patents are from China. The Non-Chinese firms are IBM, Siemens and Microsoft among the Top 20 as shown in Fig. 4.

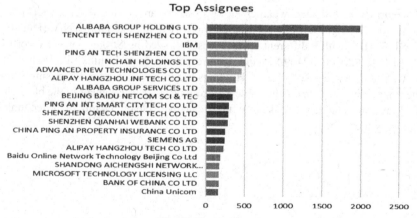

Fig. 4. Top assigners

Patents are organized based on the International Patent Classification (IPC), a universal and standardized system provided by WIPO, which enables fast assessment and search. For the sample of 1,426, total of 61 major IPC classifications are covered by the blockchain related patents. As perceived, the technology related to the computing and electric communication technique are the most focused ones. Interesting to see Health Informatics related technologies (G16H) has started to be focused more recently. The list of Top 10 IPC Subclasses has been represented in Table 2.

Table 2. Top 10 IPC subclasses.

IPC Subclass	Descriptions
G06Q	Data Processing Systems or Method's
H04L	Transmission of Digital Information, e.g. Telegraphic Communication
G06F	Electric digital data processing
G06K	Recognition of Data; Presentation of Data, Record Carries, Handling Records Carriers
H04W	Wireless communication networks
G06N	Computer systems based on specific computational models
G16H	Healthcare Informatics, i.e. Information and Communication Technology [ICT] Specially Adapted for the Handing or Processing of Medical or Healthcare Data
G07C	The time or Attendance Registers; Registering or Indicating the Working of Machines; Generating Random Numbers; Voting or Lottery Apparatus
G07F	Coin-Freed or Like Apparatus
H04N	Pictorial Communication, e.g. Television

We further investigated whether the top owners are having diverged technology focus or not. The highest IPC subclass used was by Koninklijke Philips N.V. (Patent No. US10811771B1) with 9 different occurrences; followed by Strong Force Tx Portfolio 2018 LLC (US20200272469A1) and 2 more patents from Koninklijke Philips N.V. Lbxc Co Ltd as well as Rolls Royce Holdings Plc follow thereafter. Surprisingly, none of the companies on the list in the Table 3 are among the Top assignees of the blockchain related patents. Detailed analysis in the future can give a clearer picture of the technology adoption by the companies.

Table 3. Companies with diverged technology focus

No	Publication Number	Assignees	IPC Subclass										Total IPC Subclasses
			G06Q	H04L	G06F	G06K	H04W	G06N	G16H	G07C	G07F	H04N	
1	US10811771B1	Koninklijke Philips N.V.		1		1	1	1					9
2	US20200272469A1	Strong Force Tx Portfolio 2018 Llc	1	1	1	1		1					7
3	US20200364187A1	Koninklijke Philips N.V.	1		1		1	1					6
4	US20200358183A1	Koninklijke Philips N.V.					1	1					5
5	W02020209413A1	Lbxc Co Ltd	1	1				1	1				5
6	US20200193464A1	Rolls Royce Holdings Plc	1	1		1		1					5
7	US10733160B1	State Farm Mutual Automobile Insurance Co.	1	1	1	1				1			5
8	US20200233398A1	General Electric Company		1	1								5
9	KR2141219B1	Suh Doug Geun & Seo Jeong-Seong	1		1			1					5
10	KR2149245B1	Innodigital Co Ltd & Hanshin University	1	1	1		1						5
11	EP3761255A1	Abb Asea Brown Boveri Ltd.	1	1							1		5
12	CN111667318A	Guangzhou 9skychina Information Technolo	1	1	1	1		1					5
13	CN111476656A	Shenzhen Zliaji Network Technology Co Ltd	1	1	1						1	1	5

Figure 5 presents the occurrences of the technologies within the sample for this study. These IPCs are the 4th level of the IPC categories which can give a detailed description of the major technologies needed for the efficient and effective operation of blockchain.

The network diagram in Fig. 6 is the most important presentation in the sense that it shows the interlinkages among the IPC Codes within the blockchain domain. Complementary technologies can be identified using this network. As perceived, the top technologies are found to be interlinked with each other.

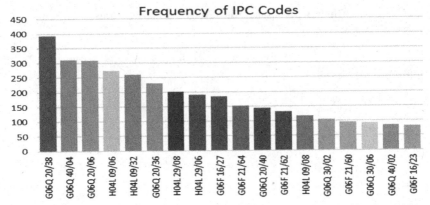

Fig. 5. Displays the contributions made by each category in the IPC classification within the collected patents.

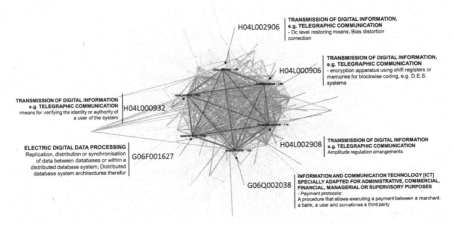

Fig. 6. IPC Codes within the blockchain domain.

Figure 7 presents the distribution of the 4th level IPC Codes within the respective top assignees. This figure can help the analyst to identify the competitors and collaborator within the same technology fields. Further analysis of this details can provide an idea on the possible M&A activities among the companies for gaining competitive advantages.

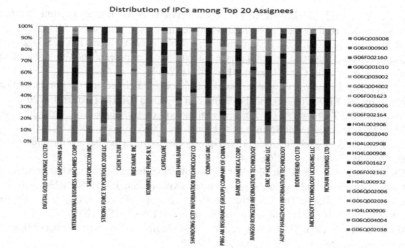

Fig. 7. The distribution of the 4th level IPC.

5 Conclusion

This paper analysed 1,426 patents related to blockchain to explore the technology focus within the blockchain landscape. One of the interesting findings, among others, is that the diverged technology focused companies are not among the top assignees, and findings of the paper can be helpful for potential M&A activities leading to competitive advantage. This paper is a pilot study for an extensive study and to develop technology map for the emerging area like blockchain.

Acknowledgement. This work was funded by Xiamen University Malaysia Research Fund (XMUMRF) under grant numbers XMUMRF/2021-C8/IECE/0025 and XMUMRF/2022-C10/IECE/0043.

References

1. Szabo, N.: Building Blocks for Digital Markets through Smart Contracts (2018)
2. In Bitcoin: A Peer-to-Peer Electronic Cash Structure, Nakamoto, S. discusses the system's foundations. Cryptography Mailing list (2009). https://metzdowd.com
3. Miraz, M.H., Donald, D.C.: Atomic cross-chain swaps: development, trajectory and potential of digital token swap facilities. Ann. Emerg. Technol. Comput. **3**(1), 42–50 (2019)
4. Hussain, A.A., et al.: An in-depth analysis of blockchain technology implementation in Bangladesh: a review based on existing literature. Ann. Progress. Technol. Comput. **6**(1), 1–30 (2022)
5. Qu, Q., et al.: On spatio-temporal blockchain query. Futur. Gener. Comput. Syst. **98**, 208–218 (2019)
6. Chernov, A., Chernova, V.: Global blockchain technology market analysis-current situations and forecast. In: Economic and Social Development: Book of Proceedings, pp. 143–152 (2018)

7. Dylan, Y., et al.: Blockchain Technology Overview. NIST Interagency/Internal Report (NISTIR), National Institute of Standards and Technology, Gaithersburg, MD (2018)
8. Xu, M., Chen, X., Kou, G.: A systematic review of blockchain. Financ. Innov. **5**(1), 27 (2019)
9. Zhang, Y., et al.: Fluorene-centered perylene monoimides as potential non-fullerene acceptor in organic solar cells. Org. Electron. **21**, 184–191 (2015)
10. Zheng, Z., et al.: An overview of blockchain technology: architecture, consensus, and future trends. In: 2017 IEEE International Congress on Big Data (BigData Congress) (2017)
11. Foroglou, G., Tsilidou, A.-L.: Further applications of the blockchain. In: 12th Student Conference on Managerial Science and Technology (2015)
12. Gao, F., et al.: A blockchain-based privacy-preserving payment mechanism for vehicle-to-grid networks. IEEE Network **32**(6), 184–192 (2018)
13. Peters, G.W., Panayi, E., Chapelle, A.: Crypto-currencies trends and blockchain technologies: A monetary theory and regulation perspective. arXiv preprint arXiv:1508.04364 (2015)
14. Kosba, A., et al.: Hawk: The blockchain model of cryptography and privacy-preserving smart contracts. In: 2016 IEEE Symposium on Security and Privacy (SP) (2016)
15. Akins, B.W., Chapman, J.L., Gordon, J.M.: A whole new world: Income tax considerations of the Bitcoin economy. Pitt. Tax Rev. **12**, 25 (2014)
16. Kravitz, D.W., Cooper, J.: Securing user identity and transactions symbiotically: IoT meets blockchain. In: 2017 Global Internet of Things Summit (GIoTS) (2017)
17. Noyes, C., Bitav: Fast anti-malware by distributed blockchain consensus and feedforward scanning. arXiv preprint arXiv:1601.01405 (2016)
18. Kuo, T.-T., Kim, H.-E., Ohno-Machado, L.: Blockchain distributed ledger technologies for biomedical and health care applications. J. Am. Med. Inform. Assoc. **24**(6), 1211–1220 (2017)
19. Mettler, M.: Blockchain technology in healthcare: the revolution starts here. In: 2016 IEEE 18th International Conference on e-Health Networking, Applications and Services (Healthcom) (2016)
20. Witchey, N.J.: Healthcare transaction validation via blockchain, systems and methods. Google Patents (2019)
21. Abeyratne, S.A., Monfared, R.P.: Blockchain ready manufacturing supply chain using distributed ledger. Int. J. Res. Eng. Technol. **05**, 1–10 (2016)
22. Korpela, K., Hallikas, J., Dahlberg, T.: Digital supply chain transformation toward blockchain integration (2017)
23. Moosavi, J., et al.: Blockchain in supply chain management: a review, bibliometric, and network analysis. Env. Sci. Pollut. Res. 1–15 (2021)
24. Tian, F.: An agri-food supply chain traceability system for China based on RFID & blockchain technology. In: 2016 13th international conference on service systems and service management (ICSSSM). IEEE (2016)
25. Turk, Ž, Klinc, R.: Potentials of blockchain technology for construction management. Procedia Eng. **196**, 638–645 (2017)
26. Casino, F., Dasaklis, T.K., Patsakis, C.: A systematic literature review of blockchain-based applications: current status, classification and open issues. Telematics Inform. **36**, 55–81 (2019)
27. Adamuthe, A.C., Thampi, G.T.: Technology forecasting: a case study of computational technologies. Technol. Forecast. Soc. Chang. **143**, 181–189 (2019)
28. Altuntas, S., Dereli, T., Kusiak, A.: Forecasting technology success based on patent data. Technol. Forecast. Soc. Chang. **96**, 202–214 (2015)
29. Abbas, A., Zhang, L., Khan, S.U.: A literature review on the state-of-the-art in patent analysis. World Patent Inf. **37**, 3–13 (2014)
30. Baumann, M., et al.: Comparative patent analysis for the identification of global research trends for the case of battery storage, hydrogen and bioenergy. Technol. Forecast. Soc. Chang. **165**, 120505 (2021)

31. Cho, Y., Daim, T.: Technology forecasting methods, in research and technology management in the electricity industry: methods, tools and case studies, In: Daim, T., Oliver, T., Kim, J. (eds.), pp. 67–112. Springer, London (2013)
32. Choi, J., et al.: A study on the patent analysis for effective technology forecasting. In: Proceedings – ICIDT 2012, 8th International Conference on Information Science and Digital Content Technology, pp. 88–91. [6269232] (Proceedings – ICIDT 2012, 8th International Conference on Information Science and Digital Content Technology; vol. 1) (2012)
33. Dou, H., et al.: Patent analysis for competitive technical intelligence and innovative thinking. Data Sci. J. **4**, 209–236 (2005). https://doi.org/10.2481/dsj.4.209
34. Firat, A., Woon, W., Madnick, S.: Technological forecasting–A review. Composite Information Systems Laboratory (CISL). Massachusetts Institute of Technology (2008)
35. Li, X., et al.: Forecasting technology trends using text mining of the gaps between science and technology: the case of perovskite solar cell technology. Technol. Forecast. Soc. Chang. **146**, 432–449 (2019)
36. Choi, Y., Hong, S.: Qualitative and quantitative analysis of patent data in nanomedicine for bridging the gap between research activities and practical applications. World Patent Inf. **60**, 101943 (2020)
37. Geum, Y., et al.: Technological convergence of IT and BT: evidence from patent analysis. ETRI J. **34**(3), 439–449 (2012)
38. Trappey, C.V., et al.: Using patent data for technology forecasting: China RFID patent analysis. Adv. Eng. Inform. **25**(1), 53–64 (2011)
39. Bamakan, S.M.H., et al.: Blockchain technology forecasting by patent analytics and text mining. Blockchain: Rese. Appl. **2**(2), 100019 (2021). https://doi.org/10.1016/j.bcra.2021.100019
40. Yang, C.B.: Role of patent analysis in corporate R&D. Pharm. Pat. Anal. **1**(1), 5–7 (2012)
41. Yoon, B., Park, Y.: Development of new technology forecasting algorithm: hybrid approach for morphology analysis and conjoint analysis of patent information. IEEE Trans. Eng. Manage. **54**, 588–599 (2007)

SocialEcho: A Social Networking Platform with Community Guidelines Violation Pre-check

Neaz Mahmud[ID], Mohammad Iqbal Hossain Emon[ID],
Md. Mahruf Hasan Beg[ID], and Md. Motaharul Islam[✉][ID]

United International University, United City, Madani Avenue, Badda, Dhaka 1212,
Bangladesh
{nmahmud191236,memon191022,mbeg191203}@bscse.uiu.ac.bd,
motaharul@cse.uiu.ac.bd

Abstract. Social media has revolutionized the way people communicate,
but it also comes with risks such as the proliferation of misinformation
and cyberbullying and violations of community guidelines. To address
these concerns, we propose the development of a social networking platform, called SocialEcho, which leverages a combination of advanced filtering techniques and third-party API services, to ensure that all user-
generated content complies with established community guidelines. Our
platform built using modern tools to create a regulated and safe space
for online communication that promotes responsible and respectful interactions among users. In addition, we have implemented an NLP-based
feature that automatically categorizes user posts into different channels,
enabling users to easily find and engage with content that aligns with their
interests. Through these features, SocialEcho enhances the user experience and promotes a more organized and structured community.

Keywords: Social media · Content moderation · Community
guidelines

1 Introduction

Social media platforms have become an integral part of people's daily lives,
with billions of users around the world using these platforms to connect with
friends and family, share information, and engage with a variety of communities.
Social media platforms function by providing users with tools to create and share
content, as well as tools to engage with other users' content. These platforms
also typically use algorithms and data analysis to curate content based on users'
interests and preferences.

However, the widespread use of social media platforms has also led to numerous challenges and issues, including the spread of misinformation, cyberbullying,
hate speech, invasion of privacy, and addiction. Social media companies have

M. H. Miraz et al. (Eds.): iCETiC 2023, LNICST 538, pp. 216–228, 2024.
https://doi.org/10.1007/978-3-031-50215-6_14

come under scrutiny for their handling of these issues, with some critics arguing that these companies have not done enough to address these challenges.

As social media platforms continue to evolve and grow, it is likely that new challenges will emerge, requiring innovative solutions to ensure that these platforms remain safe and valuable resources for users. Many researchers and developers are working on new approaches to content moderation and community management, including the use of machine learning and artificial intelligence to improve accuracy and efficiency. Additionally, there is a growing movement towards decentralized social media platforms, which prioritize user privacy and control over data and content.

While social media platforms have brought many benefits and opportunities for communication and connection, there is still much work to be done to ensure that these platforms are safe, equitable, and sustainable for all users.

A report by the World Health Organization found that cyberbullying affects around 1 in 3 young people globally, highlighting the importance of creating a safe and welcoming environment on social media, particularly for younger users who may be more vulnerable to online harassment and discrimination. In addition, a study by the Pew Research Center found that 64% of US adults believe that social media has a mostly negative effect on the way news is reported, and that 56% of US adults believe that social media platforms are responsible for the spread of false or misleading information.

While many social media platforms have implemented community guidelines to define acceptable behavior on their platforms, these guidelines often follow a one-size-fits-all approach that may not work well for specific communities or user demographics. Moreover, inconsistent enforcement of these guidelines can lead to confusion and frustration among users, and inaccurate content moderation can result in false positives and false negatives. Given that content moderation is a complex and resource-intensive process, it can be challenging for platforms to achieve consistent and effective moderation. Limited opportunities for user feedback can also hinder users from understanding and engaging with the guidelines, and a lack of transparency in the moderation process can create distrust and uncertainty.

Therefore, it is important for social media platforms to consider these issues and develop approaches to improve their community guidelines and content moderation practices. For example, platforms could explore customizing their guidelines to fit specific communities or user groups, enhancing the accuracy and efficiency of moderation, and increasing transparency and accountability by providing users with clear explanations of moderation decisions and opportunities to provide feedback. By doing so, platforms can create a more inclusive and welcoming environment for their users, while mitigating the risks associated with harmful content and behavior on their platforms.

To overcome these challenges, our social media platform, named SocialEcho, offers a customizable approach to community guidelines that can be tailored to the specific needs and themes of each community. We ensure consistent and transparent enforcement of these guidelines, which are based on clear and understandable criteria, and combine the use of third-party API services with our own custom-built algorithms for content moderation to improve accuracy and efficiency. We also provide ample opportunities for user feedback, which allows us to continuously improve our content moderation process and ensure that users have a voice in the process. Finally, we ensure transparency in the content moderation process by providing users with clear guidelines and explanations for why certain content is being moderated.

In addition to addressing the challenges of content moderation, SocialEcho also offers several potential benefits to its users. By ensuring a safe and welcoming environment, we aim to provide users with a space to share their thoughts and ideas without fear of harassment or discrimination. By using automated post filtering and fact-checking, we also help users access accurate and reliable information while preventing the spread of misinformation.

Overall, we believe that SocialEcho has the potential to be a valuable resource for users looking to engage with others and access accurate and reliable information in a safe and personalized environment.

The major contributions of this paper are summarized below:

- We have introduced a customizable approach to community guidelines that can be tailored to the specific needs and themes of each community.
- We have developed a content moderation system that uses a combination of third-party API services and our own custom-built algorithms to improve accuracy and efficiency.
- We have implemented an NLP-based feature that automatically categorizes user posts into different channels, making it easier for users to find and engage with content that aligns with their interests.
- We provide opportunities for user feedback, which allows us to continuously improve our content moderation process and ensure that users have a voice in the process.
- We ensure transparency in the content moderation process by providing users with clear guidelines and explanations for why certain content is being moderated.

This paper is organized into five sections. Section 1 is the introduction and covers our problem statement, motivation, and objectives for the project. In Sect. 2, we present a literature review and gap analysis, where we discuss similar applications and related research papers. Additionally, we analyze the gaps and shortcomings of different platforms.

Section 3 focuses on the detailed methodology, algorithm, and process flow of our project. We explain the technical aspects of our work and how we approached the development process. In Sect. 4, we showcase the implementation and results of our project. We demonstrate how our work has been realized and provide empirical evidence to support our claims.

Finally, in Sect. 5, we conclude our report and summarize our project's achievements. We also discuss future plans and potential directions for further development.

2   Related Work

This section is divided into two subsections. In similar applications, we discussed major features of popular social media platforms. In existing works, we explored different papers and discussed their adopted methods and findings.

2.1   Similar Applications

In our research, we analyzed several popular social media platforms, including Facebook, Reddit, Twitter, and Quora. Here are some of the major features of each platform:

1. **Facebook**
   - News feed: Users can view content from other users they are connected with and see related content.
   - Groups: Users can create groups to build communication networks for business or entertainment purposes.
   - Pages: Users can create pages for business, content sharing, vlogs, brands, and organizations, but they need to be verified.
2. **Reddit**
   - Content submission: Registered users can submit content such as text posts or direct links, and other users can vote on the content.
   - Discussion forums: Reddit is known for its open nature, allowing anyone to participate in discussion forums and see shared content.
3. **Twitter**
   - Tweeting: Users can write content or tweet anything, which may contain media files like photos, videos, links, and text.
   - Engaging: Tweets are posted by the users, sent to the people who follow the user, and can be searchable on Twitter search.
4. **Quora**
   - Q&A: Users can ask questions, and anyone can answer them.
   - Activity feed: People can subscribe to different categories, justify their knowledge, and see the answers at the bottom of the page.
   - Following topics: Users can follow topics and questions to receive updates according to their interests.

These platforms have different features and focuses, but they all aim to promote online communication and information sharing. Our proposed social media and community platform will utilize advanced filtering techniques and natural language processing API to ensure that user-generated content adheres to established community guidelines, promoting responsible and respectful interactions among its users.

We summarised the major features of popular social media platforms along with our system in the Table 1. In the following table, we compare the major features of popular social media platforms with those of our own social media platform. Reddit has the feature of posting content based on categories, which allows users to find content that interests them. Our platform has the unique feature of pre-filtering content, which helps to automate the process of filtering out unwanted posts, vulgar content, hate speech, and profanity.

Table 1. Comparative Analysis of Different Social Media Platforms

Feature\Platform	Reddit	Facebook	Twitter	Quora	Our Platform
Category based content posting	Yes	No	No	No	Yes
Content pre-filtering for community standard violation	No	No	No	No	Yes
Comment/reply/answer	Yes	Yes	Yes	Yes	Yes
Internal messaging system	Yes	Yes	Yes	Yes	No

2.2   Existing Works

Jiang et al. [1], presented a study that characterized community guidelines on social media platforms. They examined the decisions made by 11 significant social media sites in implementing governance and controlling inappropriate behavior through a content study of their community guidelines. In this work, they identified 66 different types of restrictions in the community guidelines, with a wide range of how these rules are covered on various platforms. Their study highlights the prioritization of certain types of wrong-doing by social media platforms and calls for more research into the formulation of regulations and content moderation procedures for specific issues, such as inciting violence and voter suppression.

The paper [2] is a systematic literature review that provides a comprehensive overview of research related to content moderation in social media platforms. The paper covers a range of topics related to content moderation, including guidelines, enforcement mechanisms, and research methods. The authors identify key challenges and opportunities in this area, as well as potential avenues for future research. Overall, the paper highlights the importance of effective content moderation in promoting healthy and respectful online communities.

The research conducted by Khan et al. [3] reviewed sentiment analysis methods and highlighted significant problems in natural language processing (NLP). They stressed the importance of addressing the major NLP challenges for the significant development of machine learning approaches. Additionally, they proposed the use of better language models that can capture context and proximity to improve sentiment analysis.

Din et al. [4] described that the transformation of online social networks (OSN) into marketplaces has raised concerns about privacy and security for users. OSN providers collect a significant amount of private and sensitive information from their clients, which could be accessed and potentially abused by data miners, outside parties, or unauthorized users. This creates a risk for OSN users, as their personal information may not be adequately protected by the service provider. It is important for OSN users to be aware of these risks and to take steps to protect their privacy and security online.

Fernandz and Perera [5] proposed that the use of social media is currently the most tempted topic of discussion. But users should be aware of the risks and consequences of utilizing social media sites. Numerous websites and applications such as Facebook, Twitter and Instagram are most trending social networking platform, In order to emphasize social media's historical context, It is a must to consider its history and its necessity.

Tafesse and Wien [6] created a framework for categorizing social media posts based on content, engagement, and identity. It includes five content, three engagement, and four identity categories. The authors believe this framework can help with social media research, content moderation, and user privacy.

Pater et al. [7] compares online harassment policies of Facebook, Twitter, YouTube, Instagram, and Reddit. Found variation in definitions, behaviors constituting harassment, and consequences. Highlights need for consistent and clear policie

Tang and Dalzell [8] proposed a two-layer model for classifying hate speech on social media platforms. The model can identify whether a post is hateful or not, as well as the specific type of hate speech. It was trained and tested on a dataset of tweets and achieved high accuracy. The study also sheds light on the challenges of identifying hate speech online and the characteristics of different types of hate speech. The authors argue that their model can be useful for mitigating hate speech on social media platforms. Yin et al.

Djuric et al. [9] presented a method for hate speech detection that utilizes comment embeddings, which capture the semantic meaning of words in a comment. The proposed method uses a convolutional neural network (CNN) to learn the embeddings of words and phrases in comments, and then uses these embeddings to classify comments as hate speech or not. The authors evaluated the proposed method on a dataset of comments from Yahoo News, and results show that their method outperforms several baseline methods for hate speech detection. The authors conclude that comment embeddings can be an effective tool for hate speech detection.

Majid and Kouser [10] discusses the risks associated with social media and provides guidelines to ensure safe social networking. They propose measures such as strong passwords, privacy settings, caution with personal information sharing, and awareness of online scams and cyberbullying.

Yi Liu et al. [11] The authors discuss the challenges of content moderation on social media platforms and explores technological solutions such as AI and ML. It also highlights the importance of balancing user protection with freedom of expression and discusses ethical implications.

Kumari and Singh [12] note that social media platforms can undermine personal accountability due to security and privacy concerns. They suggest using technologies like network virtualization and media independence to protect user information.

Eric Goldman et al. [13] propose a new model for social media content moderation that prioritizes user safety and well-being. They suggest that platforms must show good faith efforts to moderate content to maintain their legal immunities under Sect. 230.

Shagun Jhaver et al. [14] emphasize effective governance to ensure responsible use of AI in content moderation. They suggest involving stakeholders and prioritizing transparency, accountability, and user participation.

3   Proposed System

Our approach to developing a system for automated content moderation on a social media platform involves several key steps (Fig. 1).

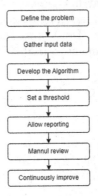

Fig. 1. Methodology of proposed system

Define the Problem. The problem is to develop an automated content moderation system for a social media platform that can detect violations of community guidelines.

Input Data Collection. The input data for the system includes user-generated content, user information (such as number of followers), any previous violations, and moderator-defined rules.

Algorithm Development. The algorithm processes the input data, sending the user-generated content to an API for analysis and calculating an overall score based on the user information, previous violations, and moderator rules.

Threshold Setting. There is a certain threshold score above which content will not be posted and notifies the user if their content is rejected. The threshold score is varying by the different parameters, especially the rules of specific community.

Reporting. If content is posted, other users can report any violations of community guidelines.

Manual Review. Reported content is sent to moderators for manual review.

Continuous Improvement. The system should be continuously improved by incorporating feedback from moderators and users to improve the accuracy of the algorithm and reduce false positives/negatives.

Overall, the methodology of our project involves a combination of automated and manual content moderation, with the goal of creating a safe and welcoming environment for users on the social media platform (Fig. 2).

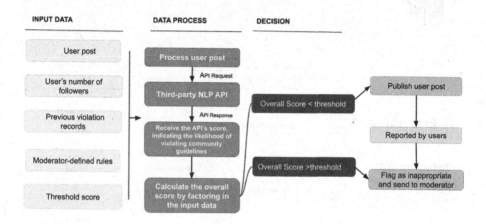

Fig. 2. Process Flow Diagram

The major feature of our project is to automate the community guidelines violation checking and content classification for posting content on a specific category. There are several types of rules which can be considered as community guidelines for social media platforms. These rules vary, but most social media platforms have some common rules which fall under community guidelines. We are working on these common rules for our project. Although a user can post images and short videos as posts, we will be filtering content based on the text, which will help us monitor user posts and comments for ensuring that community guidelines are followed (Fig. 3).

Our system will have a 3-tier architecture consisting of three logical layers: presentation, application, and database.

The presentation layer will be responsible for rendering the user interface and handling user interactions. We will be using React.js for building our front-end application and Redux for state management. The application layer will act as an intermediary between the presentation and database layers, and will be responsible for implementing the business logic of our system. This layer will use our custom algorithm for content moderation, which takes inputs from the presentation layer and sends requests to the database layer for content analysis.

The database layer will store and retrieve data, and will be responsible for managing the system's data. We will be using MongoDB for our database. Overall, our system architecture will be scalable and flexible, allowing for easy

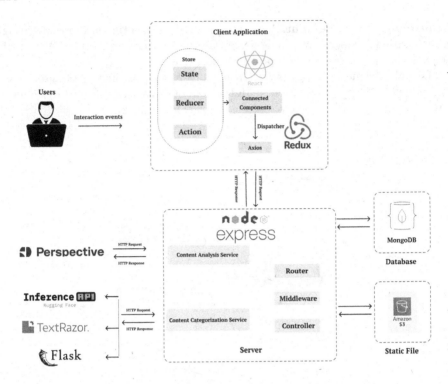

Fig. 3. System Architecture

modifications and upgrades. It will be designed with security and performance in mind, ensuring that our users' data and experience are protected.

The Content Moderation Algorithm is a procedure for evaluating user-generated content in a social media platform. It uses a combination of an API's score and a user's score based on their behavior and previous violations, as well as moderator rules, to determine if the content should be allowed to be posted or not. The algorithm calculates an overall score and compares it to a threshold value. If the overall score is above the threshold, the content is not posted, and the user is notified. If the overall score is below the threshold, the content is allowed to be posted, and other users are allowed to report any violations of community guidelines. Reported content is sent to moderators for review. The algorithm returns an overall moderation score based on its evaluation.

Content moderation, a critical aspect of our system, relies on two external API services. The first service is a content analysis API, which employs the Perspective API. This API analyzes the text content for various factors, such as toxicity, profanity, hate speech, and spam. By utilizing the Perspective API, we can accurately assess the appropriateness of user-generated content and identify potential violations of community guidelines. The second external API service is dedicated to content categorization. For this task, our system is designed to switch between multiple content categorization services based

Algorithm 1. Content Moderation Algorithm

1: **procedure** MODERATECONTENT(postText, followers, previousViolations, moderatorRules, threshold)
2:     Set overallScore to 0.
3:     Retrieve API's score, set apiScore to the returned score.
4:     Set userScore to 0.
5:     **if** followers > 1000 **then**
6:         Add 0.2 to userScore.
7:     **end if**
8:     **if** previousViolations > 0 **then**
9:         Subtract 0.2 from userScore.
10:    **end if**
11:    **for** each rule in moderatorRules **do**
12:        Adjust userScore based on the rule's weight.
13:    **end for**
14:    Set overallScore as a weighted average of apiScore and userScore, with apiScore weighted at 0.7 and userScore weighted at 0.3.
15:    **if** overallScore is above threshold **then**
16:        Do not post the user's content and notify the user.
17:    **else**
18:        Allow the content to be posted.
19:        Allow other users to report any violations of community guidelines.
20:        Send reported content to moderators for review.
21:    **end if**
22:    Return overallScore as moderationScore.
23: **end procedure**

on specific circumstances. We have integrated the Huggingface Interface API, utilizing the BART-large-MNLI pretrained model, and TextRazor as potential external services. Additionally, we have developed our own API server using the Huggingface transformer library and the BART-large-MNLI model. By leveraging these services, we can accurately categorize user posts within the specified category, ensuring appropriate content distribution and facilitating a better user experience. To facilitate the decision-making process, when a user submits a post, the content goes through the external APIs for analysis. The APIs return scores or indicators that represent the severity of violations or the degree of relevance to the specified category. Taking these scores into consideration, along with the rules defined by the content moderation service, the system determines whether to publish the post or flag it for further review.

4   Result and Analysis

In this section, we have analyzed the performance of content filtering, user experience, and discussed the limitations, challenges and future work.

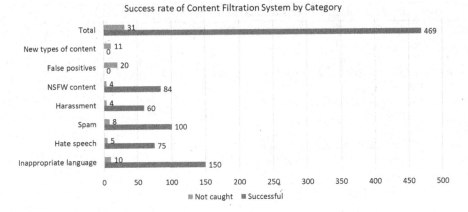

Fig. 4. Success rate of Content Filtration System by Category

4.1   Performance Evaluation of Content Filtering

For the content moderation algorithm, we created a total of 500 test posts, of which 469 (93.8%) were successfully filtered according to our guidelines. The remaining 31 (6.2%) posts were not caught by the algorithm and required manual review by moderators. Overall, we are satisfied with the effectiveness of the content filtration system, as it was able to catch the majority of inappropriate content with a relatively low false negative rate. However, we acknowledge that there is still room for improvement, and we plan to continue refining the algorithm based on feedback from users and moderators (Fig. 4).

4.2   User Experience Evaluation

We evaluated the user experience of SocialEcho based on the following criteria:

1. **Site Speed:** Users were asked to rate how fast the platform loaded and how quickly they were able to access different features on a scale of 1–10.
2. **Navigation:** Users were asked to rate how easy it was to find and use different features on the platform on a scale of 1–10.
3. **Content Filtration:** Users were asked to rate the effectiveness of the content filtration algorithm in identifying and blocking inappropriate content on a scale of 1–10.
4. **User Interface:** Users were asked to rate the overall design and layout of the platform, including the color scheme, font choices, and visual elements on a scale of 1–10.
5. **User Engagement:** Users were asked to rate how engaged they felt while using the platform, including the ability to interact with other users and create and share content, on a scale of 1–10.

We tested the usability of the SocialEcho platform with 100 users, who provided feedback on site speed, navigation, content filtration, user interface, and user engagement. The content filtration algorithm received the highest average rating of 9.1 out of 10, while navigation received the lowest rating of 7.9 out of 10, indicating room for improvement in that area. Overall, users had a positive experience with the platform, giving an average rating of 8.5 out of 10 for site speed and 8.8 out of 10 for user engagement.

4.3 Limitations and Challenges

- We faced some limitations in terms of the sample size, as only 100 users were able to test the platform during the usability evaluation.
- The evaluation was conducted in a controlled environment, which may not reflect the real-world usage of the platform.
- There were some technical challenges during the content moderation performance evaluation, as some posts were wrongly classified by the algorithm.
- Some users may have had different expectations or preferences for certain features, which could have affected their ratings.
- The user engagement evaluation relied solely on self-reported ratings, which may not accurately reflect their actual engagement on the platform.

One of the most important features that most social media platforms have been the internal messaging system, which we are not implementing. In the future, we plan to add that facility to our platform. Our platform may not be able to handle many users. To address these issues, we plan to optimize the platform's infrastructure in the future. We plan to further refining its algorithms and processes for detecting and removing content that violates community guidelines. This could involve incorporating additional data sources or third-party APIs, or developing more sophisticated machine learning models.

5   Conclusion

In conclusion, SocialEcho has been developed to offer a safer and more enjoyable social networking experience for users. Our platform uses an algorithm and third-party API services for content filtration and features a 3-tier architecture built with modern web frameworks and tools. Through user experience evaluation, we found that users were generally satisfied with the platform, but improvements can still be made in areas such as search function and user profile customization. Our content moderation algorithm had a high success rate, but ongoing updates and maintenance will be needed. Overall, SocialEcho is a positive step in creating a safer online space, and we will continue to improve the platform in the future.

References

1. Jiang, J.A., Middler, S., Brubaker, J.R., Fiesler, C.: Characterizing community guidelines on social media platforms. In: Conference Companion Publication of the 2020 on Computer Supported Cooperative Work and Social Computing, pp. 287–291 (2020)

2. Singhal, M., et al.: SoK: content moderation in social media, from guidelines to enforcement, and research to practice (2023)
3. Khan, M.T., Durrani, M., Ali, A., Inayat, I., Khalid, S., Khan, K.H.: Sentiment analysis and the complex natural language. Complex Adapt. Syst. Model. 4(1), 2 (2016). https://doi.org/10.1186/s40294-016-0016-9
4. Din, I.U., Islam, N., Rodrigues, J., Guizani, M.: Privacy and security issues in online social networks. Future Internet 10(12), 114 (2018)
5. Fernandz, H., Perera, W.S.S.: Investigation of social media security: a critical review. Int. J. Archit. Comput. (2020)
6. Tafesse, W., Wien, A.: A framework for categorizing social media posts. Cogent Bus. Manag. 4(1), 1284390 (2017)
7. Pater, J.A., Kim, M.K., Mynatt, E.D., Fiesler, C.: Characterizations of online harassment: comparing policies across social media platforms. In: Proceedings of the 2016 ACM International Conference on Supporting Group Work, GROUP 2016, pp. 369–374. Association for Computing Machinery, New York (2016)
8. Tang, Y., Dalzell, N.: Classifying hate speech using a two-layer model. Stat. Public Policy 6(1), 80–86 (2019)
9. Djuric, N., Zhou, J., Morris, R., Grbovic, M., Radosavljevic, V., Bhamidipati, N.: Hate speech detection with comment embeddings. In: Proceedings of the 24th International Conference on World Wide Web, WWW 2015 Companion, pp. 29–30. Association for Computing Machinery, New York (2015)
10. Majid, I., Kouser, S.: Social media and security: how to ensure safe social networking. Int. J. Human. Educ. Res. 1, 36–38 (2019)
11. Liu, Y., Yildirim, P., Zhang, Z.: Social media, content moderation, and technology (2021)
12. Kumari, S., Singh, S.: A critical analysis of privacy and security on social media (2015)
13. Lefouili, Y., Madio, L.: The economics of platform liability. Eur. J. Law Econ. 53, 319–351 (2022). https://doi.org/10.1007/s10657-022-09728-7. Post-Print hal-03711652, HAL
14. Jhaver, S., Ghoshal, S., Bruckman, A., Gilbert, E.: Online harassment and content moderation: the case of blocklists. ACM Trans. Comput.-Hum. Interact. 25(2), 1–33 (2018)

Green-IoT Based Automated Field Maintenance System

Jubayer Hossen, Abir Chowdhury, Md. Tasnimul Hassanm, Israt Jahan Ukti, Md. Rishad Islam, and Md. Motaharul Islam[✉]

United International University, United City, Madani Avenue, Badda, Dhaka 1212, Bangladesh
{jhossen191254,achowdhury191255,mhassan192049,iukti191138, mislam191134}@bscse.uiu.ac.bd, motaharul@cse.uiu.ac.bd

Abstract. Nowadays fields are seen everywhere around us like in schools, colleges, universities, parks, stadiums, and many more places. But the maintenance cost is very expensive and they also consume many resources like electricity, water, fuel, manpower, etc. Our main target is to use those resources efficiently and create an automation system for the field. The traditional maintenance system of a field requires a lot of workers and they need to handle everything manually. They water randomly in the field without worrying about which part of the field will need water. This process wastes a lot of water and electricity. Also, we want to implement a system that measures grass growth in that field. Workers do not use the grass trimmer efficiently because they don't know where the grass is actually grown. So, a lot of fuel or electricity is wasted during that process. We want to overcome those problems. Our proposed idea is that we will create an automation system that will detect field moisture, grass growth and it will report the field condition to a device.

Keywords: Green IoT · Field · Grass · Automation · Moisture

1 Introduction

At present, the key issue in the current domain is the utilization of resources like manpower and water which is lacking in many parts of our country. There have not been any significant technological advancements or automation being made in the university, school, or stadium field sector as compared to other sectors. Fields need to be monitored on a regular basis. The use of the developed framework is to reduce wastage by automating the entire field monitoring system. To promote sports and environmental sustainability, sporting venues and stadium arenas are implementing ground-breaking green measures. The sustainability movement has gained support from numerous locations all around the world to preserve the environment. There are several ways to accomplish this, including strategies to lower carbon emissions, lower noise pollution, build sustainable water systems that use less water, and use solar and wind energy to

M. H. Miraz et al. (Eds.): iCETiC 2023, LNICST 538, pp. 229–242, 2024.
https://doi.org/10.1007/978-3-031-50215-6_15

generate electricity. With so many possibilities, becoming green is a fiercely contested race. Stadiums are competing with one another to produce venues that are both excellent for sporting events and environmentally friendly [1]. Green IoT with sustainable designs is promised to reduce operating costs, and energy expenditure and reduce environmental pollution. IoT will have a great influence on how we refuge particular challenges in our everyday lives, and it will admittedly make our lives easier and better [2]. The field of a public or private school, university, or stadium is a very important resource. It can be used in many ways. It can give economic benefits. So it has to be very conscious about the maintenance of this important resource. The problem at hand revolves around the inefficient utilization of resources in the university, school, and stadium fields. Despite the advancements in technology and automation in various sectors, the field maintenance sector has lagged behind, leading to wastage and suboptimal resource management. The lack of regular monitoring exacerbates the issue, as it becomes challenging to identify and address resource inefficiencies and potential environmental concerns.

To address this problem, our proposed framework aims to automate the field monitoring system, reducing wastage and improving resource utilization. By implementing sustainable measures and leveraging Green-IoT technologies, the goal is to contribute the preservation of the environment. This includes reducing carbon emissions, water consumption, and incorporating renewable energy sources.

This adoption of sustainable designs and Green-IoT technologies is expected to reduce operating costs, energy expenditure, and environmental pollution. By incorporating IoT solutions, the framework can tackle specific challenges in our daily lives, making resource management easier and more efficient. Recognizing the significance of fields as valuable resources that can provide economic benefits, it is crucial to prioritize their maintenance and employ conscious practices to ensure their long-term sustainability.

The main contribution of our research are-

- We have proposed a framework that intends to automate the field monitoring system, addressing the inefficient use of resources like electricity and water. The framework can assist minimize waste and enhance overall resource usage by automating the monitoring process.
- With our proposed framework stadiums and sporting venues can implement innovative green strategies including tactics to minimize carbon emissions, create sustainable water systems, and generate electricity using solar energy.
- Our proposed framework aims to close the gap of the field maintenance industry that has lagged behind when it comes to developments. By utilizing Green-IoT technologies, our proposed system offers to lower operating expenses, energy use, and environmental damage.
- Our framework enables routine and efficient field monitoring by automating the field monitoring system. This promotes optimal resource usage and lowers wastage by enabling the identification and prompt remediation of resource inefficiencies.

– Our proposed system offers a green IoT-based sustainable field and a sustainable city also.
– We have proposed a framework that strives to guarantee the long-term sustainability and financial viability of fields in public or private schools, universities, and stadiums by implementing sustainable practices and effective resource management.

In the following section, we have included a literature review in Sect. 2. After that, in Sect. 3, we discussed our methodology part. A case study of our project is included in Sect. 4. And finally, in Sect. 5, we have covered our conclusion part.

2   Literature Reviews

We have explored some papers related to our research topic and found some important details of it. From those, we have selected a few numbers of papers that are related to our proposed work.

We read an article [3] that basically represents sensors and base computers that make use of the Internet of Things to provide online real-time information on grassy airfield conditions. In addition, they discussed a two-sensor system for the measurement of soil moisture and grass height which is based on the analysis of wheel-grass interaction as well as the prospective GARFIELD system functionality. Two types of sensors are included: a field TDR sensor and an optical sensor where the sensors are self-powered, autonomous, and able to make measurements outdoors instantly. Besides, using the sensors won't disturb airfield traffic and will not interfere with aircraft operations. Data transmission between the sensors and the base computer is an important part of the measurement technology presented here.

Another article [4] provides a concise review of the use of various biotechnologies in smart cities and the methods for incorporating them into the Internet of Things. In addition to discussing biosensors for environmental management, they provided a brief summary of future biotechnology that may be used in green smart cities.

In this article [5], they created a scenario about how IoT has made a significant impact on the traditional supply chain, as well as on society as a whole. It has improved convenience and comfort, as well as providing a more convenient and comfortable environment. The purpose of this paper was to examine co-word trends and development in the IoT research areas related to the Internet of Things. Besides, Researchers retrieved 758 papers from the WOS database, which covers 2000–2014. This research revealed seven clusters utilizing co-word analysis, including "IoT and Security," "Middleware," "RFID," "Internet," "Cloud computing," "Wireless sensor networks," and "6LoWPAN." These clusters represent the conceptual structure of the IoT. This research implemented a co-occurrence matrix based on Pearson's correlation coefficient to cluster the words using the hierarchical clustering approach in order to grasp these intellectual structures. This research used a multidimensional scaling analysis and the PROXCAL method to illustrate these conceptual structures. Additionally, the IoT intellectual structure is studied through multidimensional scaling and schematizing correlations in the context of clustering techniques.

2.1 Gap Analysis

After reviewing the other literature, we have found that there are other projects that offer similar technology but offer very different facilities compared to ours. With our underground sensor, measuring the moisture is easier and cheaper to maintain. The other literature [3] provides sensors on the surface that can be damaged during the games played on the field, but our project avoids those damages. There is also another projects [6] that use IoT to develop smart cities, but never have they used such technologies in terms of maintenance of fields. So our technology is unique in case of using such technologies to efficiently monitor the state of the fields.

3 Methodology

Our aim is to cover the entire field under automation. To achieve this we plan to visualize our field in a two-dimensional matrix. In each matrix, we will place sensors to sense the moisture of soil and detect grass height. Now, if any block in the matrix has low moisture we will get a notification that "This block has low moisture please water this block", and also If a block in the matrix does not have the expected grass height we will receive a notification that the block needs mowing. By creating the two-dimensional matrix we can cover the full field under automation Fig. 1.

3.1 Preliminaries

In this section, we have discussed what components will be required in this project. The details of the components are given below:

- **Soil Moisture Sensor:** We have used a YL-69 soil moisture sensor for detecting the moisture of the soil. A straightforward technique for determining the moisture content of soil and related materials is the soil moisture sensor. Utilizing the soil moisture sensor is rather simple. The two substantial exposed pads serve as the sensor's probes and, when combined, as a variable resistor. The better the conductivity between the pads is, the lower the resistance and the higher the SIG out will be as a result of the soil's moisture content [7].
- **4G Dongle:** We have used a SIM7600X soil moisture sensor for detecting the moisture of the soil. The SIM7600 series is the LTE Cat 1 module that supports wireless communication modes of LTE-TDD/LTE-FDD/HSPA+/GSM/GPRS/EDGE etc. It supports maximum 10 Mbps downlink rate and 5 Mbps uplink rate [8].

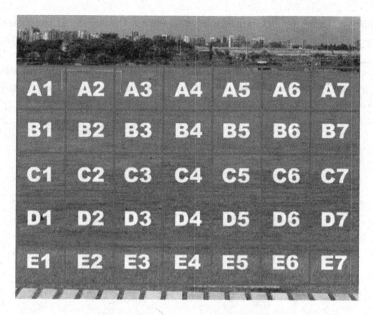

Fig. 1. Designing Two-Dimensional Matrix on the Field of United International University

- **Arduino:** Arduino refers to an open-source electronics platform or board and the software used to program it. We have used the microprocessor in order to receive the value of the sensors [9].
- **Motor Driver:** To control the rotation, power, and speed we need a motor driver. We have used the L298 motor driver. This L298N Motor Driver Module is a high-power motor driver module for driving DC and Stepper Motors. This module consists of an L298 motor driver IC and a 78M05 5V regulator. L298N Module can control up to two DC motors with directional and speed control [10].
- **Touch Sensor:** We need a touch sensor in order to detect the height of the grass. We have used the TTP223B touch sensor. The TTP223B touch sensor is a touch pad detector IC that offers 1 touch key [11].

Some other components we will need like, DC Motors, Breadboards, Wires, Solar panels, Batteries, etc.

3.2   Proposed System

Our biggest challenge is how we will place the sensors as the sensors are fragile. If we place the sensor outside of the field then a person can get hurt and also the sensors can break. After facing that problem we have found a solution. The Solution is explained below: All the sensors, micro-controller, and batteries will be stored underground and a metal plate will protect them. The moisture sensor will be placed underground. But in order to detect the height of the grass touch sensor needs to get out. So, for that, motor 1 in Fig. 2 will rotate. This will work like a linear actuator. Because of the rotation, the linear rotating rod will push the metal plate. After that, motor 2 in Fig. 2 will rotate and the rotating rod will get out the touch sensor to detect does the height of the grass is expected or not. We will fix a size for the grass.

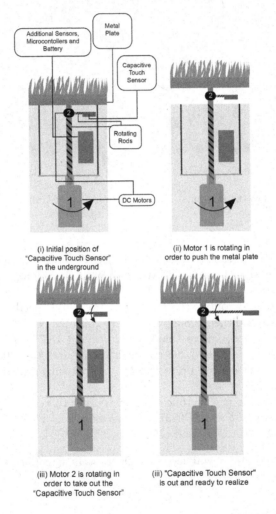

Fig. 2. The Pop-up mechanism to bring out the touch sensor

If the touch sensor touches the grass then the grass of that block needs to be cut demonstrated in Fig. 3(ii) but if not then do not need to cut demonstrated in Fig. 3(iv). But in some cases, it might happen that one side of the block has bigger grass and the other side of the block has smaller grass like Fig. 3(i). So, in

1. $Threshold\_value\_grass = 2cm$
2. $Threshold\_value\_moisture = 15\ to\ 30\%$
3. $While(true)$:
4. $for\ visiting\ m\ row\ of\ a\ matrix$:
5. $for\ visiting\ n\ column\ of\ the\ matrix$:
6. $moisture\_val = output\ from\ moisture\ sensor\ A1$
7. $turn\ on\ motor\ 1\ clockwise\ DigPort3\ =\ 1$
8. $sleep\ 8\ sec$
9. $turn\ off\ motor\ 1\ DigPort4\ =\ 0$
10. $turn\ on\ motor\ 2\ clockwise\ DigPort5\ =\ 1$
11. $sleep\ 5\ sec$
12. $turn\ off\ motor\ 2\ DigPort6 = 0$
13. $set\ the\ RPM\ of\ motor\ 1\ =\ 10$
14. $turn\ on\ motor\ 1\ clockwise\ DigPort3\ =\ 1$
15. $sleep\ 0.2\ sec$
16. $turn\ off\ motor\ 1\ DigPort4\ =\ 0$
17. $grass\_check\ =\ output\ from\ the\ touch\ sensor\ DigPort7$
18. $if\ moisture\_val\ <\ Threshold\_value\_moisture$:
19. $if\ connectivity\ isavailable$:
20. $send\ warning\ of\ low\ moisture$
21. $else$:
22. $connection\ error$
23. $if\ grass\_heigh\_check\ ==\ 1$:
24. $if\ connectivity\ is\ available$:
25. $send\ a\ warning\ of\ the\ grass\ height$
26. $else$
27. $connection\ error$
28. $turn\ on\ motor\ 2\ anti-clockwise\ DigPort5 = 1$
29. $sleep\ 3\ sec$
30. $turn\ off\ motor\ 2\ DigPort6\ =\ 0$
31. $set\ the\ RPM\ of\ motor\ 1\ =\ 500$
32. $turn\ on\ motor\ 1\ anti-clockwise\ DigPort3\ =\ 1$
33. $sleep\ 4.8\ sec$
34. $turn\ off\ motor\ 1\ DigPort4\ =\ 0$
35. end

4   Case Study to Automate a Field

We have selected the field of United International University for our case study. We have divided the field into 35 grids and now the cost analysis of the field of United International University. The prices of the components are given below (Table 1):

Grid size= 2 square meters

– Soil moisture sensor: YL-69 price = 99 BDT
– 4G Dongle: SIM7600X = 3500 BDT

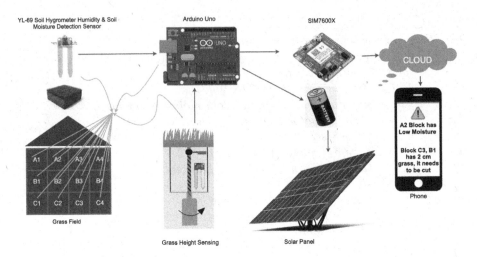

Fig. 5. Architecture of our project

Table 1. Cost per grid:

Name	Quantities	Rate	Total
YL-69	1	99	99
SIM7600X	1	3500	3,500
Arduino	1	700	700
L298	1	195	195
TTP223B	1	80	80
Motor	2	450	900
Battery (12v)	1	400	400
Wire	–	50	50
Others	–	30	30
		Cost	5,954 BDT

- Micro-controller: Arduino = 700 BDT
- Motor driver: L298N price = 195 BDT
- Touch sensor: TTP223B = 80 BDT
- Motor: Price = 450 BDT
- Battery: Battery 12 v price = 400 BDT
- Wires: Wire price = 50 BDT

Cost of each grid = 5,954 BDT
300-watt solar panel price is 16,500 BDT
If the field had 35 grids.
Then, total cost = 35 × 5,954 + 16,500 = 224, 890 BDT approximately.

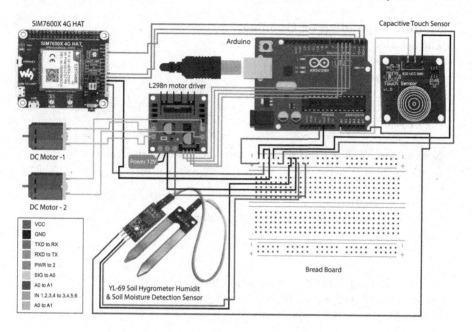

Fig. 6. Circuit Diagram of our project

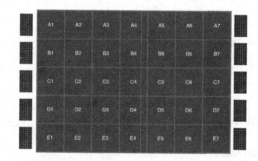

Fig. 7. Solar panels are installed at the edge of the field

4.1 Time Analysis to Detect the Grass Height

In this section, we calculated how long it would take our module to find out if the field has the expected grass height.

We have used two 500 rpm DC motors.

   Motor 1 = 500 rpm
   Motor 2 = 500 rpm
   1 rotation = 0.01 m

Those motors will rotate 500 times in one minute.

   500 times = 1 (min) x 60 (s)
   1 time = 60/500 = 0.12 s.

Module Expanding or Opening:

The rotation needs to cover 0.4 m:

    0.01 m = 1 rotation

    1 m = 1/0.01 rotation

    0.4 m = $(1 \times 0.4)/0.01$ rotation = 40 rotation

Total time to cover 0.4 m length:

    T1 = 40×0.12 = 4.8 s

Now motor 2 will expand with the sensors. The rotation needs to cover 0.25 m:

    0.01 m = 1 rotation

    1 m = 1/0.01 rotation

    0.25 m = $(1 \times 0.25)/0.01$ rotation = 25 rotation

Total time for motor 2:

    T2 = 25×0.12 = 3 s

Now we decreased our motor 1's speed by using a motor driver and set the rpm to 10 in order to get the accurate information from the touch sensor.

    10 times = 1 (min) x 60 (s)

    1 time = 60/10 s

    T3 = 6 s

Module Shrinking or Closing:

Now motor 2 will rotate anti-clockwise.

    T4 = 3 s.

Again, the rpm of the motor will increase to 500 rpm.

Now motor 1 will rotate anti-clockwise. It takes T5 = 4.8 s

Total time to the task:

    T = T1 + T2 + T3+ T4 + T5

    = 4.8 + 3 + 6+ 3 + 4.8

    = 21.6 s

So, we need 21.6 s to scan or detect the grass height of a grid.

5   Conclusion

We introduced a mechanism that keeps track of the growth of the grass and the amount of moisture in fields. It also requires fewer resources, including electricity, gasoline, water, and other resources. Utilizing these resources effectively and creating a field automation system are our key goals for this project. It contributes to the development of a sustainable, IoT-based green economy and city. Our main objective is to make efficient use of natural resources and reduce manpower by developing an automated system for the field. This project has the potential to create both a green IoT-based sustainable field and a sustainable city. Currently, we just test our model in a certain field and it comes with great results. In the near future, we will test it broadly in other fields in different locations and at different times for better results. Also, we consider another algorithm in the near future for comparison.

References

1. Mohanraj, I., Ashokumar, K., Naren, J.: Field monitoring and automation using IOT in agriculture domain. Procedia Comput. Sci. **93**, 931–939 (2016). https://doi.org/10.1016/j.procs.2016.07.275
2. Green IoT: Sustainable Design and Technologies - Speranza. https://www.speranzainc.com/green-iot-sustainable-design-and-technologies. Accessed 03 June 2023
3. Pytka, J., Łyszczyk, T., Gnapowski, E.: Monitoring grass airfield conditions for the GARFIELD system. In: 2018 5th IEEE International Workshop on Metrology for AeroSpace (MetroAeroSpace), pp. 85–90 (2018). https://doi.org/10.1109/MetroAeroSpace.2018.8453558
4. Gotovtsev, P.M., Dyakov, A.V.: Biotechnology and Internet of Things for green smart city application. In: 2016 IEEE 3rd World Forum on Internet of Things (WF-IoT), pp. 542–546 (2016)
5. Yan, B.N., Lee, T.S., Lee, T.P.: Mapping the intellectual structure of the Internet of Things (IoT) field (2000–2014): a co-word analysis. Scientometrics **105**, 1285–1300 (2015). https://doi.org/10.1007/s11192-015-1740-1
6. Obanawa, H., Yoshitoshi, R., Watanabe, N., Sakanoue, S.: Portable LiDAR-based method for improvement of grass height measurement accuracy: comparison with SfM methods. Sensors **20**, 4809 (2020). https://doi.org/10.3390/s20174809
7. YL-69 Soil Moisture Sensor at Rs 60/piece in Mumbai — ID: 12778810133. https://www.indiamart.com/proddetail/soil-moisture-sensor-12778810133.html. Accessed 03 June 2023
8. SIM7600X Module 4G Wireless Solutions — SIMCom Wireless Solutions Co., Ltd. https://www.simcom.com/product/SIM7600X.html. Accessed 03 June 2023
9. What is Arduino? - Definition from Techopedia. https://www.techopedia.com/definition/27874/arduino. Accessed 03 June 2023
10. L298N Motor Driver Module Pinout, Datasheet, Features & Specs. https://components101.com/modules/l293n-motor-driver-module. Accessed 03 June 2023
11. CAPSENSE Controllers. https://www.infineon.com/cms/en/product/microcontroller/sensing-controller/capsense-controllers. Accessed 03 June 2023
12. Murphy, D., et al.: GrassQ - a holistic precision grass measurement and analysis system to optimize pasture based livestock production (2019). https://doi.org/10.13031/aim.201900769
13. Mcsweeney, D., Coughlan, N., Cuthbert, R., Halton, P., Ivanov, S.: Micro-sonic sensor technology enables enhanced grass height measurement by a Rising Plate Meter. Inf. Process. Agric. **6**, 279–284 (2018). https://doi.org/10.1016/j.inpa.2018.08.009
14. Dalley, D., et al.: Technologies for measuring grass/crops. In: Proceedings of the South Island Dairy Event, p. 10 (2009)

15. Gupta, S., Devsani, R., Katkar, S., Ingale, R., Kulkarni, P.A., Wyawhare, M.: IoT based multipurpose agribot with field monitoring system. In: 2020 International Conference on Industry 4.0 Technology (I4Tech), Pune, India, pp. 65–69 (2020). https://doi.org/10.1109/I4Tech48345.2020.9102637

16. Achary, R., Rohan, R., Riya, K., Pavan, V.: Effect of temperature and relative humidity on onion farms and its monitoring by using IoT based smart farming system. In: 2022 International Conference on Communication, Computing and Internet of Things (IC3IoT), Chennai, India, pp. 1–6 (2022). https://doi.org/10.1109/IC3IOT53935.2022.9767884

17. Ahmad, N., Hussain, A., Ullah, I., Zaidi, B.H.: IOT based wireless sensor network for precision agriculture. In: 7th International Electrical Engineering Congress (iEECON), Hua Hin, Thailand, pp. 1–4 (2019). https://doi.org/10.1109/iEECON45304.2019.8938854

18. Rao, G.B.N., Rao, K.V., Kamarajugadda, R., Reddy, A.A., Rani, P.P.: Smart farming for agriculture management using IOT. In: 2023 9th International Conference on Advanced Computing and Communication Systems (ICACCS), Coimbatore, India, pp. 540–544 (2023). https://doi.org/10.1109/ICACCS57279.2023.10112839

19. Karthikamani, R., Rajaguru, H.: IoT based smart irrigation system using Raspberry Pi. In: Smart Technologies, Communication and Robotics (STCR), Sathyamangalam, India, pp. 1–3 (2021). https://doi.org/10.1109/STCR51658.2021.9588877

20. Reya, N.F., Ahmed, A., Islam, T.Z.M.M.: GreenPy: evaluating application-level energy efficiency in Python for green computing. Ann. Emerg. Technol. Comput. (AETiC) 7(3), 93–110 (2023)

21. Farjana, M., et al.: An IoT-and cloud-based E-waste management system for resource reclamation with a data-driven decision-making process. IoT 4(3), 202–220 (2023)

Author Index

Printed in the United States
by Baker & Taylor Publisher Services